To Colin,
   a memento

ammbm for [...]
for Aprils Indomania. )
   all best,
      Tom.

# Aryans and British India

# Aryans and British India

Thomas R. Trautmann

UNIVERSITY OF CALIFORNIA PRESS

Berkeley / Los Angeles / London

University of California Press
Berkeley and Los Angeles, California

University of California Press
London, England

Copyright © 1997 by The Regents of the University of California

Library of Congress Cataloging-in-Publication Data


Trautmann, Thomas R.
  Aryans and British India / Thomas R. Trautmann.
    p.  cm.
  Includes bibliographical references and index.
  ISBN 0-520-20546-4 (alk. paper)
  1. Indo-Aryans—History.   2. India—History—British occupation,
1765-1947.   I. Title.
  DS425.T68  1997                                            96-34953
  954.03'1—dc20                                                   CIP

Printed in the United States of America

1  2  3  4  5  6  7  8  9

*In memory of*
*A. L. Basham*
*British Sanskritist*
*historian of India*
*guru*
*friend*

# Contents

# Illustrations

# Preface

For some years it has been my strange and agreeable destiny to teach the history of ancient India at the University of Michigan, which is located, roughly, on the other side of the world from India. For the most part, the background knowledge of India my students bring with them to my classes is fairly limited unless, as is increasingly the case, they are themselves of Indian, or Pakistani, or Bangladeshi, or Sri Lankan descent.

At an early point in the course I explain how Sanskrit entered India from the direction of Iran, and was spoken by people who called themselves "Arya." Many students will not have heard of Sanskrit before, and few of them are aware that the modern languages of North India and Sri Lanka, descendants of the Sanskrit language in which the ancient scriptures of Hinduism were written, are related to the languages of Europe including English, all of them being members of the Indo-European family of languages. Again, few will know that Persian is also a member of the Indo-European language family and is not closely related to Arabic, even though it is written in a version of the Arabic script. It is only to be expected that students will be unaware of this order of facts when the ambient information stream not only is ignorant of them but so often supplies misinformation: Just a few weeks back I read in a newspaper a survey of the reactions of Arab countries to recent developments in the Middle East—beginning with Iran! The unexpected grouping of languages in the Indo-European family, deriving from the work of Orientalists of two centuries ago, is often as surprising today as it was to the pioneers of Indo-European linguistics.

All my students, however, have heard the name Aryan. Unfortunately we do not have to leave our own country, or even our own state, to find this name used by groups advocating the politics of racial hate. And so I find myself having to explain, shortly into my survey course on ancient Indian history, the following facts: *Aryan* is from *Arya* (*ārya*), a Sanskrit word used in early times by the Sanskrit speakers to refer to themselves in contrast with other groups from whom they differed. It was also used by the Iranians, the name of whose country means "land of the Aryas." Some scholars have claimed that the name for Ireland, Eire, is the same word, and that given the wide and early distribution of the word, Arya must be the name all the early speakers of Indo-European languages used for themselves. This is doubtful, but even if it is true there is no reason to think that these Indo-European speakers formed a racially unitary and pure group. The principal markers of Aryan identity are cultural (religion and language) and not physical or racial.

My problem as a teacher of Indian history is that the fascist appropriation in modern times of this ancient Sanskrit word and the politics of racial hatred with which it has become inextricably associated gives the word a strong charge that acts as a kind of interference when one wishes to tell the history of ancient India rather than the history of twentieth-century European and American racial politics. But while this prior knowledge of the modern fascist sense of the name Aryan that my students bring to class with them has a negative effect on the narrative of ancient Indian history, constituting a kind of distorting magnet that has to be corrected for, in another way the need to deal with it is an opportunity to apply historical knowledge of ancient India to the rational illumination of contemporary life in a small but crucial way. The Aryan idea, after all, is one rather important item of contemporary culture that a historian of ancient India has some special knowledge of, and it offers a person in my obscure corner of the Academy an opportunity to bring reason to bear on the problem of racial hatred, however limited the effect is bound to be.

That said I must hasten to stipulate that the story of fascism and racial hate groups is illuminated only indirectly in this book, and hovers at its margins, as it were. The central story is not about how the narrative of ancient Indian history and the ethnology of India relate to Nazism, but rather how they relate to the British of British India, more specifically to the British Sanskritists who supervised the construction of that history and ethnology. In the story of British colonialism the

Aryan or Indo-European idea has a quite different drift, complementary to its function in the story of fascism, acting (as I shall argue in this book) as a sign of the *kinship* of Britons and Indians. It is an idea that created the history of India while it revolutionized European notions of universal history and ethnology. Taken as a whole, the Aryan idea in European thought was productive of much that is false and evil, but also of much that is good and of lasting value. We are obliged, I think, to recognize that these qualities do not inhere in the idea itself but in the varying functions that the idea serves, and to be attentive therefore to the purposes toward which, at any given time, the idea is directed.

In writing this book I have been unusually blessed by helpful friends and supportive institutions. Many friends offered ideas, references and criticisms: N. J. Allen, Stephen Alter, Tom Bentley, Madhav M. Deshpande, Nicholas B. Dirks, Jean-Claude Galey, Richard Gombrich, Roger Lardinois, David N. Lorenzen, Billie Melman, Peter Pels, Tapan Raychaudhuri, Sanjay Subramaniam, Romila Thapar, Theodore W. Trautmann and James C. Turner. Figure 5 was taken by R. H. Barnes; figures 4, 6, and 7 are courtesy The Conway Library, Courtauld Institute of Art. John Hamer did the computer artwork in figures 2 and 3. To all of them I offer my heartfelt thanks. I thank the University of Michigan for sabbatical leave, the LSA Faculty Fund for research support, and the Institute for Social and Cultural Anthropology and Wolfson College, Oxford, for visiting fellow status in 1990–91 when the research for this book got under way. I am obliged to the École des Hautes Études en Sciences Sociales for a term of teaching there in the spring of 1993 (under a faculty exchange program with the History Department of the University of Michigan), during which I tried out the substance of the book in Jean-Claude Galey's seminar. I am grateful to my colleague David Bien and his counterpart at the École, André Burguière, for help in making this visit possible. In 1993–94 I held the Steelcase Research Professorship of the Institute for the Humanities at the University of Michigan, which enabled me to complete the research and write the book. I am grateful to the Institute and its director, James Winn, for a most productive and pleasant year, and to colleagues in the Fellows' Seminar for their helpful comments on my work. Finally I should like to thank the students of History 454, "The Formation of Indian Civilization," whose interest and concern about the Aryan idea stimulated me to write this book.

A. L. Basham, to whom the book is dedicated, was my teacher at the

School of Oriental and African Studies of the University of London. A poet and novelist first, he became a Sanskritist and then a historian of ancient India (see Trautmann 1988). He is a late example of the group of which I write, the British Sanskritists, a group that took form in the times of Charles Wilkins and Sir William Jones, in the latter half of the eighteenth century. But Basham was also very much a transition figure, involved in the decolonization of Indianist knowledge at the time when British India came to an end in the creation of independent republics of India and Pakistan. One sees this clearly in his critique of the arch-imperialist histories of India written by Vincent Smith (Basham 1961:266–274), and in the contrast between Smith's *Early history of India* (1904, fourth edition 1924) and Basham's *The wonder that was India* (1954, third revised edition 1967) that superceded it, a book widely read and translated into several languages, which became the standard survey of ancient Indian history for its time. The accomplishment that gave Basham the most satisfaction, however, was of having supervised the Ph.D.'s of about a hundred students from South Asia who subsequently occupied positions in history departments of universities all over the Subcontinent. He died in India while holding a fellowship, named after Sir William Jones, from the Asiatic Society, and is buried there. Those who were privileged to be his students remember him with deep affection.

# CHAPTER I

# Introduction

*For the new theory of Language has unquestionably produced a
new theory of Race. . . . There seems to me no doubt that
modern philology has suggested a grouping of peoples quite
unlike anything that had been thought of before. If you examine
the bases proposed for common nationality before the new
knowledge growing out of the study of Sanscrit had been
popularised in Europe, you will find them extremely unlike those
which are now advocated and even passionately advocated in
parts of the Continent. . . . That peoples not necessarily
understanding one another's tongue should be grouped together
politically on the ground of linguistic affinities assumed to prove
community of descent, is quite a new idea.*

Sir Henry Sumner Maine,
*The effects of observation of India on modern
European thought*

In 1875, when Britain was at the height of its power in
India, Sir Henry Maine addressed the question of the effects of India as
object of study upon European thought in the Rede Lecture delivered
at the University of Cambridge. He opened by observing the strong
contrast in the reception of Indian matters in England and on the Continent. In England (which then ruled the whole of India, more or less)
Indian topics were regarded as the epitome of dullness, while in other
European countries (excluded from colonial rule of India by England's
monopoly) India was regarded as providing the most exciting of new
problems, holding out the promise of new discoveries. The source of

this intellectual effervescence was the new theory of language that arose from acquaintance with Sanskrit, the ancient language of India—which is to say, the theory of an Indo-European language family comprising (roughly) Sanskrit and its descendants in North India and Sri Lanka, Persian, and the languages of Europe. But what was at issue was more than language—it was ethnology. Modern philology, Maine argued, had suggested a grouping of peoples quite unlike anything that had been thought of before—before, that is, Europeans began to study Sanskrit in the eighteenth century. The bases proposed for common nationality prior to the European study of Sanskrit were very different from those which were now passionately advocated in parts of the Continent. The new ethnology was led by the classifications of languages. Sir Henry's own work in comparative jurisprudence was based upon this ethnological idea, for his researches were directed to the comparison of the laws of Indo-European–speaking peoples in ancient times. Increasingly it was race that appeared to be the object of the ethnology of Indo-Europeans: "For the new theory of language has unquestionably produced a new theory of Race" (Maine 1875:9). The people who were the first speakers of languages of the Indo-European language family had long since come to be called, by a name taken from Sanskrit, Arya (*ārya*) or Aryan.

The Indo-European or Aryan concept is the focus of this book. This concept has certain formal properties of its own that have been more or less stable from its inception in the eighteenth century to the present, as I shall shortly describe. But the premise from which this book sets out is that, notwithstanding this stability of form, the concept has a very different aspect when it is looked upon from different perspectives; specifically that it has a different meaning for the British, their gaze directed toward their empire in India, than it does for those elsewhere in Europe. This requires us to take not only a "formalist" but also a "perspectival" approach to the matter; that is, we must not only analyze the structure of the Indo-European conception as a perduring object but also consider the different readings of it, looking especially at England and the Continent as different readers of a text or having varying perspectives on the same object. Maine puts the Indo-European idea at the center of the excitement about India he perceives on the Continent, and we would be right to infer that in England, where Indian subjects were regarded as dull, it was comparatively neglected. That is true, but there is much more to be said about the British "take," which had its own twist.

The special character of the British concept of the Aryan came to me as an epiphany from a stone inscription written in Sanskrit, which I found in a most unexpected place: Oxford, where I had been reading for many weeks in the Bodleian Library. I was looking at eighteenth- and nineteenth-century British writings on the non-European world, but I began to focus more and more on writings about India, the subject in which I am most at home. Following their conquest of Bengal in the middle of the eighteenth century—the beginnings of their Indian empire—the British had urgent need to answer certain questions: Who are the Indians? What is their place among the nations of the world? What is their relation to us? These are questions that had belonged to the realm of universal history and that would come to belong to an inquiry named ethnology. Conquest provoked the questions, and it also provided the means for a more intimate knowledge of India by which they could be answered. A new Orientalism came into being that was centered on India and, for a few decades, the production of it was practically a monopoly of the scholars of British-Indian Calcutta before it was established in Europe.

Increasingly I had been thinking that India was, for the development of ethnology in Britain, not merely a source for British ethnological discourse which the accidents of history had put in its way, but the very center of its debates. In British eyes India presented the spectacle of a dark-skinned people who were evidently civilized, and as such it constituted the central problem for Victorian anthropology, whose project it was to achieve classifications of human variety consistent with the master idea of the opposition of the dark-skinned savage and the fair-skinned civilized European.[1] To this project India was an enigma, and the intensity of the enigma deepened in the course of the nineteenth century, bursting into scholarly warfare over the competing claims of language and complexion as the foundation of ethnological classifica-

---

1. This notion and the problematic place of India in it appears to have a very long genealogy, extending back to Islamic writers of an early period, for whom Indians were a source of wisdom and science as well as black descendants of Ham. For example, Ṣāʿid ibn Aḥmad Andalusī, in his eleventh-century ethnology (1068:11), says that the Indians were the first nation to have cultivated the sciences, and that although black, Allah ranked them above many white and brown peoples. The opposition of negritude to science doubtless has to do with the darkening face of slavery in the international slave trade, both European and Middle Eastern, as elucidated in a masterly article by William McKee Evans (1980), "From the land of Canaan to the Land of Guinea: The strange odyssey of the 'Sons of Ham.'" We will return to this problem and these authors in the concluding chapter.

tion. India, thus, was the site of a *Methodenstreit* among Victorian Britons who were in the process of creating a "science of man" that concerned the respective claims of language and physique. By century's end a deep and lasting consensus was reached respecting India, which I call the racial theory of Indian civilization: that India's civilization was produced by the clash and subsequent mixture of light-skinned civilizing invaders (the Aryans) and dark-skinned barbarian aborigines (often identified as Dravidians). The racial theory of Indian civilization has proved remarkably durable and resistant to new information, and it persists to this day. It is the crabgrass of Indian history, and I should like to uproot it.

It seemed to me that there might be more than the obvious to be found in an examination of British ethnologies of India in the period of empire and the creation of anthropology as a specialized science. It seemed possible, if one respected the tension between the cognitive and the ideological, the scientific and the political (instead of simply reducing the one to the other), to make discoveries—to find new things that were not merely answers contained in the question.

There was first, though, the question of a cup of tea. This was not to be had, I soon decided, from the machine in the gloomy readers' common room in the bowels of the nearby Clarendon Building. The History Faculty Library, in the Old Indian Institute Building, offered better tea, amiable porters, and history students for company. As it happens, there is a foundation stone with Sanskrit verses inscribed in modern Nagari script at the entryway, but it was only after passing it many times that I stopped to read it. The first and last verses struck me forcibly:

> śāleyaṃ prācyaśāstrāṇāṃ jñānottejanatatparaiḥ |
> paropakāribhiḥ sadbhiḥ sthāpitāryopayoginī || 1 ||
> [ . . . ]
> īśānukampayā nityam āryavidyā mahīyatām |
> āryāvartāṅglabhūmyoś ca mitho maittrī vivardhatām || 4 ||

Beneath the stone inscription is a brass plate, inscribed with the official English translation:

This building, dedicated to Eastern sciences, was founded for the use of Aryas (Indians and Englishmen) by excellent and benevolent men desirous of encouraging knowledge. . . . By the favour of God may the learning and literature of India be ever held in honour; and may the mutual friendship of India and England constantly increase!

श्रालेयं प्राच्यशास्त्राणां ज्ञानोत्तेजनतत्परैः ।
परोपकारिभिः सद्भिः स्थापितार्यौपयोगिनी ॥ १ ॥
श्राल्वर्टेडुर्डितिख्यातो युवराजो महामनाः ।
राजराजेश्वरीपुत्रक्षत्रप्रतिष्ठां व्यधात्स्वयम् ॥ २ ॥

अङ्करामाङ्कचन्द्रेऽब्दे वैशाखस्यासिते दले ।
दशम्यां बुधवारे च वास्तुविधिरभूदिह ॥ ३ ॥

ईशानुकम्पया नित्यमार्यविद्या महीयताम् ।
आर्यावर्ताङ्गलभूम्योश्च मिथो मैत्री विवर्धताम् ॥

This Building, dedicated to Eastern sciences, was founded for the use of
Aryas (Indians and Englishmen) by excellent and benevolent men desirous
of encouraging knowledge. The High-minded Heir-Apparent, named Albert
Edward, Son of the Empress of India, himself performed the act of inauguration. The ceremony of laying the Memorial Stone took place on Wednesday, the tenth lunar day of the dark half of the month of Vaiśākha, in the
Samvat year 1939 (= Wednesday, May 2, 1883). By the favor of God may
the learning and literature of India be ever held in honour; and may the mutual friendship of India and England constantly increase!

Figure 1. Sanskrit inscription in the Old Indian Institute Building, Oxford.

What is so curious about this inscription is the use of the Sanskrit
word *ārya* in novel and contradictory ways that repay a closer look. To
begin, the building is "for the use of Aryas" (*āryopayoginī*), and the
official translation instructs us that this is to be taken in an inclusive
sense, to mean both Indians and Englishmen. In other European set-
tings and in other times a sign saying "for the use of Aryas" would
be taken to have an exclusive sense, denying entry to Jews, Gypsies,
and non-whites generally. Yet both senses of *Arya* or *Aryan*, the inclusive one of the Oxford inscription and the exclusive one of the ideolo-
gists of racial hatred, come from different perspectives on the same construct, the idea of an Aryan people (whether conceived as a race or not),
which is the human substrate of the family of languages called Indo-
European.[2]

2. Joan Leopold was the first to see the significance of the Oxford inscription. Her
articles speak directly to several of the issues of this book and have been helpful guides to
the sources (Leopold 1970, 1974a, 1974b).

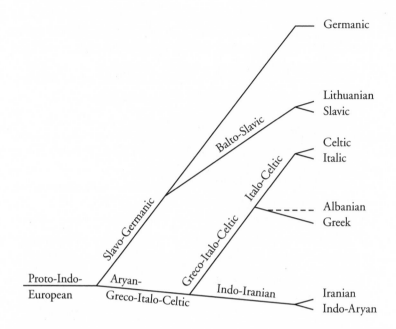

Figure 2. Schleicher's family tree of Indo-European languages.

Although the word *ārya* is a Sanskrit one, the construct in question is unmistakably European and by no means native to Sanskrit. It comes from the European study of Sanskrit in the eighteenth and nineteenth centuries. The discovery that Sanskrit was very similar to ancient Greek and Latin, and more distantly to the modern languages of Europe, led to the unexpected groupings of languages and peoples to which Sir Henry Maine alludes. The relationships among the Indo-European languages are understood by means of a genealogical diagram or family tree as in the one published by August Schleicher in 1861 (figure 2). Thus the Indic languages (Sanskrit and its descendants in North India and Sri Lanka) are closely related to the Iranian languages; they are more distantly related (reading up the diagram) to Greek and Albanian, the Celtic (e.g., Irish, Welsh) and Italic (Latin and the Romance languages, e.g., French, Spanish, Italian, Rumanian), the Balto-Slavic group (including Russian), and the Germanic group (including English). Relations of near and far are calibrated by the branching structure of the family tree, and the whole expresses a conception of the progressive differentiation and radiation across Eurasia of languages from a common ancestral language. This ancestral language is called Proto-Indo-European. It is a scholarly construct of a language for which we have no direct trace and which is known wholly by inference from the shared features of the languages of this family. What makes the family relation of these languages surprising and unexpected is that they do not form a single geographical area. Languages of the Indo-Iranian branch form one region (Iran, Afghanistan, Pakistan, India, Sri Lanka, Bangladesh), the others another (Europe and parts of the former Soviet Union), and the two regions are separated by a wedge consisting of Turkey and the Arabic-speaking countries (figure 3).

Other language groups fall outside this figure, including the Semitic languages such as Hebrew, Arabic, Aramaic, and Amharic, and the Hamitic languages of North Africa. There are several ways the relations among distinct language families might be understood, but the dominant trend within comparative philology or historical linguistics is to say that the relationships of these (or any other family of languages in the world) to the Indo-European languages is remote, perhaps more remote than philological study at a given time can demonstrate, in that they are all branchings of a common tree at a level deeper than that of the Proto-Indo-European node, which is the starting point of the Indo-European tree. Indeed, several scholars of the nineteenth century believed what could not then be shown, and what historical linguists of today demonstrate: The Indo-European and Semitic families (to take a historically salient example) are historically related at a deeper level. The ideal end of the historical-linguistic project is to subsume all the languages of the world into a single family tree. It is easy to show that this impulse continues to run strong. One thinks immediately of the work of Joseph Greenberg to unify the various language families of Africa (1955) and of the Americas (1987), or of the "Nostratic" superfamily posited by V. M. Illich-Svitych (see Manaster Ramer 1993).

Thus the figure of the family tree or *Stammbaum* is not confined to the Indo-European idea but pervades historical linguistics as its master image. It becomes necessary at this point to temporarily take leave of the Oxford inscription in order to take up the formalist side of the inquiry. There are several important matters of the structure and history of this master image that need to be stated right at the outset, even though much of what I say here will be substantiated only in chapters to come.

The matter is so important because the tree image not only serves as the master image for historical linguistics but also has been of major

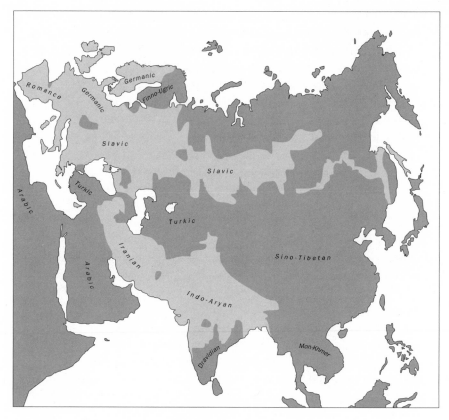

Figure 3. Map of the Indo-European languages.

importance in ethnological discussion and in Darwinian biology. As I have argued elsewhere, British (and American) ethnological thought in the eighteenth and nineteenth centuries was guided by two master figures, the tree and the staircase. The first is the branching tree-of-nations image that ethnologists share with linguists, and the second is the stepped staircase of progressive succession of forms, the "scale of civilization" that subtends the notion of the stages of social evolution (Trautmann 1987, 1992a). The stage theory of social evolutionism that so dominated the anthropology that emerged in the 1860s and 1870s in Britain is very well known to us and constitutes our shared sense of the anthropological past. But we have little collective recollection of the very great power of the tree image, which (as I shall be arguing in this book) dominated British ethnological thinking from Sir William Jones to James Cowles Prichard—that is, roughly from 1780 to 1850. While the tree remains a powerful paradigm in historical linguistics and in biology (which has recently given it a new-old name, "cladistics"), it has long since faded from ethnology, and an effort of the imagination is required to recover a sense of its former dominance. Each of these ideas has a long pedigree. The scale of civilization is an elaboration of Aristotle's scale of nature, and the tree of nations is from the Biblical book of Genesis attributed to Moses, whence I speak of "Mosaic ethnology" as the kind of ethnological thinking that has this treelike structure. It is sometimes suggested that linguistic and ethnological usage of the tree idea derives from biology, specifically comparative physiology, but Charles Darwin makes it quite clear in his great chapter on classification in *On the origin of species* (1859) that the influence runs from linguistics/ethnology to biology (see chapter 2).

Coming now to the structure of the tree image, we see on examination that the family tree in question (as in figure 2, for example) is of a peculiar type, one in which there are no marriages to tie up the ends of a descent structure which, therefore, ramifies endlessly. It is a kinship structure of unilineal type, like the patrilineages of the Nuer social structure to which E. E. Evans-Pritchard (1940) gave the name segmentary lineage. *Segmentary* is a somewhat opaque term, but it becomes clear if one considers its source, Emile Durkheim's *Division of labor* (*De la division du travail sociale,* 1893). Durkheim wished to contrast two types of society (call them complex and simple) based on his conception of the two fundamental types of solidarity. Organic solidarity is the kind of social cohesion that comes about through the division of labor, by the interdependence it establishes among subgroups of specialists, whereas mechanical solidarity is the weaker form of social cohesion arising from the similarity to one another of the members of a simpler kind of society that lacks a division of labor. The ideal type of a simple society based on mechanical solidarity would be one in which there is no specialization of functions and in which the internal divisions of the society (moieties, clans, marriage classes) are homogeneous in structure and content, like the segments of a worm. Hence the term *segmentary,* which Durkheim got from the zoologists. Building on Durkheim's work, Evans-Pritchard's concept of the segmentary lineage characterizes the ideology of a society segmented into lineages, but one in which there is neither a state to create solidarity by force nor a specialization of economic functions integrating the groups through structures of exchange.

The segmentary lineage is a certain kind of genealogical figure in which (to put it briefly) relations among the living are understood and calibrated for nearness by reference to common ancestry, with the result that everyone within the structure (which could be the entire human race, as is potentially the case for linguistic trees) is related to everyone else, and everyone of the same generation is a sibling or cousin of a specifiable degree. In societies with a segmentary way of thinking the function of such calibration of nearness is to determine with whom and against whom to side in a dispute: "My brother and me against my cousin; my brother and my cousin against my distant relation," and so forth. It is not a question of self versus other, but of a universe of thought in which *everyone* is imagined to be kin, albeit sometimes warring kin, internally divided by a gradation of nearness with as many grades as may be required. The totality of the figure is built up of segments, each one of which is alike in structure to every other irrespective of scale: Larger units comprise smaller units that are of the same structure.

Thinking of this kind is important to our inquiry because it is characteristic of the story of the descent of Noah in the Bible, whence universal histories among Jews, Christians, and Muslims have had, over many centuries, a segmentary character, which they impart to the ethnological and linguistic discussions that are the object of this book. Not only is the segmentary lineage an *object of* ethnological thought, it also has been an important thought structure *for* ethnological thought through a very long period, beginning with Biblical times and continuing into the nineteenth century (although it has been overtaken by other forms and become largely forgotten within anthropology).

In our own time segmentary thinking retains a place in linguistics, but in ethnology it is largely replaced by the familiar Hegelian binary of Self versus Other (Hegel 1807), as deployed by the structuralists, particularly Claude Lévi-Strauss, who taught us how to use it. It is undoubtedly a very useful tool of analysis. Any congeries of relations (segmentary trees included), no matter how complex, can be analyzed into so many nesting oppositions of self/other at successive levels of generality. The segmentary idea is quite different. Instead of difference it assumes sameness (kinship), which it then partitions along a calculus of distance. Thus every position within the segmentary universe is both self and other at one and the same time, but the system allows for infinite modulations between oneself and the most distant point in that universe. It takes nothing away from the method of binarism (which I use) to say that it has become overworked these days by virtue of its own success, which has grown even greater under postmodernism than it had been under structuralism. There are, however, analytic tasks for which the old segmentary way of thinking has proven and continues to prove indispensable.

Like any principle of classification, the segmentary idea derives its great power to order large amounts of information into a general scheme of things from its ability to simplify, and the information that is left aside in order to make these simplifications is itself of a characteristic kind. Every analytic has its shortcomings, and it is important to be aware of what exactly they are. To impose the radiating logic of segmentation upon language history or ethnological classifications one has to remove or ignore or deal in other ways with the phenomena produced by convergence of languages and peoples in the formation of new languages and new peoples. Specifically, the segmentary logic of the family tree of languages or of nations prevents and disallows the idea of *mixture* as a creative principle.

In segmentary systems inclusion and exclusion are not given by the structure alone, but are relative to the social location of any particular episode of conflict; that is, they are determined by the relative positions of everyone to the parties in conflict, solidarity following segmentary nearness.[3] It is in this sense, it seems to me, that the inclusiveness or exclusiveness that attaches to the word *Aryan* is not given by the structure independently of the situation. And—returning to the inscription at the Old Indian Institute—as our text so plainly shows, British rule of India imparts to the word an inescapably inclusive significance for Britons of that period.

The single passage I have quoted together with its officially sanctioned translation, "for the use of Aryas (Indians and Englishmen)," would be enough, without any further information, to establish that the word *Arya* is here used in a sense that it did not have in older Sanskrit literature, and that the inscription cannot predate the nineteenth

---

3. There is of course a large bibliography on segmentation. I have relied on Paul Dresch's *Tribes, government, and history in Yemen* (1989), an exceptionally fine treatment of segmentary principles, together with his important 1988 article, "Segmentation: Its roots in Arabia and its flowering elsewhere." Segmentation, in the end, has a forking genealogy: The lexeme (and part of the semantics, the idea of mechanical solidarity) leads back to Durkheim and thence to the segmentary structures of zoology, but the structure of segmentary *lineages* as an anthropological concept derives from certain societies of the Middle East and the Biblical concept of the tree of nations that I discuss in chapter 2.

century. The inscription was in fact composed by the Boden Professor of Sanskrit at Oxford, Monier Monier-Williams, as we know from other sources, but even if we did not know this we would guess from the construction of *Arya* in the first stanza that its author was a practitioner or at least an admirer of the comparative philology of the nineteenth century. The middle verses from the inscription would confirm this conjecture, at least as to the time horizon: The act of inauguration was performed by the high-minded heir apparent, named Albert Edward (*ālbarṭ-eḍvarḍ iti khyāto yuvarājo mahāmanaḥ*), son of the Empress of India (the *rājarājeśvarī*, Victoria). The date is given as Wednesday, the tenth lunar day of the dark fortnight of the month of Vaiśākha, Samvat 1939, which is to say, A.D. 2 May 1883.

But *ārya* also occurs, twice, in compounds in the second of the two verses I have quoted, in quite a different sense. In those places the official translation implies that it means not Indians and Englishman (that is, the Aryan or Indo-European people), but Indians alone and in opposition to the English. Thus we are given *āryavidyā*, "Aryan learning," a compound devised for the occasion to refer to the "language and literature of India," and *Āryāvarta* (anciently North India), in the new meaning of India as a whole, contrasted to *Aṅglabhūmi*, a translation of the name England. This is of course inconsistent with the inclusive sense that the author intends for *Arya* in the first stanza.

Professor Monier-Williams was perfectly aware of the prephilological referents of the word *ārya* in Sanskrit literature, for they are given in his *Sanskrit-English dictionary* (Monier-Williams 1899). Looking up the entry for *Arya* we find the following significations: a respectable or honorable or faithful man, an inhabitant of Āryāvarta; one who is faithful to the religion of that country; name of the race that immigrated from Central Asia into Āryāvarta, opposed to *an-ārya, Dasyu, Dāsa* (although here we would have to say that the use of the word *race* and the reference to Central Asia comes from European ideas and not from Sanskrit texts); in later times the name of the first three castes, Brāhmaṇa, Kṣatriya, Vaiśya, as opposed to Śūdra; in Buddhism, a man who has thought on the four chief truths of Buddhism (the *āryasatyas*) and lives accordingly; someone behaving like an Aryan, worthy of one, honorable, respectable, noble; of a good family; excellent; wise; suitable. . . . Monier-Williams would have known, too, that in a Sanskrit text an Englishman would be—insofar as an Englishman would figure in a work of Sanskrit—a Mleccha (outcaste, barbarian), or Yavana (Ionian, Greek, Westerner), conceivably a Hūṇa (judging from *Hūṇa-*

*pati,* "Hun lord," for the French general Dupleix in the eighteenth century), or perhaps the Aṅgla implied by the *Aṅgla-land* of this inscription—but by no means an Arya. If the Old Indian Institute had fallen to ruin and we had only the Sanskrit inscription on the foundation stone to go by we would reach a very different reading of it than that which the official translation imposes on us. We would presume internal consistency in the use of *Arya* and come to the conclusion that a building had been built in central Oxford for the use of Indians, and that Englishmen must keep out! This is not altogether fanciful, for Monier-Williams himself said that the very name Indian Institute tended to be taken in that way (Indian Institute 1887).

The broader usage of the term *Arya* is largely due to Friedrich Max Müller, who took the word from Sanskrit and applied it to the family of languages now called Indo-European and the peoples speaking them. As we shall see in the next chapter, the concept of the Indo-European language family had been clearly articulated by Sir William Jones in 1786 as a group of related languages consisting of Sanskrit, Latin, Greek, Gothic, Celtic, and Old Persian, codescended from a lost ancestral language, although he did not give this language family a name. The "original stock" that spoke the ancestral language he simply called Indian or Hindu. In the early nineteenth century the name for the language family and its peoples varied among four main choices. From the Bible narrative of Noah and his three sons, Shem, Ham, and Japhet, came the name Japhetic for this family; unlike the coordinate names Semitic and Hamitic, which are still in use for language families, the name Japhetic did not last long. German philologists preferred "Indo-Germanic," devised by Heinrich Klaproth in 1823 (see Schwab 1984:184), but non-Germans resisted. The English linguist Arthur Young proposed "Indo-European" as early as 1813, and it eventually displaced the other terms (Young 1813). But "Aryan" had a long innings.

What made "Aryan" seem appropriate was that it was not only the name Sanskrit speakers gave themselves, but it was also used by the speakers of Old Persian; indeed, the name Iran is derived from a genitive plural of this word, meaning "(land) of the Aryas" (the *Ariana* of Greek sources, equivalent to Sanskrit *āryāṇām*). Some thought that the name Arya was not confined to the Indo-Iranian branch of the Indo-European family but was also found, for example, in the name for Ireland, Eire. Thus it was argued that "Aryan" was the self-designation not only of those who spoke ancient languages of the Indo-Iranian branch of the Indo-European family but, since it was found as well in the most distant branches of the Indo-European linguistic family tree, also of the ancestral Proto-Indo-European language. To these considerations Max Müller brought others. He observed that Zoroastrian sources oppose Iran, land of the Aryas, to Turan, the Central Asian land of nomads, and he proposed a Turanian language family to comprehend the latter, the core of which consisted of languages we would call Turkik. He explained the name Turan as connected with the "swiftness of the horse" (via Sanskrit *turanga*, "horse," that is, *tura* + *ga*, "swift-goer"), whence it refers to the nomadism of the Central Asian enemies of Iranians. Under this construction, "Turan" is neatly opposed to "Aryan," which he connected with plowing (cf. Latin *arare*, "to plow"); thus, for him, Aryans are people who practice agriculture and who self-consciously named themselves as farmers over against the nomadic pastoralists who were their neighbors and enemies (Max Müller 1861:248). These etymologies are no longer taken seriously, but they express the sense widely held by those who use "Aryan" to mean a people in a higher state of social evolution.

For us, as children of the twentieth century, the name Aryan has different, far more sinister connotations. Associated forever with the Nazi atrocities of the recent past, it continues in the present through racial hate groups who use it to evoke the full force of the racist idea: mental differences among races that are original and unchangeable; the superiority of whites; the preservation of the racial purity of whites by separation from Jews, blacks, Asians, and others. Through these associations the name Aryan joins the memory of deeds that have defined for us the farthest extreme of human evil with one of the great and enduring intellectual accomplishments of modern times, the discovery of Sanskrit's relation to the languages of Europe and through it the creation of historical linguistics. It is hardly surprising therefore that the use of "Aryan," so popular up to World War II, is now poison for linguists and has given way completely to "Indo-European." "Aryan" lingers among them only where it is directly justified, namely in relation to India and Iran, specifically in the name Indo-Aryan for languages of the Indian branch of the Indo-European family and occasionally as a name for speakers of the lost common language of the Indo-Iranian subfamily.

The long shadow of the death camps casts itself backward, darkening the aspect of nineteenth-century linguistic and ethnological thought. The Aryan concept is the central idea of twentieth-century fascisms, and the fact that it was developed by scholars raises the question of the role scholars have played in preparing the way for these appropriations. Ethnological ideas belong inescapably to the realm of moral reasoning, and their misuses are properly subject to moral evaluation. The need to combat the appropriations of science by Nazis, segregationists, and hate groups has led to the writing of a number of books exploring ways in which linguists and ethnologists have provided the materials for such appropriations and in some cases participated willingly in them.[4]

The story of this book, however, is a different Aryan story. It has a shape all its own and is by no means a simple inversion of the better-known one. It is at the outset, if I may call it that at the risk of being misunderstood, a love story. I mean to use "love" as a cover term of very large reach, as the genus of which the many species include not only erotic love but also such forms of human solidarity as familial love (including the mechanical solidarity of brothers in a segmentary line-age), friendship, the affection of master to servant, and the loyalty of servant to master. This Aryan story is a story of love in several senses. In the first place it inquires into the relation of Briton and Indian to each other and gives unexpected news: We are long-lost kin; we are Aryan brethren, to use the phrase of Max Müller. The colonial encounter of the two nations thereupon takes on the sense of one of those television programs in which orphans separated at a tender age are reunited many years after—the Aryan love story as family reunion. In the British vision of India, then, the Aryan idea always has the function of being a sign of the kinship between the two nations. Since this is so, the Aryan idea and the Orientalism that sustains it tend to be associated with discussion of the ways in which Indians may be bound to British rule by some

4. Léon Poliakov's *The Aryan myth* (1974) is very good treatment of the Aryan concept and anti-Semitism, written from a depth-psychology viewpoint. Martin Bernal's ambitious *Black Athena* (1987; to comprise four volumes) touches this issue, in that the author makes the case that anti-Semitism was the primary reason European scholars of the nineteenth century abandoned the idea of the Egyptian origins of Greek civilization in favor of the newly discovered Indo-European connection. However, the argument in that strong form seems quite wrong for, as we shall see, India and Egypt were not opposed but intertwined in the beginnings of the Indo-European idea, and remained so until the non-Indo-European character of the Coptic language of Egypt became clear and the hieroglyphics were deciphered. If anything, nineteenth-century European and Euroamerican discussion of Egypt, so far from driving a wedge between the ancient Egyptians and the Greeks, tended rather to make the Egyptians white, uniting them with the Greeks and driving a wedge between them and black Africans. This is especially so in the notorious *Types of mankind* of J. C. Nott and George R. Gliddon (1854). The recent book of Maurice Olender is a very good survey of European philology and ethnology from J. G. Herder to Ignaz Goldziher: *The languages of paradise: Race, religion and philology in the nineteenth century* (1992).

form of love, whether of solidarity, of "firm attachment," loyalty, or friendship. We see that function in the last verse of Monier-Williams's inscription, calling for the friendship (*maitri*) of the two nations.

Now, everything depends on what exactly "friendship" (or any other species of love under conditions of colonial rule) may mean to the British and the Indians in expressions of this kind. In the case in hand we can consult the speech that Monier-Williams gave in 1884 at the ceremony marking the opening of the completed half of the Indian Institute building that he had done so much to bring about. He makes it very clear that this is not a friendship of equals.

It was always his desire, Monier-Williams said, "that the Indian Institute should have, so to speak, two wings, one spreading itself to foster Eastern studies among Europeans, the other extending itself to foster Western studies among Indians" (Indian Institute 1887:46). The Europeans in question were the Indian Civil Service Probationers at Oxford, who were given a yearly stipend of £150 by their London masters, the Civil Service Commissioners, and were housed in Oxford colleges while they were studying in the Indian Institute and sitting examinations in London. They would be, he hoped, "well trained physically, morally, and mentally, well formed in character, well informed in mind, well instructed in Indian languages, law, and history, carefully imbued with a respect for those they will have to govern, free from all tendency to self-conceit and arrogance of manner, capable of governing themselves that they may govern others, able to be firm, yet not overbearing, conciliatory, yet not weak, patterns of justice and morality, models of Christian truth, rectitude, and integrity" (1887:40). Thus the meanings of love, of Britons toward Indians: love as paternalism without arrogance.

Monier-Williams's hopes of having fellowships for Indians attached to the Indian Institute were not being realized, however, and he felt the disappointment acutely. His reasons for wanting to assist young Indians to attend Oxford derived from an analysis of Indian needs that is, to my mind, astonishing: Indians, he claims, have inadequate family life and lack the benefits of English public schools. "From what I have seen of the youthful natives of India in their own country," he says, "and from my knowledge of the debilitating effects of Indian home life, and the absence of all strengthening influences like those of our Public School system, I am convinced that no young Indian is fit to stand alone at an English University . . . [and] will return to India deteriorated in character rather than improved" (1887:47). Strange as that diagnosis sounds today, it was part of the standard British Protestant critique of the Indian family as a source of moral decay, first formulated by William Wilberforce (1813). Whatever we may make of the diagnosis, the fact is that the parties did not meet, and the intended "interchange of the literary wealth of Asia and Europe . . . repaying with interest the wisdom and knowledge received centuries ago from the East" (Indian Institute 1887:46) on common ground did not happen. Something was always coming between the British and the Indians and preventing their friendship. In the end was not that something the colonial relation itself?[5]

The whole argument with its contradictory elements of love and coercion sounds like a distant echo of the classic statement of Warren Hastings, architect of the Orientalist policy, in the preface to the first English translation of the *Bhagavad Gītā* by Charles Wilkins, published in 1785:

Every accumulation of knowledge, and especially such as is obtained by social communication with people over whom we exercise a dominion founded on the right of conquest, is useful to the state: it is the gain of humanity: in the specific instance which I have stated, it attracts and conciliates distant affections; it lessens the weight of the chain by which the natives are held in subjection; and it imprints on the hearts of our own countrymen the sense and obligation of benevolence. (*Bhagavad Gītā* 1785:13)

Whereas Hastings wrote modestly and realistically of conciliating affections that were distant and recognized that the bond between Briton and Indian was a heavy chain that could, at best, be lightened, his Orientalist successors spoke of love and brotherhood as if colonial rule was a happy family reunion and coercion had nothing to do with it. A central issue for the British in their arguments over Indian policy was how the Indians might be made to love the British regime. In the paradigm wars the British fought among themselves over India, the

---

5. Nicholas Dirks recalls the frustrated friendship of Aziz and Fielding in E. M. Forster's *A passage to India:*

The novel concludes with a kind of natural closure that reiterates the inscription of colonialism in India's landscape. For in spite of an extraordinary past of intimacy and support, Aziz and Fielding could not be friends, would not be friends, not until the Indians had driven "every blasted Englishman into the sea." In the words of the final paragraph: "The horses didn't want it—they swerved apart; the earth didn't want it, sending up rocks through which riders must pass single file; the temples, the tank, the jail, the palace, the birds, the carrion, the Guest House . . . : they didn't want it, they said in their hundred voices, 'No, not yet,' and the sky said, 'No, not there.' " Not until the antinomy of native nature and colonial culture was dissolved through the closure of colonialism itself would Aziz and Fielding be in a position to engage with each other as genuine friends. (Dirks 1992:2).

Orientalists embraced the Indo-European idea and were identified with the politics of love; those who rejected the politics of love rejected the Indo-European idea, and Orientalism, as well.

I hope I have said sufficient to make it clear that I do *not* mean that British Orientalism promoted affection between Britons and Indians as a matter of fact. I am speaking rather of Orientalist *representations*. I mean to say that British Orientalists devised a theory of their own activities (further discussed in the next chapter) that involved *claims* about promoting affection between ruler and ruled and a political *rhetoric* of love. The Indo-European concept was foundational for this position, and accordingly the nearness of kinship between Briton and Indian tended to be stressed by Orientalists. At a more general level, to anticipate a misunderstanding of another sort, I am *not* saying that the effect of the Indo-European or Aryan concept was to promote British affection for Indians. The Aryan idea stood as a sign of kinship and the political rhetoric of love; those who rejected the rhetoric of love, and they were many, tended also to ignore or attack the Aryan idea, to deny a close kinship of Britons and Indians, and to oppose the Orientalists. I shall give examples of this anti-Orientalist rejectionism in chapter 4.

This study lies within the territory opened up for exploration by Bernard S. Cohn, which he has called the construction of the colonial sociology of India. I think of such notable papers as "Notes on the history of the study of Indian society and culture" (1968), "The command of language and the language of command" (1985), and "The census, social structure and objectification in South Asia" (in Cohn 1990:224–254), some of which were given in seminar and became widely influential long before their publication. The achievement of this fine body of work is to have shown that the knowledge of India that is current today is the product of the colonial situation and to have elucidated the process of its production by a wide variety of types such as Orientalists, missionaries, and administrators, and by state institutions such as the census. In this book I will focus more narrowly upon the Orientalists, specifically the British Sanskritists, because (as I believe and will try to show) it was they who supplied the theoretical structures that dominated and directed the construction of ethnologies of India.

The importance of Cohn's work lies in the fact that it is very good history and, because the object of study is the built-up structure of sociological constructs about India, that it is at the same time a critique and reconstruction of existing knowledge, bringing expertise to bear in the reformulation of itself. In the same vein are some notable works of historiography, such as David Lorenzen's "Imperialism and the historiography of ancient India" (1982) and writings of Romila Thapar, culminating in her recent book, *Interpreting early India* (1993).

In the meantime, Edward Said's *Orientalism* (1978) has appeared, bringing a harsher critique to bear. Coming from outside the guild and concerned with the Middle East rather than India, it is nevertheless a book that has brought about a revolution of opinion among Indianists. Like all revolutions it has been divisive and violent in its effects.

Said's argument, briefly, is an extension to the colonial world of Michel Foucault's concept of power/knowledge: that power and knowledge implicate each other (Foucault 1979). The two terms are particularized by Said to colonial power and Orientalist knowledge, or Orientalism. Put in this bare way, the Saidian thesis would be perfectly agreeable to the British Sanskritists of whom I shall be speaking, who were all of them empire loyalists and for whom the relation of their intellectual work to the governance of India was by no means concealed or shamefaced. What has generated a large and growing literature on Orientalism is not the bare fact of that relation, which lay open to view and did not need to be unmasked, nor again the fact that the ethnological thinking of the present has its origins in a colonial past, which has always been evident. What constituted the success of Said's book was that it exploded the comforting sense of "that was then and this is now" and implanted in its place a sense that "all academic knowledge about India and Egypt is somehow tinged and impressed with, violated by, the gross political fact" (1978:11). Since the appearance of Said's book, we cannot discuss current knowledge of Asia without a far more acute sense of the relevance to it of the colonial conditions under which such knowledge came into being than that which we have held.

For those whose training was in the Orientalist tradition, the Saidian attack was something of a surprise. Does studying the ancient languages of Asia hold out the prospect of lucrative careers and an abundance of jobs among which to choose or influence in the formation of government policy? If anything, the public image of Orientalism before Said was that of Proust, for whom (in his great novel) the Professor of Sanskrit alternates with the Professor of Tamil as the very type of the dry old stick, the ineffectual academic, the purveyor of arcane knowledge who has few students. Scholars are used to such cruel jibes from the great writers, but the changed image of Orientalism in Said—from dreamy obscurantism to the intellectual Foreign Legion of Europe—was a shocking reversal.

What needs to be kept in mind when weighing the claims of the book is that for Said—and this is a crucial move—Orientalism is not limited to the intellectual product of Orientalists. Said's Orientalism includes as well (as we could expect from a literary critic) the Orientalism of poets, and painters, and more. Orientalism is "the corporate institution for dealing with the Orient—dealing with it by making statements about it, authorizing views of it, describing it, by teaching it, settling it, ruling over it: in short, Orientalism as a Western style for dominating, restructuring, and having an authority over it" (1978:3). In the end, for Said, Orientalism is any European pronouncement about the Orient that is made with a show of authority. The Saidian expansionary redefinition of Orientalism unites the productions of Orientalists and non-Orientalists, both of the colonial past and of the postcolonial present.

Said's concept of Orientalism can be illustrated with a contemporary example. Henry Kissinger, in the chapter in his memoirs on "The India-Pakistan Crisis of 1971," has this to say about South Asia:

Bordered on the south by the Indian Ocean, on the north by the Himalayas, and on the west by the Hindu Kush mountains that merge with the heavens as if determined to seal off the teeming masses, and petering out in the east in the marshes and rivers of Bengal, the Indian subcontinent has existed through the millennia as a world apart. Its northern plains simmer in enervating heat in summer and are assailed by incongruous frost in winter; its lush south invites a life of tranquillity and repose. Its polyglot peoples testify to the waves of conquerors who have descended upon it through the mountain passes, from neighboring deserts, and occasionally from across the sea. Huns, Mongols, Greeks, Persians, Moguls, Afghans, Portuguese, and at last Britons have established empires and then vanished, leaving multitudes oblivious of either the coming or the going. (1979:842)

The passage is remarkable for the way in which the burden is carried by the adjectives: *teeming, enervating, incongruous, lush, polyglot, oblivious;* almost by themselves they sketch a view of Indian civilization—shaped by climate and landscape, unchanged by history—that comes straight out of the eighteenth century. The writer has more in the same vein, and worse, but I will spare readers the painful details. Enough has been given, I think, to conclude that in the corridors of power where ideas may have very real consequences there do indeed circulate general views of Indian civilization that, although they strike one as parodies, have a genealogical affiliation with things that Orientalists have written over the centuries. It is this order of facts that makes Said's argument persuasive and the inflationary redefinition of Orientalism seem well founded, linking the non-Orientalist Kissinger of the present with the knowledge production of a colonial past.

Even if one finds it persuasive, however, considerable problems arise when one wishes to translate Said's book into the terms of South Asia. In the first place he limits his argument to discussion of the French and British in their relation to the Arabs, which is constructed as but one "case" of the more general phenomenon he calls Orientalism, and inevitably the specificities of that particular triangular relation shape generalizations about Orientalism in ways that will not be applicable to the "case" of India under British rule. In the second place the work is one of polemic, meant to stir things up and set discussion going in a new direction (and in this it has been immensely successful), but of course the tools of polemic are rather blunt instruments and are not always used with the best of manners. What is needed to make the book useful for India is a double translation, out of the terms of the Middle East and into those of South Asia, and from polemic into analysis.[6]

This effort is well under way, and one of the most notable results came out of the 1988–89 South Asia Seminar at the University of Pennsylvania, namely the collection of papers edited by Carol Breckenridge and Peter van der Veer titled *Orientalism and the postcolonial predicament* (1993). One gathers from the preface that the book did not come about without personal turmoil, disagreement, complaints of Orientalist-bashing, and published opposition, so that its pro-Saidian contents are by no means the whole story of the Indianist response. Another direct response is Ronald Inden's *Imagining India* (1990), an ambitious attempt to apply a Saidian reading to the four big topics of Indology—caste, Hinduism, the village, and kingship—and it does so with learning and vigor. The root-and-branch extremity of its criticism is disarming: Inden flays practically everyone in sight, including close colleagues and even his own earlier work. Quite different is Wilhelm Halbfass's *India and Europe: An essay in understanding* (1988), a superb study of the place of India in the Western philosophical tradition and the effect of the latter upon Indian philosophy. This is a topic that could be subjected to a Saidian analysis, but in fact Said does not merit so much as a single entry in the index. The wide space between these landmarks tends to show how vague the Saidian thesis is, and how underdetermined and various its applications to India are bound to be.

The problem of translating Said into Indian terms, as I see it, goes

---

6. James Clifford's review of Said strikes me as the one that gets both the strengths and weaknesses of the book just right (1988:255–276).

something like this: One begins by observing, with David Ludden (1993), that Foucault's power/knowledge and Said's colonialism/Orientalism are badly underspecified. These formulations offer us a direction in which to pitch our attention but very little guidance about what to do with what we find. To say that colonialism and Orientalism are mutually entailed does not get us very far. What about the Orientalist study of Europeans before colonial rule, as exampled by the Orientalism of diplomacy, Christian missions, trade, and the "philosophical traveler"? How does Said's thesis help us understand the special enthusiasm of the Germans for Orientalist study? In these and other ways we are left asea.

As to the "case" of India, at first blush it exemplifies the Saidian thesis even better than does the Middle East. To show the full-blown conjuncture of Orientalist and scientific information gathering with colonialism in the Middle East, Said must start with Napoleon's expedition to Egypt, which came rather late and did not last very long. European colonialism of an extensive and durable kind is established much earlier in India (in the mid-eighteenth century) than in the Middle East. What is more, its conjuncture with Orientalism was originary and deep. The government formed by Warren Hastings after the conquest of Bengal was committed to an Orientalist policy of respecting Indian religion and law and committed thereby to developing and controlling knowledge of them through knowledge of Indian languages. The formation of the Asiatic Society in 1784 to promote the scientific study of Asia, and the issuance of the Society's famous journal, *Asiatic researches,* and the founding of the College of Fort William in 1800 for the education of civil servants in the seat of colonial government insured that an overlapping roster of persons, British and Indian, were jointly engaged in the advancement of Orientalist knowledge, the teaching of Indian languages to servants of the East India Company, the operation of the courts administering Hindu and Muslim law, and the construction and execution of government policy along the lines of Orientalist conceptions. Said would have made his case better by putting India at the center of it.

Nevertheless, it is exactly this close connectedness of Orientalists with government in British India that makes the fuzziness of the Saidian formulation troublesome in another way, one having to do with his expansion of the concept of Orientalism. Orientalists are those whose knowledge of Asian history, religion, and so forth are grounded in mastery of Asian languages, and in the ordinary way Orientalism is the knowledge that Orientalists produce. But, for Said, Orientalism is the whole, more or less, of Western authoritative pronouncements on Asian societies.

There is nothing inherently wrong with such inflationary redefinition of a familiar word, which happens all the time. But it creates the problem that new and older senses of this word trip up one another in discussions of India. Let us tag these two meanings so that we can distinguish them in discussion; call them Orientalism[1] (knowledge produced by Orientalists, scholars who know Asian languages) and Orientalism[2] (European representations of the Orient, whether by Orientalists or others). In India the British Orientalists were by no means a unitary group, but Orientalists constituted the core of a distinct policy group who, as I have said, had been dominant since the time of Hastings and who had devised the Orientalizing policy. This group constituted a faction promoting education in the vernacular languages; these "Orientalists" were in opposition to the "Anglicists," Evangelicals, and others who promoted English as a medium of instruction. The Anglicists were also involved in the production of knowledge of a kind Said calls Orientalism. In this case Orientalism[1] was one party to a dispute within Orientalism[2], and the Saidian expansion of Orientalism, applied in this context, tends to sow confusion where there once was clarity.

Something like this seems to have happened in Inden's book, *Imagining India*, when the author makes the surprising claim that the writings of James Mill and G. W. F. Hegel on India constituted hegemonic texts for Indology (Inden 1990:43–48), which is tantamount to making them the authors of Orientalism for the Indian "case." But neither Mill nor Hegel learned an Indian language or set foot in India, and although they both read deeply in the scholarly productions of Orientalists available to them in European languages, they used their secondhand knowledge to fashion arguments *against* the authority of the Orientalists and the enthusiasm for India with which it was associated. Thus Mill's essay "On the Hindoos" in his *History of British India* (1817) attacks Orientalism[1], in the person of Sir William Jones and the India hands generally, as being too partial to Indians, insufficiently theoretical, and lacking in the kind of philosophical judgment that is cultivated by long study in Europe (see chapter 4, this volume). And Hegel, reviewing all that Europeans had discovered about Indian thought, concluded that there was no philosophy, indeed no theory, outside Greece and Europe, and that India's marginality in the history-of-philosophy narrative was thereby effectively settled—and with it the marginality of Orientalism[1] in

German philosophy (see Halbfass 1988:chap. 6). Both Mill and Hegel are undoubtedly major architects of Orientalism[2], that is, Orientalism *sensu* Said, but in these matters Orientalism[2] is in *opposition* to Orientalism[1] and the Orientalists who produced it. Moreover, it is by no means the case that Mill and Hegel were hegemonic for Indology—that is, Orientalism[1]. Thus not only do we have the confusion of two senses of Orientalism, but the relation between the two is not a simple one of inclusion or of part to whole. Orientalism of the Saidian variety that we find in Mill, or Hegel, or, ultimately, Henry Kissinger is parasitic of the Orientalism produced by the Orientalists, but it is often hostile to it at the same time. Said himself is well aware of such conflicts within his Orientalism, but what he wants to draw attention to is the common ground that unites the opposing parties. We need to redraw the distinction in order to understand the production of the Orientalists, which has a coherence and ideology of its own. Thus the relation of the two kinds of Orientalism needs to be problematized and investigated.

The application of Said's thesis to India also faces a problem of a more general kind. Said declines to examine the *value* of Orientalist scholarship, dismissing it, moreover, not as an open question, but with prejudice. He asserts that "Orientalism is more particularly valuable as a sign of European-Atlantic power over the Orient than it is as a veridic discourse about the Orient" which it claims to be, and that its durability shows it to be "more formidable than a mere collection of lies" (1978:6). The accomplishments of Orientalism[1]—the Orientalism of the Orientalists—that remain viable, of which the great decipherments of the Egyptian hieroglyphics and the cuneiform writings of old Mesopotamia are the premier examples, appear in his work only in the form of mockery, of a silly argument made by reactionaries to justify imperialism. What he parodies, to be sure, is real: The idea that Orientalism is colonialism's monument, a noble and enduring edifice that justifies the otherwise sordid and evanescent taking of profit, is an old one. We find, for example, the following sentiment in a *Monthly review* article on a work of the British Orientalists of Calcutta, written at a time when the British Indian empire seemed a temporary commercial advantage that would soon be lost.

We always contemplate with renewed satisfaction the ingenious labours of our countrymen in the East. We consider them, in the aggregate, as constituting the monument more durable than brass, which will survive the existence and illustrate the memory of our Eastern dominion. After the contingent circumstances to which we owe our present preponderance in that country shall have ceased to operate, and the channels of Indian knowledge and Indian wealth shall have again become impervious to the western world, the Asiatic Researches will furnish a proof to our posterity, that the acquisition of the latter did not absorb the attention of their countrymen to the exclusion of the former; and that the English laws and English government, in those distant regions, have sometimes been administered by men of extensive capacity, erudition, and application. (*Monthly review* 1797:408)[7]

Even so, Said's simple inversion of the idea of Orientalism as monument-of-colonialism is hardly satisfactory. It seems to betray a feeling that one cannot seriously weigh the value of Orientalism's substance without running the risk of finding some of it good and, in that measure, a justification of a regime of colonial power. This strikes me as the central unresolved moral dilemma of a book that is above all a work of moral assessment, in that it passes judgment on Orientalism while refusing to pass judgment on its substance. But any view one holds or may construct about India is built and will continue to be built in part upon the work of Orientalists of the last two centuries, so that the continual reassessment of that body of work is something we cannot refuse. We cannot do without a critical and expert winnowing of that work.

Are these two features connected—the two features, that is, of expanding the meaning of Orientalism so that it includes anti-Orientalist productions and of passing judgment on Orientalist knowledge while refusing to assess its content? I cannot help thinking that they are. Said's expanded definition of Orientalism, in that it joins "describing" with "dominating" the Orient, is an argument in the form of a definition, a conclusion concealed in the introduction, a destination in a starting point. Its argument, as I hope I have made clear, is a serious one and deserves examination, but the examination must include, I would have thought, what actual Orientalism—that is to say, Orientalism[1]—actually contains. In that enterprise a knowledge of Sanskrit and of ancient Indian history will not necessarily be a disadvantage.

7. The anonymous article in the *Monthly review* is attributed to Alexander Hamilton, an important British Sanskritist, by the editor in his own set of the journal, as described in Nangle (1955); but I have to add that there are internal reasons for doubts, including several references to the author's previous articles in the *Monthly review* which the editor attributed to someone else. There is no sign of the Sanskrit and Persian learning that is so marked a feature of Hamilton's other reviews of Orientalist productions. The viewpoint here seems to be that of a stay-at-home Briton.

Accordingly I need to make it clear that the Orientalism I will be examining in this book is Orientalism[1]. Within that more limited category I will focus even more narrowly, concentrating upon the British Sanskritists to the exclusion of others whose knowledge of, say, Persian or Hindustani qualifies them for inclusion in the Orientalist category strictly construed. I believe that doing so will enable me to show things that can be discovered in no other way, in particular that it was the British Sanskritists who provided the theoretical foundation of the British ethnologies of India. I will engage with the technical content of this knowledge as well as with its relation to power.

The book which, more than any other, forms the foundation of this study is one that Said himself introduced to the Anglophone world in 1984, but that runs in rather a different direction from his own: Raymond Schwab's *The Oriental renaissance* (1984), first published in French in 1950.[8] This extraordinary book—extraordinary in its richness of detail, its passion, its beauty—takes its title from the conception, which came into being at the beginning of the nineteenth century and a bit before, that Europe would undergo a second renaissance through the study of the Orient, especially through the study of Sanskrit and the Veda, much as the study of Greek was the cause of the first Renaissance. Thus India and Sanskrit were the defining center of a new Orientalism, stimulated by the translation of the *Avesta* by Abraham Hyacinthe Anquetil-Duperron in 1771, the various translations of Sir William Jones and his associates in the Asiatic Society at Calcutta, and followed by the founding of Asiatic societies in Europe. The older Orientalism based on the study in Europe of Hebrew, Arabic, and Persian continued, but the ensuing Indomania gave the Oriental renaissance a new Indian center.

Schwab follows the enthusiasm for India on the Continent and (in part) the United States. But he also notes the paradox of Britain:

The Oriental Renaissance—though not Indic studies themselves—had only an ephemeral career in the same England to which it owed its origin. Later the debt of several writers, especially the Lake Poets, to the Hindu revelation became clear, and the shadow of its impact on London was evident in Chateaubriand when he returned from exile. But the fire in England was soon damped. Great Britain could not, or would not, be the hearth for such a renaissance. Thereafter, even in Indic Studies, the Victorians procured their best workers only by appealing to the German universities. This had

8. See also Said's "Raymond Schwab and the romance of ideas" in *The world, the text, and the critic* (1983:248–267).

already been the case with Rosen, who was born in Hanover and died a professor of Sanskrit at London. It was, above all, the case with Max Müller, who was born in Dessau in 1823 and died a professor of comparative linguistics at Oxford in 1900. Ultimately, England was to welcome many more Orientalists than she gave birth to. (1984:43)

The process by which, in British eyes, Sanskrit and the Orientalist study of India came to seem something foreign, an inexplicable enthusiasm of the Continent (especially a German one), to the degree that it was sometimes forgotten that it was British in origin, is evident at many points in the record we will be studying, including the passage from Sir Henry Maine with which this chapter opened. The British paradox, including the fact that Oriental studies languished in Britain and that Britain did not produce enough Orientalists to meet its own low level of need, is a phenomenon for which, again, the Saidian conception of Orientalism does not prepare us; it does not help us explain, more especially, the inverse relation between colonialism and the production of Sanskritists as between Britain on the one hand and the Continent on the other. Schwab gave only a few words to the question of its mechanism. The British paradox and its causes must be a major problem for this story of the Aryans and British India.

CHAPTER 2

# The Mosaic Ethnology
# of Asiatick Jones

Well before the middle of the nineteenth century the
Indo-European concept had come to seem essentially foreign to Britons, identified with the Continent generally and German scholars in
particular; the enthusiasm for Sanskrit and the antiquities of India,
which comprised the core of the "Oriental Renaissance," likewise
seemed to belong to the other side of the Channel by which Europe
was cut off from Britain. Yet in some ways the unfamiliar sound Britons
were hearing was the echo of their own voice, reshaped by an alien
landscape. For it had largely been British scholars who created the European enthusiasm for India—the British scholars of newly conquered
Bengal who in 1784 formed the Asiatic Society at Calcutta. The Indo-
European concept, which was given its name by an Englishman, Arthur
Young, had been first proposed by another, Sir William Jones, the founder and first president of the Asiatic Society, in his famous pronouncement of 1786.

Before setting out for India in 1783 Jones had made a great reputation
for himself as a prodigy of Orientalism, having published a number of
books, including translations from Persian, Arabic, and Turkish, starting at the age of twenty-three. He had to abandon Orientalism to take
up the law in order to free himself from the dependent life of a tutor to
an aristocratic family. The conquest of Bengal by the East India Company and the beginnings of its role as a governing power created a need
for judges at Calcutta, appointed by the Crown. He applied for a judge-
ship, thinking to save much of his salary and retire to the life of an independent scholar on a small country estate in England. His application

was eventually successful, and he married, was knighted, and shipped out for India, but he died in India after a decade, just short of his goal. He was not the *creator* of the new Orientalism, which, under the patronage of Warren Hastings, was well along in the process of taking shape when he joined it, but by his own scholarly contributions he set a high standard for it and by forming the Asiatic Society he gave it institutional structure. His fame assured that its work would be noticed in Europe, and indeed it was.[1]

The journal of the Society, *Asiatick researches* (the "k" was soon dropped), made a great hit in Europe, as may be seen from the reprints and translations that were published in response to a celebrity that it attained soon after its first volume was printed in Calcutta in 1788. Pirated editions appeared in London in 1796, 1798, and 1799, and other editions appeared in 1801 and 1806 (two editions by different publishers were issued in that year). A four-volume German translation by Johann Christian Fick and Johann Friedrich Kleuker was published at Riga in 1795–97, and French translations by A. Labaume were published in Paris in 1803 (one volume) and 1805 (two volumes). The works of Jones, who died in India in 1794, ten years after the founding of the Society and at a time when the clamor for its works was rising, were also in great demand: The six-volume quarto edition of 1799 was followed in 1807 by a thirteen-volume edition in a smaller format. Undoubtedly the most celebrated single production of the Calcutta Sanskritists was Jones's translation of the ancient Sanskrit drama *Śakuntala,* published at Calcutta in 1789, reprinted in 1790 (London), 1796 (London and Edinburgh), and 1805 (in the *Monthly anthology* of Boston), translated into German by Georg Forster in 1791, into French by A. Buguière in 1803, and into Italian from the French (from the English, from the Sanskrit!) by Luigi Doria in 1815. Goethe's poem on the *Śakuntala,* and the effect of the Indian play upon the writing of his *Faustus,* providing the idea for the prologue in heaven, are well known. Those whose thirst for the facts of publishing history is not slaked by this recital may consult Gar-

---

1. The standard biography of Jones is that of Garland Cannon, *The life and mind of Oriental Jones: Sir William Jones, the father of modern linguistics* (1990), although S. N. Mukherjee's *Sir William Jones: A study in eighteenth-century British attitudes to India* (1983) is still the best study of his Indological work. The subtitles indicate the differing orientations of the two biographies. A. J. Arberry's earlier pieces are also worth reading: *British contributions to Persian studies* (1942) and *British Orientalists* (1943), and John Shore's *Memoirs of the life, writings, and correspondence of Sir William Jones* (1805) is of historical interest for its presentation of Jones as a Christian and a patriot. Cannon's scholarship on Jones is extensive and includes a bibliography (Cannon 1979) and the fine edition of Jones's letters (Jones 1970), which are indispensable.

land Cannon's (1979) bibliography of Jones or the catalogs of the great national libraries for more. The point, surely, is made: The work of the Calcutta Sanskritists had a tremendous vogue in Europe in the closing decade of the eighteenth century and the opening decades of the nineteenth.

## The Authority-Claim of the New Orientalism

What was occurring was a titanic shift of authority. The Asiatic Society gave institutional form and definition to a group of scholar-administrators who were fashioning a new claim for authority over that of the older Orientalism, a claim that largely succeeded. The vogue for the new Orientalism virtually eclipsed the earlier writings on India that had been authoritative hitherto, including such works as the Dutch missionary Abraham Roger's *Open door to heathendom,* widely known through the French translation of 1670, *La Porte ouverte, pour parvenir à la connoissance du paganisme caché;* Henry Lord's *A display of two forraigne sects in the East Indies* (1630); the *Lettres édifiantes et curieuses* of the Jesuits (1702–77); the writings of the travelers, especially François Bernier (1968), and those of the savants. Writings such as these which had been authoritative in their day were thrown into the shade, and Calcutta became the fount of the new knowledge. The European fascination with China that was so marked in the seventeenth and early eighteenth centuries gave way to a fascination with India.

In the beginning, Persian was the principal medium through which the approaches to India's ancient past were made. The first works of the new Orientalism, prior to the formation of the Asiatic Society at Calcutta, were mostly translations from Persian: Anquetil-Duperron's translation of the *Zend-Avesta* (1771) with the help of Parsi scholars in India; John Zephaniah Holwell's *Interesting historical events, relative to the provinces of Bengal* (1765–71), which relies on Persian sources in part, although it also contains what purport to be translations from a mysterious ancient Hindu text, *Chartah Bhade Shastah* (Sanskrit, *Catur Veda Śāstra*), a work not heard of since; Alexander Dow's translation of Firishtah's Persian *History of Hindostan* (1768); and the *Code of Gentoo laws* (1776), translated by Nathaniel Brassey Halhed from a Persian translation of a Sanskrit digest of Hindu law compiled by pandits on commission from the East India Company. The translation by Francis

Gladwin of Abuʾl Fazl's Persian account of Akbar's government, the
Āʾīn-i Akbarī (1783–86), gave European readers a Mughal perspective
upon India. It was through his publications on Persian and Arabic literature that Sir William Jones had made a formidable reputation for
himself as an Orientalist well before coming to India and taking up
Sanskrit; these included the translation of the history of Nadir Shah
into French for a prize offered by the king of Denmark (1770; English
and German versions, 1773); a *Grammar of the Persian language* (1771),
written especially for the use of the East India Company and a most
successful work, going into nine editions by 1829 and French (1772) and
German (1773) translations; the *Poeseos Asiaticae commentariorum libri
sex* (1774); a translation of the pre-Islamic Arabic classic poems, *The
Moallakát* (1782a); and *The Mohamedan law of succession* (1782b), a translation of an Arabic treatise by Ibn al-Mulaqqin, also intended for the
use of the East India Company.

Hindustani (or Hindi-Urdu) was the other principal language
through which Englishmen dealt with Indians in Bengal, since few
knew Bengali. Halhed was one of the first to truly master it, and in
his *Grammar of the Bengal language* he says that hitherto Europeans
"scarcely believed that Bengal ever possessed a native and peculiar dialect of its own, distinct from that idiom which, under the name of
*Moor's* [Urdu], has been supposed to prevail all over India" (1778:ii).
Thereafter, via Persian, Hindustani, and Bengali, and with the help
of the pandits, the British quickly came into direct knowledge of the
source itself: Sanskrit. Halhed, in the introduction to his translation of
the so-called *Code of Gentoo laws* (1776:xxiii ff.), had already given the
first sketchy account in English of the structure of Sanskrit, which he
calls in his grammar of Bengali the "grand Source of Indian Literature,
the Parent of almost every dialect from the Persian Gulph to the China
Seas" (1778:iii). His remarks excited interest on account of its acute observations as to similarities of Sanskrit with Greek and the promised
richness of Sanskrit literature. The raja of Krishnagar, he announced,
"has in his own possession Shanscrit books which give an account of a
communication formerly subsisting between India and Egypt; wherein
the Egyptians are constantly described as disciples, not as instructors,
and as seeking that liberal education and those sciences in Hindostan,
which none of their own countrymen had sufficient knowledge to impart" (1778:v). (This notion of a connection between the ancient civilizations of India and Egypt will, as we shall see in this chapter and the
next, play a considerable role in British enthusiasm for Indian studies.)

Charles Wilkins, however, is rightly reckoned the first of the British Sanskritists; his translation of the *Bhagavad Gītā* appeared in 1785. When Jones arrived in India in 1783 he intended to leave Sanskrit in Wilkins's able hands, but a year after his arrival he succumbed to the temptation and took it up.

The new Orientalism was based on direct interchange with the pandits in India, who as well as being teachers of language and scholarly interlocutors to aspiring Orientalists were also, in several cases, employed by the East India Company as experts on the Hindu law. Some engaged in the production of new texts under British patronage or encouragement. J. Duncan Derrett's survey (1968) lists nearly fifty Sanskrit treatises of law known or conjectured to have been produced for the British. The first of these was the *Vivādārṇavasetu,* the "bridge across the ocean of litigation" (troubled water indeed for the British administration) compiled by eleven pandits from 1773 through 1775, translated into Persian by Zayn al-Dīn ʿAlī Rasaʾi, and translated (from the Persian) into English by Halhed as the *Code of Gentoo laws.* Two other digests of the Hindu law with similar watery names were commissioned by Jones, the *Vivādasārārṇava* of Trivedi Sarvoruśarman and the *Vivādabhaṅgārṇava* of Jagannātha Tarkapañcānana, this latter translated after Jones's death by Henry T. Colebrooke in 1797 (Derrett 1968; Lingat 1973:121). Rādhākānta Śarma's epitome of history from the Purāṇas, *Purāṇārthaprakāśa,* was written at the instance of Warren Hastings, the governor-general, in 1784; Jones refers to it and to having discussed it with the author. It, too, was translated into Persian (by Zuravar Singh) and, by Halhed, into English (see L. Rocher 1986:217). In the first volume of *Asiatic researches* Jones published a translation of a short treatise on Sanskrit literature communicated by Govardhan Kaul (Jones 1788).

In its own propaganda, the new Orientalism drew authority from its knowledge of the languages of India and opposed it to that of the travelers and missionaries. The traveler's claim to authority is simpler: "I was there." It is, at bottom, the authority of the eye-witness. It is striking that the ancient Greek travelers' accounts of India, those of the Alexander historians and the Hellenistic ambassadors to the Mauryas, rest implicitly or explicitly upon direct seeing and give us no particulars of the linguistic means by which their knowledge of Indian religion, government, and social organization were acquired; ancient critiques of their knowledge, unlike modern ones, do not probe the implied linguistic competence but only call the veracity of the witness into question, as when Strabo says that all the writers on India were liars.[2] There is, then, something in the claims of the new Orientalism as it opposes itself to the travelers' accounts. These claims are not as powerful against the missionaries, who generally took pains to learn the languages.

One of the first statements of this new authority claim comes from Holwell—ironically, to be sure, given that he left the question of the linguistic medium of his supposed translations of the supposed ancient *Shaster* so obscure and dubious. In a sustained critique of the travelers, ancient and modern, Holwell blames on them and their ignorance of the languages the fact that "all the modern writers represent the *Hindoos* as a race of stupid and gross *Idolaters*" (1765–71, 2:6). In doing so he draws a line between his own work and that which went before, and he associates knowledge of Indian languages with sympathetic description.

A mere description of the exterior manners and religion of a people, will no more give us a true idea of them; than a geographical description of a country can convey a just conception of their laws and government. The traveller must sink deeper in his researches, would he feast the mind of an understanding reader. His telling us such and such a people, in the East or West-Indies, worship this stock, or that stone, or monstrous idol; only serves to reduce in our esteem, our fellow creatures, to the most abject and despicable point of light. Whereas, was he skilled in the languages of the people he describes, sufficiently to trace the etymology of their words and phrases, and capable of diving into the mysteries of their theology; he would probably be able to evince in us, that such seemingly preposterous worship, had the most sublime rational source and foundation. (1765–71, 2:9)

This kind of argument becomes a trope of the new Orientalism. For example, we meet it again a half-century later when the Orientalist Alexander Hamilton reviews *A journey from Madras, through the countries of Mysore, Canara and Malabar,* whose author, Francis Buchanan, "possessed no means of communication with the natives but through an interpreter" (1808:90) and whom, accordingly, he proceeds to skewer. Buchanan's proceeding was to depart at dawn of each day, travel eight or nine miles, pitch camp, and summon local inhabitants for questioning on their agricultural practices, social organization, and religious beliefs—with results as reliable, says Hamilton, as if

---

2. Strabo, *Geography* (1949), 2.1.9. This discussion draws on ideas about authority and authority claims from writers as different as Amos Funkenstein, "History, counterhistory, and narrative" (1993), and James Clifford, "On ethnographic authority" (in 1988:21–54).

an officer, armed with a letter from the Secretary of State, [were] to arrive in a village in Yorkshire, and, assembling the inhabitants, by means of a constable, [were] to question them respecting their prospects in this life, and their hopes in the next. . . . But if any misapprehension arose, little time was allowed for its correction; for the next day's sun usually found Dr. Buchanan on his road to the next station, complaining, probably, the whole way, of "the inveterate liars and beastly stupidity" he had met with. (1808:90)

Hamilton then generalizes the connection between Orientalist knowledge of languages and the drawing of sympathetic portraits:

We cannot associate long and intimately with our fellow-men, without a sincere and reciprocal attachment being exited. . . . We discover good qualities where we did not expect to find them,—wit under the mask of dulness, and benevolence under an ungracious exterior. The whole man becomes known to us; and the interest thus excited proves, that, in the aggregate, the good qualities usually preponderate. Whenever, therefore, a very worthy man has adopted unfavourable impressions of a whole people, we should first inquire into his opportunity of knowing them. We have no hesitation in stating the faculty of conversing with them as an indispensable qualification; and of this Dr. Buchanan was totally destitute. (1808:31)

By contrast, "When we read the valuable productions of those great Oriental scholars, whose attainments have placed England on a footing with the Continent in that particular,—those of a Jones, a Wilkins, a Colebrooke, or a Halhed,—we uniformly discover in the Hindus a nation, whose polished manners are the result of a mild disposition and an extensive benevolence" (the same). To know is to love, says this Orientalist trope, and language is the gate of knowing.

As against the traveler's testimony of the eye, which reveals only the exterior of things, the Orientalist has access, through language, to the deeper meaning of things, to the intentionality of those he is attempting to understand and describe, which is the ultimate fount of all Orientalist authority. Linguistic capacity is the indispensable means for the new knowledge, and as it is the standard of authority in the claims of the new Orientalism against the travelers, so too is it the standard to which appeal is made in disputes among Orientalists. So rapidly does the new knowledge advance that within a very short span of time the previous scholarly productions are vulnerable to the criticisms of the more recent ones, and the grounds for criticism are usually mastery of the linguistic means or access to authoritative persons and texts. Thus one year after Holwell's "Religious tenets of the Gentoos" (1765–71,

2:1–101) appeared in print, denouncing all Western accounts of India
that went before, Dow, in his preface to Firishtah's *History of Hindos-*
*tan,* titled "Dissertation concerning the customs, manners, language,
religion and philosophy of the Hindoos," echoed the sentiment, saying
that modern travelers had "prejudiced Europe against the Brahmins,
and by a very unfair account, have thrown disgrace upon a system of religion and philosophy, which they did by no means investigate" (Firishtah 1768:xxii). Yet he also found himself "obliged to differ almost in
every particular concerning the religion of the Hindoos" as described
by Holwell (1768:xxix). And it is undoubtedly Holwell he means in another passage when he says,

Some writers have very lately given to the world, an unintelligible system
of the Brahmin religion; and they affirm, that they derived their information from the Hindoos themselves. This may be the case, but they certainly
conversed upon that subject with the inferior tribes, or with the unlearned
part of the Brahmins: and it would be as ridiculous to hope for a true state
of the religion and philosophy of the Hindoos from those illiterate casts,
as it would be in a Mohammedan in London, to rely upon the accounts of
a parish beadle, concerning the most abstruse points of the Christian faith;
or, to form his opinion of the principles of the Newtonian philosophy, from
a conversation with an English carman. (1768:xxxvii–xxxviii)

The language-based authority structure of the new Orientalism me-
diated between its universalism, as a part of the Republic of Letters,
and the claims of national pride and religious difference. Holwell's critique of the travelers is, in large part, a critique of missionaries "chiefly
of the *Romish* communion," although the burden of the critique is
borne by language. The inaptness of the criticism insofar as it applies to
Catholic missionaries, who were often rather good at learning the language, makes my point: The new criterion must serve as surrogate when
other, inadmissible motives intrude. As to national pride, the most famous case is William Jones's fiery denunciation of Anquetil-Duperron's
translation of the *Avesta* in a pamphlet, *Lettre à Monsieur A\*\*\* du*
*P\*\*\*, dans laquelle est compris l'examen de sa traduction des livres at-*
*tribués à Zoroastre* (1771), in which he lost his usual Olympian calm in
an attack occasioned by what he perceived to be a slur upon the scholarship of his nation and his university. The trashing of Anquetil's scholarship was misplaced if not unprovoked and had the effect, the experts
tell us, of stalling the advancement of Avestan studies for a goodly period—such being the power of the language criterion when wielded
perversely by someone of recognized authority.

Religion and national difference perhaps combined in the slang-
ing match that divided the missionary Paulinus a Sancto Bartholomaeo
and the British Sanskritists after Jones's death. Fra Paulinus, Carmelite
author of a Sanskrit grammar, a Sanskrit dictionary, and many other
Indological works in the 1790s, had a talent for harsh invective which
he applied liberally to Jones, Wilkins, Halhed, and Anquetil. Alexander
Hamilton replied in kind:

That Paulinus was unacquainted with the Sanscrit language, of which he
has published a dictionary, it seems paradoxical to assert. It is nevertheless
true, that in his travels, he betrays a complete ignorance of that language,
and quotes books for facts that are not to be found in them. His Sanscrit
dictionary (which we have in vain endeavoured to procure) is, we will venture to assert, a dictionary of the Malabar idiom, which bears the same
relation to the Sanscrit that Italian does to Latin, or the vernacular dialect
of modern Athens to the language of Aristotle and Plato. (1802:30–31)

Ludo Rocher, who has studied the works of Paulinus closely, has shown
that this criticism is based on misunderstanding (see Paulinus a Sancto
Bartholomaeo 1790:xviii–xix). Paulinus's rendering of Sanskrit often
shows the influence of Tamil phonology (*T* for *D*, *G* for *C* or *K*, ro-
manized, moreover, in an Italian orthography), just as that of the Calcutta Sanskritists is influenced by the Bengali phonology of their pandits. This kind of confusion can be seen as early as Holwell, who says
that the "Viedam" is followed by the Hindus of Malabar and the Coro-
mandel coast and who is unaware that this is the same as his (Bengali)
"Bhade" (i.e., *Bed*, rhymes with *made*), that is, Sanskrit *Veda*, with reflexes of *Vedam* in South India and *Bed* in Bengal.[3]

   The intrusion of national feeling into the Republic of Letters tracked
the clashes of real nations. Schwab is right to insist that Anquetil's
*Avesta* translation should be numbered among the first achievements
of the new Orientalism.[4] But the conquest of Bengal came about in the
course of a worldwide rivalry between the British and the French, which
decided, in the end, that India (along with North America) was to be

   3. That, at any rate, is what I propose. P. J. Marshall's glossary equates Holwell's
"Bhade" with Skt. *vada*, "word," implying a different pronunciation, which is certainly
possible, but it is hard to know what to make of the title in that case. Marshall's excellent
volume, *The British discovery of Hinduism* (1970), reprints extracts from Holwell, Dow,
Halhed, Hastings, Wilkins, and Jones.
   4. Schwab's first venture into the history of Orientalism was a superb biography of
Anquetil-Duperron (1934) which, although superceded by that of Jean-Luc Keiffer (1983),
continues to be very well worth reading.

under British rule and that French interests there would not be allowed to expand beyond a few small enclaves. The conquest had the double effect of giving the British conditions under which the new Orientalism might flourish and denying them, largely, to the French, at least so long as the new Orientalism was based on direct tuition by pandits conducted in India. Even a slight acquaintance with the discourse on India of the French missionaries, savants, and lumières, aided by Sylvia Murr's fine analysis (1983), shows that the finalities with which the British Orientalists engaged in their colloquies with the pandits of Bengal were ones they had brought with them, that had often been first aired on the pages of the *Lettres édifiantes* or the memoirs of the Académie des Inscriptions: to determine who the Indians were and their relation to sacred history; to establish their religious views and their relation to the Christian revelation; to determine their antiquity and whether their sciences came from the Greeks, or the Egyptians, or were original with them. The writings of Gaston-Laurent Coeurdoux, who spent his entire adult life in South India as a missionary, have been rescued from oblivion by Murr (1987); they constitute a lost continent of learning, one that remained largely unpublished because of the twofold check of the suppression of the Jesuit order and the eclipse of French power in India. After the death of Père Coeurdoux, bits of this corpus were published by Anquetil and, as Murr has discovered, the well-known book of the Abbé Dubois, *Hindu manners, customs and ceremonies* (1906, first published in 1817), plagiarized one of Coeurdoux's manuscripts (Murr 1977, 1987). Coeurdoux's work would have been an important voice for the new Orientalism, but by the time it appeared in Dubois it was outdated. Max Müller noticed that the Abbé Dubois's book had an air that "really belongs to a period previous to the revival of Sanskrit studies in India, as inaugurated by Wilkins, Sir William Jones, and Colebrooke" (in Dubois 1906:v).

## The Ethnological Project of Sir William Jones

The premier text for the Indo-European concept belongs to the third of the presidential addresses with which Jones marked the anniversary of the Asiatic Society. It is regularly cited in histories of linguistics as a landmark on the passage from the prescientific to the scientific stage of the discipline. I cite it yet again, and develop my theme as a commentary upon the text:[5]

The *Sanscrit* language, whatever be its antiquity, is of a wonderful structure; more perfect than the *Greek*, more copious than the *Latin*, and more exquisitely refined than either, yet bearing to both of them a stronger affinity, both in the roots of verbs and in the forms of grammar, than could possibly have been produced by accident; so strong indeed, than no philologer could examine them all three, without believing them to have sprung from some common source, which, perhaps, no longer exists: there is a similar reason, though not quite so forcible, for supposing that both the *Gothick* and the *Celtick*, though blended with a very different idiom, had the same origin with the *Sanscrit;* and the old *Persian* might be added to the same family, if this were the place for discussing any question concerning the antiquities of *Persia.* (1807, 3:34–35)

The modernity of the formulation is remarkable. The grouping of Sanskrit, Greek, Latin, Gothic (Germanic), Celtic, and Old Persian through mutual resemblance, the resort both to lexicon and grammar as bases of comparison, the conception of these languages as codescendants of a lost ancestral language, which we call Proto-Indo-European—these are exactly the views historical linguists hold today. It fits Schleicher's tree diagram very well (figure 2) and identifies ancient languages that represent most of the major branches of the Indo-European tree except the Slavic, which Jones believed, wrongly, belonged with the languages of Central Asia. In some respects the formulation is more modern than those of some writers after Jones in the early nineteenth century, such as Friedrich Schlegel, for whom, in his famous essay *Über die Sprache und Weisheit der Indier* (*On the language and wisdom of the Indians,* 1808), Sanskrit itself was the Indo-European *Ursprache* rather than, as Jones rightly has it, its descendant. The only decidedly unmodern notes are struck by the words "perfect" and "copious," alluding to the developmental view of language typical of the age, as theorized by John Locke in his *Essay concerning human understanding* (1689:433; see Trautmann 1992a:210–211). According to this view, civilized languages are "copious" in their vocabulary and "regu-

5. Jones's anniversary discourses were initially published in the first four volumes of *Asiatic researches.* They may also be found in the two editions of Jones's *Works* (1799 and 1807, the latter reprinted in India in 1976) and collected together in a separate volume (1824). I shall be citing the third volume of the 1807 edition of the *Works,* which is the most widely available in research libraries. The discourses I am mainly concerned with are the third through the ninth, delivered between 1786 and 1792.

lar" in structure; the languages of savages are correspondingly "scanty" and "rude." In these attributions Jones is saying that Sanskrit is a civilized language, on a par with Latin and Greek and even surpassing them in some respects.[6]

The sense of precocious modernity emanating from Jones's address is an effect of the place it has been given in the story of the rise and progress of linguistic science. Its function in this narrative is as a partial discovery of a truth to be fully revealed by the comparative philology that was later created, of a pointer to what was to come after: the adumbration of Indo-Europeanist comparative philology by Franz Bopp and Rasmus Rask in works they published in 1816 and 1818, respectively, the discovery of law-like regularities of sound changes in Indo-European languages inaugurated by Jacob Grimm, and so forth.[7] In the narrative logic of "before" and "after," Jones's text stands for the breaking through of science from prescience, and it is an anticipation of greater things to come.

There are several good reasons, however, why we should think of Jones as being a prisoner of the narrative of the rise of linguistics and attempt to rescue him from it. It may seem retrograde to do so after what I have said about the centrality of the mastery of languages to the authority claims of the new Orientalism. But as Jones himself said, "I

---

6. Halhed had said something similar:

The Shanscrit Language is very copious and nervous, but the Style of the best Authors wonderfully concise. It far exceeds Greek and Arabick in the Regularity of its Etymology, and like them has a Prodigious Number of Derivatives from each primary Root. The grammatical Rules also are numerous and difficult, though there are not many Anomalies. (1776:xxiii)

All of this goes to show the stereotyped character of a "polished" language: copiousness of vocabulary, regularity of grammatical rules. Halhed also came close to formulating the Indo-European conception:

I have been astonished to find the similitude of Shanscrit words with those of Persian and Arabic, and even of Latin and Greek: and these not in technical and metaphorical terms, which the mutation of refined arts and improved manners might have occasionally introduced; but in the main ground-work of language, in monosyllables, in the names of numbers, and the appellations of such things as would be first discriminated on the immediate dawn of civilization. (1778:iii–iv)

Jones, as we shall see, was very clear that Arabic does not show evidence of a relationship with Sanskrit. For more on the Halhed-Jones comparison see Rosane Rocher 1980b.

7. This characterization relies on the introduction to Aarsleff 1982, which addresses the foundational histories of linguistics, namely those of Rudolf von Raumer, Theodor Benfey, Holger Pedersen, and Vilhelm Thomsen. Selections from the pioneering works of Bopp, Rask, Grimm, and others are published in Lehmann 1967.

have ever considered languages as the mere instruments of real learning and improperly confounded with learning itself" (1807, 3:7); the instrumental role of language in an enterprise that has other ends could not be more clearly expressed. We are not surprised, then, when he says he does not wish to be regarded as a linguist, and although we must grant that he used the word in the sense of "a knower of many languages" and is not referring to a discipline that takes language as its object of study (which had yet to be created), the telling point is that the vast range of the things on which he wrote—religion, chronology, astronomy, music, history—is not contained within linguistics and cannot be captured by the narrative of its progress.[8]

None of this is compelling, however. The dead have no rights over what narratives they appear in, and their wishes on this head or any other are of no account; *we* will decide what stories they must be part of, and they must show up willy-nilly and play the parts we assign them. The main reason for abandoning the "rise of linguistic science" narrative, which frames the text we have cited and delivers its modern and modernizing meaning, is the sense of shock it engenders when we follow the text back to its source, the third anniversary discourse. As soon as we step outside the passage in question we stumble over all manner of things that do not meet the expectations the modernist representation raises, that are not rendered intelligible by it, and that cannot be included in its narrative. Not the least of these is the inclusion of Egypt in the Indo-European group, and also, although only tentatively, the Chinese and the Japanese, the Incas and the Aztecs.

Although the Jonesean corpus has been in print for a very long time, and much has been written about him including a number of good biographies, I believe that we can come to a new understanding of Jones, one that departs significantly from the existing treatments, which emphasize his contribution to linguistics and to scientific Orientalism. We can do so by examining his central project on the assumption that he conceived it as *ethnological* in character and following it to its sources.

It is my argument that Jones's proposal of the Indo-European language family is better understood when we recognize that the character of Jones's project was primarily ethnological, not linguistic; that his

---

8. It should be added that for Jones and his contemporaries the different languages are more or less transparent media through which one can get at the human mind which is, at bottom, everywhere the same. The attribution of deep cultural significance to language differences is not yet evident, nor is the (Whorfian) notion of the capacity of language to determine thought. They come with the full tide of Romanticism.

ethnology is of a kind that we may call Mosaic, that is, an ethnology whose frame is supplied by the story of the descent of Noah in the book of Genesis, attributed to Moses, in the Bible; that its proximate sources were the ethnological writings of Jacob Bryant and Sir Isaac Newton; and that Jones and the new Orientalism of the Calcutta Sanskritists need to be included in the narrative of the history of ethnology.[9] Indeed, as we shall see, the Jonesean ethnology was a model for subsequent British and British-Indian ethnologies.

## AN ETHNOLOGICAL PROJECT

Jones's text on Indo-European is embedded in the "Anniversary discourses," which Jones envisioned as a set and which were so published in his *Works* and in a separate volume after his death titled *Discourses delivered before the Asiatic Society* (1824). It is in the third discourse that he sets out upon his ethnological plan, which is to investigate the five principal nations who have divided the vast continent of Asia among them: the Indians, the Chinese, the Tartars, the Arabs, and the Persians (1807, 3:27–28). He devotes a discourse to each on as many anniversaries of the Society, "the last of which will demonstrate the connexion or diversity between them, and solve the great problem, whether they had *any* common origin, and whether that origin was *the same*, which we generally ascribe to them" (1807, 3:28). These five discourses (to which he added another on the "borderers, mountaineers, and islanders of Asia") each reviewed four kinds of evidence—language and letters, religion and philosophy, architecture and sculpture, and arts and manufactures—creating a six by four grid over which the matter of the discourses was distributed. Language is instrumental to the ethnological goal, which is to show the common origin of the five Asian nations. Even so the amount of linguistic evidence brought forward is surprisingly small. One reads the anniversary discourses expecting to find lists of cognate words demonstrating the common origins of languages, but the examples are very limited. Jones makes the reason clear: The anniversary discourses were no place for dry lists of words. If brevity had not been his object, he said at the end of the eighth discourse, the matter of his discourses "might have been expanded into seven large

9. Hans Aarsleff (1967:chap. 4) was the first to call attention to the ethnological character of the anniversary discourses. I have discussed the Mosaic ethnology in an earlier book (Trautmann 1987), and George Stocking discusses it under the name of Biblical anthropology (Stocking 1987).

volumes with no other trouble than that of holding the pen; but (to borrow a turn of expression from one of our poets) 'for what I have produced, I claim only your indulgence; it is for what I have suppressed, that I am entitled to your thanks' " (1807, 3:184).

## A MOSAIC ETHNOLOGY

Although the Biblical frame is not brought to the foreground until the summing up in the ninth discourse, it is present at the very outset in the aspiration to determine whether the origin of the Asian nations is "that which we generally ascribe to them" (1807, 3:28), which is to say, whether it accords with the Mosaic account in the opening books of Genesis in the Bible. In the event, Jones shows in his discourses that the Persian nation surely, and the Chinese probably, are not original stocks but branches of the Hindu or Indian nation, leaving three original stocks in Asia: Hindus or Indians, Arabs, and Tartars. He then identifies these with the three sons of Noah—the Indians with Ham, the Arabs with Shem, and the Tartars with Japhet. It becomes clear in the ninth discourse that the entire project is one of forming a rational defense of the Bible out of the materials collected by Orientalist scholarship, more specifically a defense of the Mosaic account of human history in its earliest times. The unnamed antagonist throughout is Voltaire, who used the new Orientalism, especially that of Holwell and Dow, to quite different ends.

Jones brought this project with him to India, and he situated his work in series with other rational defenses of Moses, specifically those of Newton and of Bryant. The ethnological writings of Newton and Bryant, barely touched on in the Jones biographies, need to be understood clearly if we are to grasp the content and deeper significance of the anniversary discourses for their author and his audience.

Newton's contribution was a curious and controversial one, published posthumously as *The chronology of ancient kingdoms amended* (1728). He held that the Egyptians had invented astronomy in the time of Amon (who for Newton was effectively the first ruler of a united Egypt), and that it spread thence, together with a new idolatrous religion based upon the worship of deceased leaders, to Africa, Europe, and Asia, giving rise to the celestial sphere of the ancient Greeks, Chaldeans, and others. Thus science and paganism arose from one source and constituted a unitary system. Through a tissue of evidence, he identified the celestial sphere of the ancients mentioned in Eudoxus with the Argonauts' expedition. Since the Eudoxus fragment specified the position of the zodiac at the solstices and equinoxes, it was possible to recalculate the date of the primitive sphere, and of the Argonauts, to 936 B.C., which would be forty-three years after the death of Solomon and some five centuries more recent than the generally received chronology of the time. The proposed chronological revolution "squeezed Greek history into the first millennium and exalted the Hebrews for their greater antiquity, thus at once humbling the heathen and vindicating the diffusionist thesis of the [Church] Fathers," specifically that of Clement of Alexandria, who tried to show that Greek philosophy and culture were derived from Hebrew sources (Manuel 1959:98–100; Newton 1728).

Bryant's "new system" is contained in his three-volume *Analysis of antient mythology,* published in 1774–76 (republished in six volumes in 1807). He, too, wishes to reconcile sacred and secular history, and his system is by and large an elaboration of Newton's. Bryant's fundamental innovation upon Newton's argument is to identify Amon, the author of Egyptian civilization, with the Ham of the Bible. Believing that only the Mosaic account of earliest times had preserved the "native truth from which the Gentiles were continually receding" (1807, 4:436), and that pagan mythology was a corrupted telling of true history, he proposes to recover the original truth behind the myths, which had been lost to the Greeks themselves, by means of etymology, as the only possible thread by which to find one's way through the labyrinth. Thus his project is to show that the pagan mythologies and historical traditions speak with one voice and are at bottom one mythology from one original people and that the history they tell is consistent with the Mosaic narrative.

The gist of Bryant's learned, tedious volumes is that the Egyptian worship of their god Amon was in fact the worship of their half-forgotten ancestor Ham. The Hamians or Amonians comprised the Egyptians, the Greeks and Romans, and others (including the Indians), all of whose national religions were thus interpreted as the corrupted remembrance of their ancestry and of the incidents of their history, including the Biblical flood and the Tower of Babel. The Hamians or Amonians were the first of mankind to decline from natural religion into idolatry, but they were also the first inventors of the arts of civilization. Bryant's identification of these peoples as Hamites rests upon an endless series of etymologies of which the foundational one, Amon = Ham, will suffice as an example.

Jones's relation to Bryant and his new system is highly ambivalent. To put it simply, he strongly disapproves of Bryant's etymological methods but embraces his conclusions. He believes that Bryant was right for the wrong reasons, and his project largely reworks the same ground to establish a firm foundation for the Bryant thesis. We need to consider for a moment both the thesis and the method.

What is new and remains unusual about Bryant's system is how he locates the Greeks and Romans in the Mosaic ethnology. Traditionally these are regarded as descendants of Japhet, the Greeks being identified specifically with Javan of that line, presumably "Ionian" (comparable to Persian "Yauna" and Sanskrit "Yavana"). Bryant, however, groups the Egyptians and the Indians (although in truth he has very little to say about the Indians) together with the Greeks and Romans as Hamians, more specifically Cuthites (descendants of Chus or Cush, son of Ham). The Egyptians certainly figure as descendants of Ham in the Mosaic account, under the name Mizraim, and indeed the Egyptians of today call their country Misr. But Bryant explicitly rejects the prevailing identification of Ionians with Javan, and says that the race of Javan were earlier inhabitants of Greece, whereas the true Greeks (Dorians, Achaeans, and Hellenes, generally) were Cuthites.

This was decidedly a new way of looking at things, and it entailed a new reading of the Mosaic narrative. In Bryant's reading, the general dispersal of nations occurred after the flood but *before* the Tower of Babel, Shem to Asia, Japhet to Europe, Ham to Africa. The Cuthite branch of the Hamian family, however, did not submit to the divine dispensation and stubbornly remained in Asia, their king Nimrod driving Ashur (of Shem) from his lawful dominion and becoming king of Babel—"the first rebellion [against God] in the world" (Bryant 1807, 4:21–22). The next rebellious act of the Cuthite sons of Ham was the building of the Tower of Babel, wherefore God *temporarily* confused their languages, causing them to disperse to the various countries they occupied in ancient times. The Cuthites were the first to rebel against God and to fall into idolatry, whence the unity of all pagan mythology, which can be deciphered if one knows the key; they were also the first inventors of the arts and sciences, such as astronomy and navigation, whence the story of the Cuthites' dispersal is the story of the beginnings of civilization everywhere, and of the unity of pagan mythology and science. Jones's adumbration of the Indo-European concept is based on Bryant's thesis, although he moves the Indians center stage and argues the evidence quite differently.

Jones's critique of Bryant is worth following in some detail, because it comes to the heart of his own method. Consistent with the authority claim of the new Orientalism, his objection to Bryant's system is that Bryant knew no Oriental language but Hebrew and that the system rested therefore upon etymologies that were sometimes ill-informed and very often of the loosest kind. The matter of etymology is crucial, for the comparative philology that will grow up around the Indo-European concept is in large part a new system of etymology claiming scientific status in competition with other existing systems, and etymology is the core of the linguistic aspect of Jones's ethnology. On two occasions in the anniversary discourses he criticizes etymology as a method in Bryant's work.

At the beginning of the third discourse, as Jones embarks upon his ethnological journey, he invokes Bryant, "whom I name with reverence and affection," but goes on to criticize his method:

Etymology has, no doubt, some use in historical researches; but it is a medium of proof so very fallacious, that, where it elucidates one fact, it obscures a thousand, and more frequently borders on the ridiculous, than leads to any solid conclusion: it rarely carries with it any *internal* power of conviction from a resemblance of sounds or similarity of letters; yet often, where it is wholly unassisted by those advantages, it may be indisputably proved by *extrinsick* evidence. (1807, 3:25)

We know *à posteriori,* that is to say outside the evidence of language itself (and in the absence of the famous "laws" of Indo-European sound shifts that are yet to be devised), that English *fitz* and Spanish *hijo,* which are not at all similar, nevertheless both derive from the Latin word *filius,* "son"; that, however different they may seem, *uncle* comes from Latin *avus* and *stranger* from Latin *extra.* Similarly, French *jour* is deducible, through the Italian, from Latin *dies,* "day," and *rossignol,* "nightingale," from *lucinia,* the "singer in groves"; Italian *sciuro,* French *écureuil,* and English *squirrel* are compounded of two Greek words descriptive of the animal. These etymologies could not have been demonstrated *à priori* because no similarity remains to guide one, and yet they are true, as we know by recourse to "extrinsick evidence." Knowing these etymologies might serve to confirm other evidence of historical relationship among the speakers of the languages in question as former members of the Roman Empire. Etymology, then, lacks the power to show on its own, unaided by outside evidence, the existence of relationships among cognates that are highly dissimilar (which of course is exactly the power that the later comparative philology claims for itself); nor is it able to discriminate misleadingly similar words that are not true cognates and are unrelated, of which Jones gives a number of examples, including English *hanger,* a short pendent sword, falsely derived from the misspelling of Persian *khanjar,* a different kind of weapon (1807, 3:26). The existence of historical derivations can be shown among European languages, therefore, but not by reliance on etymology alone.

Jones's critique of etymology turns to a parody of Bryant's methods in the ninth discourse:

I beg leave, as a philologer, to enter my protest against conjectural etymology in historical researches, and principally against the licentiousness of etymologists in transposing and inserting letters, in substituting at pleasure any consonant for another of the same order, and in totally disregarding the vowels: for such permutations few radical words would be more convenient than CUS or CUSH, since, dentals being changed for dentals, and palatials for palatials, it instantly becomes *coot, goose,* and by transposition, *duck,* all water-birds, and *evidently* symbolical; it next is the *goat* worshipped in *Egypt,* and, by a metathesis, the *dog* adored as an emblem of SIRIUS, or, more obviously, a *cat,* not the domestick animal, but a sort of ship, and, the *Catos,* or great sea-fish, of the *Dorians.* It will hardly be imagined, that I mean by this irony to insult an author, whom I respect and esteem; but no consideration should induce me to assist by my silence in the diffusion of errour; and I contend, that almost any word or nation might be derived from any other, if such licences, as I am opposing, were permitted in etymological histories. (1807, 3:199–200)

Bryant was furious when he read this.

But, Jones goes on, "when we find, indeed, the same words, letter for letter, and in a sense precisely the same, in different languages, we can scarce hesitate in allowing them a common origin" (1807, 3:200). Exact etymology of this kind, then, is not only admissible but compelling, and it is in fact Jones's conception of etymologies that can stand alone as first-class proofs. I blush for him, to name the three exact equivalents he finds in Sanskrit materials to support the Hamian character of the Hindu nation and prove that Sanskrit literature is a distant echo of the events of early history recorded by Moses: The Biblical Cus or Cush answers to Kuśa, a son of King Rāma; Rāma himself is the Biblical Raamah; and the Biblical Misraim (or Mizraim), from the root *Misr,* "Egypt," corresponds to the Sanskrit *miśra,* "mixed," which is a common surname in eastern India. All these Biblical names occur in the line of Ham, son of Noah (Genesis 10:6–7). Jones believes that Indian civil society, or civilization as we would say, was instituted by Rāma shortly after the flood of Noah, and thus India is one of the oldest of civilizations. With the unearned advantage of hindsight we can say that for Jones, who did not have the knowledge of regular sound shifts that would account for cognates that look dissimilar and who was unwilling to abandon etymology, his only method was to limit himself to those etymologies showing exact correspondences and to seek "extrinsick evidence" for confirmation.

I do not wish to dwell on this weakness in Jones's argument, and I do not suggest that his argumentation is on a level with that of Bryant; it is not accidental that Jones's work is remembered and Bryant's is largely forgotten. Jones's arguments, especially the linguistic ones, are generally very acute and are informed by far better knowledge of the languages in question. We see the real strengths of his ethnology if we follow it through the constituent parts and boundaries of what we now call the Indo-European family.

Perhaps the strongest part of Jones's argument, and the most durable, is his demonstration (in the sixth discourse, on the Persians) that Persian is closely related to Sanskrit, and that it is not closely related to Arabic, loanwords apart. Having twice read Firdausi, whose *Shahnameh* is almost devoid of Arabic words, he tells us, he finds that hundreds of Persian nouns are pure Sanskrit with no more change than one finds in the modern languages of India, that very many Persian imperatives are the roots of Sanskrit verbs, and that even the moods and tenses of the Persian verb substantive are deducible from the Sanskrit by an easy and clear analogy. Moreover, the identity is even closer in a vocabulary of the old language of the Zoroastrian holy book, the *Avesta,* published by Anquetil (1771). Jones was "inexpressibly surprised" to find that "six or seven words in ten were pure *Sanscrit*" and that some of their inflections followed the rules of Vyākaraṇa, the ancient Indian grammatical science (1807, 3:118). In the pure Persian, he says, there is no trace of any Arabian (i.e., Semitic) language except what is known to have been borrowed—a crucial point, since the segmentary logic of the linguistic family tree can only function accurately upon true cognates, which must therefore be discriminated from loanwords. In the fourth discourse, on the Arabs, Jones says of Arabic that it is unquestionably one of the most ancient languages and that it yields to no language in the number of its words and the precision of its phrases (that is, it is copious and regular, hence civilized); but, it bears no resemblance in words or the structure of them to Sanskrit. He gives two examples of difference: Sanskrit, like Greek, Persian, and German, delights in compounds, which Arabic and its sister dialects invariably express in circum-locutions; and Sanskrit and other languages of the same stock have roots that are almost universally biliteral, whereas those of Arabic are triliteral. He discusses a number of possible roots and words common to Sanskrit and Arabic, but comes to the conclusion that in whatever light we view them, they seem totally distinct and must have been in-vented by two different races of men; nor, he says, does he recollect a single word in common between them, except a possibly accidental one. The formation of the Indo-European concept (here called Indian), then, takes place with the distinction from it of a similarly formed con-cept of Semitic (here called Arabian), in a single continuous act of rea-soning. The one misstep in his treatment of the Semitic–Indo-Euro-pean boundary is that he wrongly classifies Pahlavi with Arabic and not Sanskrit. His judgment on the matter seems to have been unsettled by his quarrel with Anquetil and his desire to show him wrong.

Jones's identification of the Egyptians, Ethiopians, and Phoenicians with the Hindus was of course wrong, and it would not be defini-tively put aside until the decipherment of the ancient hieroglyphics by Jean-François Champollion. He rightly supposed the Coptic language of Egypt to be the modern descendant of the language of the hiero-glyphics. Its literature is a church literature, containing many Greek loanwords (especially ecclesiastical words) and written in a derivative of the Greek script, so that it could very well appear to be related to Greek (and hence Sanskrit); its true affiliations were in fact difficult to estab-lish. But there is surely an underlying fascination with the idea of an ancient connection of India and Egypt, seen already in Halhed, that motivated this particular interpretative outcome of evidence that could have been read either way.

Other Indo-European–speaking peoples, namely the Gypsies, Cey-lonese (or Sinhalese), and Armenians, are correctly classified, although the "Sclavonians" are wrongly grouped with the Tartars as Japhetites (who are uncivilized nomads, in his implicit scheme of things), and the Javanese, Tibetans, Central Asians, and Burmese are tentatively but wrongly identified with the Indians. Even the errors are learned ones. For example, of the Javanese, Jones observes with evident pleasure that Jean Baptiste D'Anville was unable to explain why the name Jabadios or Yavadvipa found in Ptolemy's *Geography* was rendered as "isle of bar-ley" in a Latin version of the text, since it makes no sense in Latin, whereas he was able to say that this shows that the name is Sanskrit, because in it "Yavadvīpa" does indeed mean "barley island." In this he was certainly correct. There are, moreover, multitudes of pure Sanskrit words in the principal languages of the Sumatrans, he says, as may be seen "without any recourse to etymological conjecture" (1807, 3:174). This of course is perfectly true; what he did not get right is that these Sanskritic words are *borrowings* in the languages of the Indonesian archipelago, an error resulting from the absence at that period of sufficient materials to make such a determination. Since William Marsden had shown the unity of language from Madagascar to the Philippines— what today we call the Malayo-Polynesian family—Jones (wrongly) assimilated all of them to his Indian group along with Java (in the eighth discourse, 1807, 3:173–175). Again, Tibetans and other peoples influenced by Indian Buddhism have writing systems that show the syllabic structure and alphabetical order of Devanagari and other Indian scripts used to write Sanskrit, which inclined Jones to class such peoples with the Indians. His errors, in short, are those of a very learned mind acting upon insufficient information. On the other hand, the recognition that the Gypsy language was closely related to Sanskrit was a brilliant hit. To be sure, the inclusion of the Gypsies among the Indian nation was also motivated by the belief that the Gypsies came from Egypt (from which they get their name), but from the vocabulary recently published by H. M. G. Grellmann (1787), Jones could say with authority that it "contains so many Sanscrit words, that their Indian origin can hardly be doubted." He gives as examples the Gypsy words *angár,* "charcoal"; *cásht,* "wood"; *pár,* "a bank"; *bhú,* "earth"—"and a hundred more, with no parallel in the vulgar dialect of Hindustan, though we know them to be pure Sanscrit scarce changed in a single letter" (1807, 3:170–171).[10]

On the more speculative frontiers of the Jonesean ethnology, he includes the Chinese and Japanese in his Hindu nation, following Manu's text (1886) to the effect that the "Cīnas" are lapsed Kṣatriyas who had neglected the Vedic rituals (10:44). All the pandits Jones consulted agreed that Manu's "Cīnas" had settled northeastward of Bengal and must therefore be the Chinese. There is no doubt that the identification of Sanskrit *Cīna* with the Chinese, which he regarded as new and

10. Cf. Skt. *aṅgāra, kāṣṭha, pāra, bhū.* The Indian origin of the Gypsy language (Romany) had only recently been suggested:

Ruediger (1782), Grellmann (1783) and Marsden (1783) almost simultaneously and independently of one another came to the same conclusion, that the language of the Gipsies, until then considered a thieve's jargon, was in reality a language closely allied with some Indian speech. (*Encyclopaedia Britannica,* 11 ed., s.v. *Gipsies*)

It would seem that it was Jones who first demonstrated a connection with Sanskrit, a point not noticed in the histories of the question.

important, was correct (the seventh discourse, on the Chinese, 1807, 3:142–143). He also notes, shrewdly, that the order of sounds in Chinese grammars corresponds nearly with that observed in Tibet, "and hardly differs from that, which the Hindus consider as the invention of their Gods," another good point (1807, 3:35). However, the discourse on the Chinese cannot be numbered among Jones's triumphs. The Incas and Mexicans are also tentatively classed with the Indians on the slender grounds of reports that the grand festival of the Peruvians is called Ramasitoa, which Jones takes to be a reference to the Hindu god Rāma. It is clear that Jones had a "two-nation" conception of the ethnology of the New World, according to which the civilized peoples of Mexico and Peru were colonies of his Hindus (and hence Hamians), while the nomadic Indians of the Americas were Tartars (and hence Japhetites) (1807, 3:39).

Finally, I should mention Jones's position on Hindi. Of the Braj Bhasha of Mathura, which Muslim sources mention, he says, five words in six, perhaps, are derived from Sanskrit, and it appears to have been formed by the imposition of an exquisite grammatical arrangement upon some unpolished language, "but the basis of the *Hindustani,* particularly the inflexions and regimen of verbs, differed as widely from both those tongues, as *Arabick* differs from the *Persian,* or *German* from *Greek.*" The general effect of conquest, he reasoned, is to leave the language of the conquered little altered in its groundwork, "but to blend with it a considerable number of exotick names both for things and actions," as is found in the language of the Turks in Greece and of the Saxons in Britain, "and this analogy might induce us to believe, that the pure *Hindi,* whether of *Tartarian* or *Chaldean* origin, was primeval in Upper *India,* into which the *Sanscrit* was introduced by conquerors from other kingdoms in some very remote age" (1807, 3:33–34). I note for future discussion (in chapter 5) the first argument for the presence of a non–Indo-European "substratum" language in the make-up of the Indian vernaculars.

Jones recapitulates in the ninth discourse. I will summarize his conclusions as a series of numbered points.

1. The Persians, Indians, Romans, Greeks, Goths, and ancient Egyptians or Ethiopians spoke the same language and professed the same popular religion. Whether the settlers in China and Japan had a common origin with the Hindus is no more than highly probable.

2. The Jews, Arabs, Assyrians, the speakers of Syriac, and the Abyssinians had a single ancestral language wholly distinct from the former.

3. It appears that all the Tartars were of a third, separate branch totally differing from the two others in language, manners, and features.

4. God created a single pair of every living species. The original human pair was gifted by God with sufficient wisdom and strength to be virtuous and happy, but entrusted with freedom of will to be vicious and degraded. As the population grew, humans dispersed from the place of origin, and forgetting by degrees the language of their progenitor, they formed new dialects to convey new ideas simple and complex. Laws and governments were formed.

5. The three branches of the human family migrated from a central country; call this country Iran. We then have straight lines of outmigration, which do not intersect as they would if the center were placed in Arabia, Egypt, India, Tartary, or China.

6. The three branches "have shot into their present state of luxuriance in a period comparatively short" (1807, 3:191). Civilization begins twelve, or at most, fifteen or sixteen centuries before Christ.

7. For sake of argument, Jones says, he has treated the narrative of Moses as he would any other (secular) text and found its truth confirmed by outside sources, especially Sanskrit ones, namely, the story of the flood, which is also found in the *Padma Purāna;* the Tower of Babel, remembered in the story of the man-lion avatar of God (Narasimha) who bursts forth from a pillar (!); the dispersal of the nations; and so forth. Thus the truth of the Mosaic narrative is confirmed by the testimony of other nations, and its inspired nature is further proved by the predictions of the Old Testament which are fulfilled in the Gospel.

8. One old dream had to be abandoned, that of recovering the language of Noah. It is lost irretrievably. After a diligent search, Jones says, "I cannot find a single word used in common by the *Arabian, Indian,* and *Tartar* families before the intermixture of dialects occasioned by *Mohammedan* conquests" (1807, 3:199). So far from being impelled by a desire to drive a wedge between Christians and Jews, as Martin Bernal (1987) has argued,

the creation of the Indo-European concept was the outcome of a program (in which Jones was only one of the more brilliant of many participants) of recovering the lost language of Noah and of Adam through the comparison of vocabularies.

9. The branch of Yaphet (Japhet) was scattered over the north of Europe and Asia and beyond the seas, cultivating no liberal arts and having no use of letters. They are, as we say, nomadic pastoralists. The children of Ham invented letters, observed and named the stars and planets, calculated the Indian astronomical period of 432,000 years, and contrived the system of pagan mythology, partly allegorical, partly grounded on idolatrous veneration of their sages and lawgivers. The Hamian tribes of Misr, Cush, and Rama settled in Africa and India. Some of them improved the art of sailing and passed into Italy and Greece, while "a swarm from the same hive" (1807, 3:202) moved into Scandinavia, and another, by the head of the Oxus, through the passes of the Himalaya into Kashghar and Eighur, Khata and Khotan, as far as the territories of Chin and Tangut, and possibly overseas to Mexico and Peru. The progeny of Shem, who settled on the Red Sea, peopled the whole Arabian peninsula and pressed close on the nations of Syria and Phenicia. Of these events we have "no history unmixed with fable, except that of the turbulent and variable, but eminently distinguished, nation descended from ABRAHAM" (1807, 3:203).

## Finding India's Place

We must now step back and look at Jones's project in a larger frame—the project, so to say, of finding India's place. I shall be examining it under three rubrics: the Mosaic ethnology, its past and its future; time; and ancient wisdom.

### THE MOSAIC ETHNOLOGY, ITS PAST AND FUTURE

The Mosaic ethnology, of course, is not an invention of the eighteenth century. It is the common heritage of Jews, Christians, and Muslims—the Peoples of the Book, so to say—and it figures regularly in universal histories as a starting point for the classification of peoples. Its source is the first eleven chapters of the book of Genesis in the Bible, in which the nations are accounted for by a genealogy of the descent of Noah and of his three sons subsequent to the flood, when they were scattered across the earth following the confusion of their languages after they had built the Tower of Babel against God's wishes. Jones's project had its immediate antecedent in Bryant, but it was also a recent version of a very old ethnological paradigm.

Given that the approach to Hindu learning was made in the first instance through an older, Biblical Orientalism that was based upon the study of Hebrew, Arabic, and Persian, it is not perhaps surprising that we find some aspects of Jones's particular instantiation of Mosaic ethnology prefigured in Muslim sources. First was the determination that the Hindus were descendants of Ham. India was one of the many nations not named in Genesis because it did not fall in the text's narrow geographical horizon, but it had long since become a commonplace of Muslim histories that the Hindus had descended from Ham. In Dow's translation of Firishtah, for example, we have a full-blown Mosaic ethnology in which India's place is specified: Shem is progenitor of the Arabs and Persians; Japhet has sons named Turc, Chin, and Rus, from whom the Turks, Chinese, and Russians are respectively descended; and Ham begat Hind (India), Sind (Sindh, the Indus region), Habysh (Abyssinia), Zinge, Barber, and Nobah. Hind in turn had four sons: Purib, Bang (Bengal), Decan (Deccan), and Nerwaal, and these in turn had named sons who founded the great tribes (Firishtah 1768:7–9). In Abuʾl Fazl's *Akbar Nāma* (1908, 1:chap. 16), likewise, the distribution of Noah's descent is specified, and Ham has sons named Hind and Sindh; Japhet was the most just of Noah's sons, with whom the lofty lineage of the Mughal emperor Akbar was linked. Any of Jones's encounters with Muslim-Indian texts or scholars would have reinforced his application of the Mosaic ethnology to India and India's place in the Hamian line, although to be sure we do not have to look farther than Bryant for these ideas in Jones's work. However, and in the second place, there is one striking coincidence between Jones's ethnology and that of classical Islam that has not, I believe, been pointed out before. In Muslim universal histories such as the vast treatise of al-Masʿūdī (see Khalidi 1975) and the short book of Ṣāʿid ibn Aḥmad Andalusī, the ancient nations subsequent to the destruction of the Tower of Babel were seven: those of the Persians, the Chaldeans (whence the ancient

Hebrews and Arabs), the Greeks, the Egyptians, the Turks, the Indians, and the Chinese, each of which was, at the outset, of one language and one kingdom and subsequently subdivided into many nations (Khalidi 1975:88–108; Andalusī 1068:chap. 1). Leaving aside the Egyptians of Africa and the Greeks of Europe, the remaining five nations correspond to Jones's five principal nations who had peopled Asia prior to the birth of Muhammad, the subjects of the anniversary discourses. Thus there is reason to think that the frame of Jones's ethnological project had been structured long before. Finally, both these Muslim sources speak of India as the first of the seven ancient nations to have cultivated the sciences (Khalidi 1975:102–106; Andalusī 1068:chap. 5). The reputation of India as a repository of wisdom is also very old and long predates the British Indomania we will examine in the next chapter.

It was within the same Mosaic framework that French discussions of India were being carried out in the mid-eighteenth century. Murr (1983:263–265) cites opinions of this period to the effect that the brahmins were descended from Shem or Ham, whereas Père Coeurdoux, writing to the Académie des Inscriptions in about 1768 (although the text was not published until 1808 by Anquetil), derived them from Magog, son of Japhet, and routed them through Central Asia:

The Samskroutam language is that of the ancient Brahmes; they came to India from the north of that country, from Caucasia, from Tartary, which had been peopled by the descendants of Magog. Of the sons of Japhet, some spoke Greek, others Latin, still others Sanskroutam. Before their total separation, their languages were somewhat mixed because of the communication they had among each other; and there remain vestiges of that ancient intercourse, in the common words which still exist, and of which I have reported a part. (cited in Anquetil 1808:666; see also Murr 1987, 1:chap. 7)

This is a striking anticipation of the Indo-European idea, supported moreover by several lists of cognate words in Sanskrit and Latin. In addition, Père Coeurdoux's discussion of the similarities between Sanskrit, Latin, and Greek carefully considers and refutes the earlier suggestion that they are due to commerce or the Indian expedition of Alexander, arguing that we would have to believe that the Indians had lacked until then terms for fathers, mothers and brothers, and for feet, nose, and teeth (Anquetil 1808:661). His treatment lacks Jones's reference to Celtic, Gothic, and Old Persian, and its conception of historical process in language is less modern: The similarity of Sanskrit, Greek, and Latin is due to a partial *mixture* of different but (formerly) neighboring languages rather than the gradual differentiation of languages among the separated branches of a people originally speaking a common language that is now lost. Nevertheless the outcome bears a distinct resemblance to the Indo-European doctrine and goes to show not only that had Jones not gone to India the Indo-European doctrine would have been discovered by someone else but also that, in fact, it *had* been discovered, in a measure, before Jones. It shows, too, that it is not important to which branch of the descent of Noah Sanskrit, Latin, and Greek were assigned, so long as they were assigned to the same branch. What is important is the conjuncture of persons educated in Latin and Greek encountering Sanskrit and interpreting their similarities by means of the segmentary structure of the Mosaic ethnology. Under this conjuncture, the discovery of the Indo-European language family was bound to happen sooner or later.

What was rather distinctive of European pursuit of ethnological issues within this framework since the Renaissance was the attention to language and the use of word lists. G. W. Leibniz is an important figure in the formation of this project, but long before him there was J. J. Scaliger, and before him the medieval lists of the seventy-two languages of the world based on the seventy-two descendants of Noah's three sons named in Genesis according to St. Augustine in *City of God* (1950, 16.6; Borst 1957–63). Polyglot dictionaries, polyglot collections of the Pater Noster in the languages of the world, and polyglot vocabularies against standardized lists were being constructed by Europeans in the eighteenth century in the lead-up to the formation of Indo-Europeanist philology. Two such projects were being inaugurated, more or less simultaneous with and independent of that of Jones and in vastly different places: Catherine of Russia's collection of vocabularies against a standardized list (eventually published by P. S. Pallas, 1786–89), and Thomas Jefferson's proposal for the collection of such lists from American Indian languages, which was carried out by the American Philosophical Society under his protégé Stephen Duponceau (Jefferson 1782: 179–180). The Mosaic ethnology is one of those large, enduring projects that has preoccupied a large number of people over many centuries.[11]

The structure of the Mosaic ethnology as we find it in Genesis is

11. For Umberto Eco (1995), the various linguistic projects of European scholars, including comparative philology, are so many versions of the search for the perfect language. He describes this special fascination as a response to the foundational linguistic anxiety of Europe, which was born of the decay of Latin into the Romance languages, and the Germanic invasions.

segmentary (as we have seen in the previous chapter). The genealogical tree is a patrilineal one, and the units are not the nations as such but their eponymous ancestors, patriarchs whose names are the supposed sources of national names such as Eber (Hebrew) and Javan (Ionian, Greek), and, in the Muslim sources we have been speaking of, such extra-Biblical patriarchs as Hind and Sind. The radiating, segmentary character of the underlying genealogical figure requires that the specifications be unilineal, in the instance of males related through males. It is worth noting that the Hindu ethnological frame of the *jātis* (castes) which Jones met in the Sanskrit lawbook of Manu that he translated (1794), is quite different. In it we do not have a segmentary arrangement of units; rather, the social units are outcomes of the *mixed* statuses of fathers *and* mothers (although one finds something rather more analogous in the Puranic king lists). Thus we have in the Dharmaśāstra doctrine of *jātis* a theory of ethnogenesis through intermixture or marriage of persons of different *varṇas,* and secondary and tertiary intermixtures of the original ones, leading to a multitude of units, rather than the radiating segmentary structure of ethnogenesis by fission or descent. The segmentary lineage kind of society that gives rise to the Mosaic ethnology, so different from that which leads to ethnological thinking of the kind we find in Manu and related Hindu texts, seems to comprise a large region including the so-called tribal structures of the Arab world and the Blue Nile. Paul Dresch (1988), indeed, finds a link between the segmentary thinking of the Arab world, via the influence of W. Robertson Smith (*Kinship and marriage in early Arabia,* 1885), and of E. E. Evans-Pritchard's famous study of the Nuer (1940). As I have suggested in the previous chapter, it is no coincidence that the Genesis narrative with its segmentary logic comes from an area that comprehends segmentary Arab tribal charters and the Nuer segmentary lineages.

The segmentary structure of the tree of nations persists and propagates itself into the nineteenth century and beyond. For all the faults and errors of Jones's ethnology, the Mosaic frame and the method of comparing vocabularies and grammars were the necessary elements for imagining the Indo-European language family and Indo-European speaking peoples. This tree paradigm remains very much the foundation of historical linguistics to this day, although a kind of willful collective amnesia has tended to suppress its Biblical origins. The names Semitic and Hamitic persist as vestigial reminders of the real source of the "genetic" or genealogical relations among languages which historical linguists continue to study. As to the Indo-European family, the

Bryant-Jones identification for Indo-Europeans as Hamians was decidedly unusual and did not stick, but neither did the name Japhetite, so that the Biblical element in the composition of this family became less salient. In the self-conception of linguistics there came to be a strong tendency to imagine that its central conceptual structure comes from comparative anatomy and to forget that it comes from the Bible. In British ethnology, too, as we shall see throughout this book, the structure of the Mosaic family tree of nations was the central idea for the first half and more of the nineteenth century, against which the polygenist notion of separate creation of the races was distinctly unorthodox. And finally, I note that Darwin, in the chapter on classification in *Origin of species,* employs the segmentary tree as the organizing conception for the classification of species on the basis of the degree of relationship among them, and in doing so illustrates his meaning by analogy with this very ethnological figure:

It may be worth while to illustrate this view of classification, by taking the case of languages. If we possessed a perfect pedigree of mankind, a genealogical arrangement of the races of man would afford the best classification of the various languages now spoken throughout the world; and if all extinct languages, and all intermediate and slowly changing dialects, had to be included, such an arrangement would, I think, be the only possible one. . . . The various degrees of difference in the languages from the same stock, would have to be expressed by groups subordinate to groups; but the proper or even only possible arrangement would still be genealogical. (1859:422–423; see also Trautmann 1987:215)

### TIME

Integral to the Mosaic ethnology was a certain frame of time. The exercise of matching up distant nations to the nations named in the Bible also required that the unfolding of the whole ethnological story be contained within the short chronology that the Peoples of the Book allotted to the peopling of the earth after the flood of Noah. There were many calculations as to when exactly this was, but for British Protestants the matter had been settled by Archbishop Ussher in the seventeenth century. God had created the world in 4004 B.C. and the flood of Noah had taken place in 2349 B.C. That meant that the development of all ethnological variety, and the spread of the human race across the earth, had begun only four thousand years ago, and its completion had to be accounted for in a quick-tempo history.

In respect of time, India proved at once helpful and resistant to the

Mosaic ethnology. On the one hand, the flood narrative in the Purāṇas could be read, and was, as independent confirmation of the flood of Noah. Jones seized this possibility as the foundation of his ethnology, and in doing so he was able to demonstrate that the study of Hindu scripture fortified Christian truth against the skeptics. On the other hand, the ancient Indian doctrine of immense cycles of time repeating endlessly, on a titanic scale, dwarfed the time of the Biblical narrative. Dow, Halhed, and other pre-Jonesean scholars had been attracted to the possibilities of this long chronology, but Jones firmly rejected it, with such authority that a European consensus came about, joining believers and skeptics in the rejection of Indian time (for details see Trautmann 1995).

Jones's reconciliation of the story of the past in Sanskrit literature with the Biblical narrative fixes upon the list of Viṣṇu's ten avatars or "descents" into earthly form to save the good from destruction by forces of evil. The series begins with three avatars that were especially associated with the story of a worldwide flood: the fish, the tortoise, and the boar. The fish incarnation in particular seems readymade for identification with the Biblical flood, carrying Manu (the first human), his family, and the seven sages (ṛṣis) in a ship (the Ark of Noah!) fastened to a horn on his head. Jones identifies Manu with Noah, distinguishing this Manu from an earlier one, the progenitor of the human race, whom he identifies with Adam. Manu II, then, and the seven sages can be identified with the eight humans aboard the Ark in the Biblical story (Noah, his three sons, and the four wives), from whom the entire human race has since been propagated. Jones furthermore identifies the fourth avatar of Viṣṇu, the man-lion Narasiṃha, with the Biblical Nimrod, descendant of Ham. Bali, the demon who was overcome by the fifth avatar, the dwarf Vāmara, is identified with the Biblical Bel. The seventh incarnation, king Rāma of Ayodhyā, Jones identifies with the Biblical Raamah, also in the line of Ham; with him begins "civil government" in India, or as we would say, civilization. In this manner the whole series of avatars of Viṣṇu can be forced into the diluvian and postdiluvian chronology, and Sanskrit literature can be read as reporting the same historical events as does Genesis. But this reconciliation of Indian chronology with the Biblical chronology is only possible by simultaneously rejecting the vast spans of time that make up the *yugas*, *kalpas*, and *manvantaras* of Indian time cycles. The four *yugas* are squeezed into the Ussherite chronology, rejecting the traditional figures for their duration (4,320,000 years for the entire cycle of four

ages), or the traditional dating of the beginning of the Kali, namely
3102 B.C. In outline, Jones's Mosaic reading of Indian chronology may
be represented as follows (Jones 1807, 4:24,48; see Trautmann 1995):

| Adam | Manu I | Kṛta *yuga* | 4004 B.C. |
|------|--------|-------------|-----------|
| Noah | Manu II | | 2948 B.C. |
| the flood | fish, tortoise, boar avatars | | 2349 B.C. |
| Nimrod | Narasiṃha | Tretā *yuga* | 2217 B.C. |
| Bel | Bali | | 2105 B.C. |
| Raamah | King Rāma | Dvāpara *yuga* | 2028 B.C. |
| | the Buddha | Kali *yuga* | 1026 B.C. |

Both the acceptance of Hindu flood mythology as history and the rejection of Indian cyclical time as mythology are part of the unitary
project of the Mosaic ethnology.

## ANCIENT WISDOM

The final aspect of finding India's place has to do with
the idea of ancient wisdom. Jones embraces the Newton-Bryant theory
of the unity of ancient astronomy and paganism, and like Bryant he
puts all the civilized nations of antiquity in the same descent line from
Noah—that of Ham. For Jones, Hinduism was the living cousin of the
religion of the other Hamians, more especially of the ancient Greek
and Roman texts. Thus, besides supporting the Bible, Hinduism had
this second source of fascination. We see this idea worked out at length
in an early essay, "On the gods of Greece, Italy, and India" (1807, 3:319–
397; written in 1784), in which he develops a series of parallels among
Greco-Roman gods and Hindu ones. His notion of a genetic relation
between the two sets of divinities has proved a useful and durable one,
although one has to say that not one of the comparisons he proposes
has held up, and the cognate divinities among the three ancient peoples
that are accepted today are in fact few (Zeus Pater = Jupiter = Dyaus
Pitṛ; Uranos = Varuṇa; Eos = Uṣas; and one or two more).

To the Newton-Bryant thesis he adds the idea that the Greeks, Romans, Indians, and Egyptians were originally one people who separated
into many and migrated to their respective countries from a common
center in the Middle East, namely Chaldea or Iran; from India the common religion and civilization had spread eastward to China and Japan,
and perhaps also to Mexico and Peru. In their development of astronomy and the arts of navigation, among others, the Hamians or Indians

had promoted the first beginnings of civilization, while in their idolatry they had first departed from the pure original religion of Noah. This unitary idolatry or paganism would be revealed by the comparative study of mythologies. But idolatry was only the popular religion, behind which lay the original natural religion, still adhered to by the philosophers. The program of comparative religion that this vision entails, then, has a strong element in it of a search for ancient wisdom, a primitive monotheism, which Jones tends to identify with the teaching of the Veda, or rather, of the Vedānta.

All three of these elements, the Mosaic ethnology, the short Biblical chronology, and the idea of ancient wisdom, had to come together to find a place for India that would sustain the hopes of an Oriental renaissance. For there was no question in Jones's mind that Christianity was the only true religion and that Europe's talents, on the whole, surpassed those of Asia, as they had since the times of the ancient Greeks. The three faculties of the human mind were everywhere the same: memory, reason, and imagination, the sources of history, science or philosophy, and poetry (Jones 1807, 3:5–6). Asiatics excelled in imagination, and it was one of Jones's many projects to bring that imagination to the invigoration of English poetry; in doing so he played a role in the beginnings of Romanticism. Asiatic history, both civil history (human history, ethnology, the history of civilization) and natural history, of course, was of enormous value in his eyes.[12] And the study of the Indian sciences would, he thought, be of great benefit. But reason and taste were the grand prerogatives of European minds (Jones 1807, 3:12–13), and in science, he said, it must be admitted that the Asiatics are "mere children" (1807, 3:19). The great scientific accomplishments of India lay in the past, and the study of Indian science, therefore, was a contribution to history, not to current science. India, then, was by no means the sign of the future; Europe most decidedly was. This was the second point upon which Jones and the future critics of the new Orientalism were agreed. The rejection of Indian time and the superiority of European science were the two articles of common belief

---

12. For Jones, history is identified with the descriptive level and science or philosophy with the theoretical level. Thus history comprises human history and the description of the natural world (natural history). Science embraces mathematics, the natural sciences, ethics, and law as subjects that have risen to the theoretical level. Language study he put low on the intellectual scale: "I have ever considered languages as the mere instruments of real learning, and think them improperly confounded with learning itself," although they are indispensable to opening the immense mine of the literatures of Asia (Jones 1807, 3:7).

uniting Orientalists and their European antagonists (as we shall see in chapter 4).

It would be a mistake to overread this consensus or to underrate the element of ancient wisdom in the fascination India held for Jones and to read as merely antiquarian the view that India is only a museum of Europe's discarded past. This misreading shares the perspective of James Mill, Jones's great critic; it is a secular, progressive, science-based perspective, the perspective, if I may call it that, of "future wisdom." The belief in ancient wisdom, that changeless truths were revealed in the past and are recoverable only through the study of the past, is religious in character, and it can occur side by side with a "future wisdom" belief in the cumulative progress of scientific knowledge, as it did in Jones. It is hard to recapture this almost Masonic sense of the present value of India's past.[13]

If, then, it were the case that India was one of the first civilized nations of the postdiluvian world and an inventor of sciences, and if, above all, Sanskrit literature was a repository of the most ancient written records of the human kind, recording not only the popular religion of ancient paganism but the philosophers' recollection of primitive monotheism, of the natural religion taught by the unsullied light of nature to the patriarchs of the Bible and bequeathed by Noah to the ancient nations—if, in short, India were a source of knowledge of ancient wisdom—Europeans would find, as they did, that India (to borrow a phrase from Lévi-Strauss) is "good to think."

---

13. Perhaps someday someone will work out the relations between Freemasonry and the Orientalist study of India. This is one of those good ideas that is very difficult to carry out. I offer the following tantalizing passage from *The royal Masonic cyclopaedia*:

The first Masonic Lodge in India was granted in 1728 by Lord Kingston, the Grand Master, by deputation to Brother George Pomfret, for Bengal, but the Masonic position of India remained in abeyance until 1740, when the Lodge Star in the East, no. 70, was established at Calcutta. It was soon after introduced into Madras and Bombay, and the Grand Lodge of Hindustan was finally established with independent powers in 1875. The progress of Masonry in that country has been very surprising, and the natives have vied with the English and Scottish residents in spreading it abroad. At some future time, there can be little doubt that India will repay the mother country for the care shown in sowing the seeds of the Craft, the peculiar idiosyncracies of the inhabitants being of a kind calculated to foster Masonic impressions, and the great attention which the last half century, in the person of its scholars, has paid to ancient Indian literature, will afford great and enduring satisfaction to archaeologists and students of symbolism. (Mackenzie 1877:334, s.v. *India*)

CHAPTER 3

# British Indomania

~

By 1875, when Sir Henry Maine gave the Rede Lecture
on "The effects of observation of India upon European thought," the
dullness of Indian subjects to Britons had become proverbial and the
greater enthusiasm for India on the European continent had long since
been evident. It is surely a paradox that British imperial rule should have
rendered India dull to those back home, while European enthusiasm
for India raged. How did this strange state of affairs come about—or
need we even trouble ourselves to ask?

It may be thought that the differences between Britons and Indians
are so great that British Indophobia (at worst) or indifference (at best)
was inevitable and in some sense natural, and that there is no mystery
here that is in need of explaining. Indeed, the great gulf of difference
separating the two "races," the rulers and the ruled, is a staple of the
historical literature whose implicit thesis is that the nonmeeting of
minds between them was determined from long before their encounter
(e.g., Spear 1963:chap. 8). But, as I shall show in this chapter, in the
decades following the conquest of Bengal there was a significant sector
of British opinion that, entertaining quite the opposite opinion, found
in Indian culture "a deep and appealing wisdom, [and] argued that the
Indian people had a way of life that was valid for them, however different it might be from western civilization" (Embree 1962:148). This is a
capital fact, which goes to show that the proverbial dullness of Indian
subjects for the British of whom Sir Henry speaks was not a permanent
condition arising from the nature of things but has a history that we

must try to capture. More than that, the early British enthusiasm for India goes to show that there are both differences and likenesses between any two peoples and that what signifies is the determination to magnify one and minimize the other. There is always an interpretative choice to be made, and we must observe the direction and seek out the causes of those choices.

Taking a different tack, one perhaps might wish to say that an enthusiasm for India was a predictable feature of early colonial rule, when everything Indian had the aspect of novelty, and that Indophobia, equally, is the predictable face of late colonialism. There is something in this view: The mere fact of conquest pressed more heavily with the passage of time, and as it appeared to become a permanent and immovable fact it bred contempt for Indians and their civilization. But this datum is too crude; it explains nothing of the actual content either of British enthusiasm for India or opposition to it.

I am going to argue in the next chapter that British Indophobia was made, not born. To persuade readers of this, and to show that there is a problem here that wants solving, I shall develop in this chapter the evidence for the existence of a British enthusiasm for India, beginning, say, in the 1760s (shortly after the conquest of Bengal) and continuing into the early nineteenth century. British Indophobia was above all a deliberate attack upon the built-up structure of a prior Indomania; it was devised to oppose it.

In making the case for British Indomania I do not wish to make the phenomenon appear larger than it really was. Indomania was not like Beatlemania—it was not a mass phenomenon or in any sense a popular movement. It was an enthusiasm for India that was entertained by a few very well educated Britons, most of them male, and although the high visibility of its proponents gave Indomania a certain resonance among the elite in Britain, it was not able to send down roots deeply into the other strata of the British social system. The circumscription as to class and gender on the subject side had an answering circumscription on the side of the Indian object: It was the learning of male brahmins in Sanskrit, the sister dialect of the Latin and Greek that educated English gentlemen studied as the object of their enthusiasm, not the culture of Indians generally. Indomania, moreover, was directed toward the Hindus and not the Muslims of India, even though the Persian language played a large role in the recovery of this object. It was concerned more especially with Indian civilization in most ancient times, prior to the coming of the Muslims. It sought out the Hindus in the belief that here, in the layer of the Indian population that lay under the Mughal imperial structure, was a living reservoir of ancient paganism and ancient wisdom.

As to the intellectual content of Indomania, its fundamental postulate was the great antiquity of civilization in India, and enthusiasts drew upon some subset of the following propositions: that India's arts and sciences came from Egypt, or that India had colonized Egypt in ancient times and planted its civilization there; that India's civilization, in relation to that of Greece, was original and older; that in its religion was to be found not only the living representative of a unitary ancient paganism (more especially the living cousin of the paganism of Greece and Rome), but the primitive truths of natural religion from which that paganism was a departure; and that its scriptures, being very old and independent of the Bible, either supplemented or confirmed its authority.

The enthusiasm for India, then, was above all an enthusiasm for Hinduism. I shall examine this new phenomenon and its relation to Christianity at some length in the writings of the pre-Joneseans (or, more accurately, those early characterizations of Hinduism by writers who had not acquired a working knowledge of Sanskrit), and in those of Jones himself. Thereafter I shall take up some of the ramifications of Indomania: enthusiasm for the Sanskrit language, for Indian astronomy, for ancient Indian geographical knowledge of Egypt and the British Isles, and for an Indian connection with Celtomania.

## Hinduism

What P. J. Marshall (1970) calls "the British discovery of Hinduism" had a sudden onset in the second half of the eighteenth century. British merchants had been trading with India for the better part of two centuries before the Battle of Plassey turned them into territorial rulers, but the new Orientalism perceived itself in terms of a sharp discontinuity with the past. In the accounts of the 1760s—Luke Scrafton's *Reflections on the government . . . of Indostan* (1761), Holwell's *Interesting historical events, relative to the provinces of Bengal, and the Empire of Indostan* (1765–71), and Dow's introduction to his translation of Firishtah's *History of Hindostan* (1768)—is a breathless sense of having just come upon the literature of a vast and ancient religion that had been vaguely known and thoroughly distorted by all the Europeans who came before. To these accounts we can add the somewhat later work of Quentin Craufurd, *Sketches chiefly relating to the history, religion, learning, and manners, of the Hindoos* (1790) and of course the greatest of the pre-Joneseans, Halhed (whose translation of the *Code of Gentoo laws* [1776] and *Grammar of the Bengal language* [1778] I have already introduced), plus various works of non-India hands, above all the Rev. William Robertson (*An historical disquisition concerning the knowledge which the ancients had of India*, 1812; first edition, 1791). Taken together with the *Asiatic Researches* these form the core texts of British Indomania.

The portrait of the Hinduism that is discovered in these publications is highly favorable; indeed it consistently shows a disposition to put the most favorable construction upon the information the writers have managed to acquire of Hindu religion and history. The main features, which are more or less the same in all the renderings, are two: that Hinduism is basically monotheistic, and that the benevolence of its religion and laws made India a prosperous and peaceful country before foreign conquest.

## HINDUISM IS MONOTHEISTIC

Hinduism's evident use of images, so offensive to Protestant Christianity, is explained as a lapse or a secondary formation of priestcraft, not the essence of the religion. According to Scrafton, for example, the brahmins are taught to believe in one Supreme Being who has created a regular gradation of beings, some of them superior and others inferior to humans, in the immortality of the soul, and in a future state of rewards and punishments, which takes the form of transmigration into different bodies according to the lives they have previously led. But, believing that "sensible objects were necessary to make this intelligible to the vulgar, their doctrines have been taught in allegory" by the use of images (Scrafton 1761:5). We find similar sentiments elsewhere. In short, we have in this and the other texts a fundamental distinction between the monotheism of the brahmins (good) and the popular religion of images (not so good), together with a disposition to put the most favorable interpretation on the meaning and significance of images. Craufurd, for example, says that if we abstract our minds from the abuses of the Hindu religion and inquire into the spirit, we find "that it inculcates the belief in one God only, without beginning and without end" (1790:139). The result is not surprising; it follows from the initial determination to abstract the mind from "abuses" and to inquire into the "spirit" that prefigures it. The disposition to read

Hinduism as Christianity is evident both in the emphasis on common ground and the very language of description. The twofold character of Hinduism develops over time: Monotheism comes first; imagery is its later translation into a popular idiom. Thus the study of Hinduism is deflected from the present to the ancient past.

## THE RELIGION AND LAWS OF HINDUISM MADE INDIA PROSPEROUS

The moral worth of Hindu religion and the benevolence of its system of government and laws are inferred from the size and prosperity of the Indian population prior to its subjugation by foreigners. The eastern countries were the first to be inhabited, and the civilization of India—its cultivation of the arts and sciences—is taken for granted and reckoned to be the work of ages. The Indian climate and landscape are highly favorable to human habitation and agriculture. We need no greater proof, according to Scrafton, of the goodness of the government than the immense revenue of India, "many of the Gentoo provinces yielding a revenue in proportion of the extent of country equal to our richest countries in Europe" (Scrafton 1761:13). This Indian prosperity, however, tends to get located somewhere in the past, before foreign conquest. In Scrafton and Craufurd the prosperity and well-being of India is more especially illustrated by the condition of South India before the war of the English and French (Scrafton 1761:13; Craufurd 1790:89), and Scrafton considers the contemporary Hindu Maratha rulers to have "vastly deviated from the true Gentoo character" (1761:15). More generally the ills of contemporary India tend to be attributed to Muslim conquest rather than being interpreted as evidence contrary to the thesis of Indian prosperity as an outcome of the benevolence of Hindu religion and government. Here again, the discovery of Hinduism tends to displace its object into the past, even a remote past. Robertson's treatment of India is a sustained attempt to lay open to view "the ancient and high civilization of the inhabitants of India" (1812:197), the benevolent-religion-and-government theme that describes the times before Alexander.

## THE *DISCOVERY* OF HINDUISM— OR ITS *INVENTION*?

Hinduism is a loosely knit assemblage of systems of belief and ritual whose unity was only vaguely evident to the British. With

the growing appreciation that there existed a large and ancient literature in Sanskrit which, they came to believe, was the historical source
of all the non-Muslim religious systems of India, Hinduism took shape
in British minds as the religion of the native Indians, or the Gentoos, or
the Hindoos, in distinction from the Muslims; Muslims were regarded
as foreign conquerors. In Scrafton, for example, the Muslim population
consists of foreign conquerors as opposed to native Indians, and it is
broken down into Arabs, Pathans, Afghans, Mongol Tartars, and Persians, plus slaves. There is no recognition of indigenous Muslims other
than "slaves," and the numbers are hugely underrated: The Moors are
not "the hundredth part of the natives" (Scrafton 1761:20). Rural Bengal's millions of Muslims are not yet visible. Hostility to Muslim religion and rulership of India is very pronounced in Scrafton, and it is
a leitmotif of much of this literature. Most of the evils of India are
attributed to Muslim conquest and despotic rule, and the virtues of
Hindu laws and customs are contrasted favorably, as if to say that Indian
civilization will spring up once the overburden of Muslim rule is pulled
back. Consistent with that view, the Orientalist element of British government in India that begins with Warren Hastings tends to represent
that government as enfranchising the Hindus, as Rosane Rocher (1993)
has recently shown. One of the characteristic effects of the subsequent
Indophobia of the anti-Orientalists was to invert this relative valuation
of Hinduism and Islam (as we shall see in the next chapter).

Nevertheless, there are a number of good reasons to be wary of saying that the British invented Hinduism. Many of the elements of the
way in which Hinduism is construed by the British in the period of
Indomania derive from Indians and Indian sources. It cannot be an accident that the superior value of ancient times and sources in British
discussion of Hinduism is so strikingly consistent with the "degenera-
tionist" character of brahmin views of the historical process, involving
among other things a decline in virtue and religion as the golden age
of the Kṛta *yuga* recedes and the present age of iron (the Kali *yuga*),
in which it is our misfortune to live, lengthens. Moreover, the view of
Muslims as having come from outside India and the Hindus as natives,
and the contrast of religion between the two, is very likely to have been
gotten from Indians themselves, especially from Indian Muslims and
Persian-language histories of India. The very (Persian) word *Hindu* for
an inhabitant of India and follower of a certain religion shows that the
conception predated British contacts with India. In any case the British
conception of Hinduism as the religion of the natives of India is well
along in its development in the seventeenth century, when Henry Lord

wrote an account of what we would recognize as Hinduism, calling it the sect of the Banians—the merchant caste with whom the English trades were most familiar—whom he calls "the ancient natives of India" (Lord 1630). To adopt the view that the British had no conception of Hinduism before the new Orientalism we are reviewing here would be to fall in with the propaganda of its own authority claims.

To convey a fuller sense of the content of early British Indomania I should like to examine some of the writers in greater detail, namely Holwell, Dow, and Halhed, with a brief return to Jones. I begin with John Zephaniah Holwell because he is one of the earliest exponents of British enthusiasm for the Hindu religion and because his is, in some ways, the era's most extreme example. Holwell came to believe, and publicly declared, that the Hindu scriptures completed the Biblical revelation and supplied its hitherto hidden meaning.[1]

Holwell's account of Hinduism is somewhat baffling because, although the description bears a family resemblance to the thing described, the texts to which he refers are—how shall I put it?—not otherwise known, before or since. There are three sets of writing that comprise what he called the Shastah (Śāstra) or Hindu scriptures. The details of his account are confusing, but it is important to try to disentangle them. According to Howell, the first and earliest text is the *Chartah Bhade Shastah* of Bramah, meaning (according to Holwell) "four scriptures of divine words of the mighty spirit" (i.e., Brahmā). This would be something like *Catur Veda Śāstra* in Sanskrit, an odd title since it combines two classes of Sanskrit literature that are distinct, Veda and Śāstra. It is a confused reference, one supposes, to the four Vedas. The second text, a paraphrase of the first, composed a thousand years later and called the *Chatah Bhade* of Bramah, or the six (Skt. *ṣaṣ;* cf. *ṣaṣṭha,* "sixth") scriptures of the mighty spirit, whose referent (the six Vedāṅgas or Vedic sciences? the six Darśanas or philosophies?) is entirely obscure. Finally, five hundred years later the Goseyns and Battezaaz brahmins published the third text, a commentary on the latter, in eighteen books, the *Aughtorrah Bhade Shastah,* or the eighteen (Skt. *aṣṭādaśa*) books of divine words; this, from the number, should be the eighteen major

---

1. Holwell's exposition of Hinduism is found in the second volume of his *Interesting historical events, relative to the provinces of Bengal, and the Empire of Indostan* (1765–71), published in 1767, especially chapter 4, "The religious tenets of the Gentoos, followers of the Shastah of Bramah," upon which I draw for the matter in the next two paragraphs. His more speculative constructions of the bearing of Hindu doctrine on the interpretation of Christianity come in the third volume, published four years later.

Purāṇas. Of these three texts, the first contains the primitive truth, pure and unadulterated; the second contains the beginning of polytheism; and in the third, the original teaching is covered over in ritualism and myth. This last caused a schism between North and South India, the south following, rather, the Viedam (= Veda!), based upon the second text, but in fact further corrupted; Holwell does not seem to understand that his *Bhade* is the same word as his *Viedam,* the one under a Bengali pronunciation, the other a Tamil one. The original pure teaching is utterly lost except to three or four Goseyn families, he says, who expound it from the Sanskrit. Holwell claims to have owned two copies of the Shastah (which, exactly?), and although the originals and translations were lost in war in 1756, Holwell, in ways not made clear, redid translations of parts of the text and published them in his book, recovering from it the fundamental doctrines of the brahmins.[2] It is all rather murky and more than a little suspicious. It is a little more helpful when Holwell tells us that he took help from informants of the scribal (Kāyasth) caste.

The fundamental doctrine of the brahmins from these imprecisely specified sources is, in brief, as follows: God, the Eternal One, created angelic beings: first Birmah, Bistnoo, and Sieb (Brahmā, Viṣṇu, Śiva), then Maisasoor (Mahiśāsura), then all the Debtah-Logue (*devatāloka*). Led by Maisasoor, many of the Debtah rebelled against God, who condemned them to perpetual punishment, but, at the intercession of Bistnoo, God tempered the punishment with the possibility of earning a return to grace. The rebellious angels were to pass through a series of rebirths as different beings in a series of fifteen boboon (*bhuvana*) or worlds of punishment and perfection, arriving at length at human form on earth, with the possibility of achieving their salvation. All humans, then, and all animals too, are fallen angels seeking to regain paradise. Hinduism, in Holwell, reads like Milton with transmigration.

Having stated the Hindu doctrine as he understands it, Holwell ventures to "launch out into the ocean of hypothesis and speculation upon

2. Howell writes: "It is well known that at the capture of *Calcutta,* A.D. 1756, I lost many curious *Gentoo* manuscripts, and among them two very correct and valuable copies of the *Gentoo Shastah* . . . [and] a translation I made of a considerable part of the *Shastah,* which had cost me eighteen months hard labor" (Holwell 1765–71, 2:3). He continues, at a later point, "I resumed my researches with tolerable success; which, joined to some manuscripts recovered by an unforseen and extraordinary event (that possibly I may hereafter recite) enables me to undertake the task I now assign myself" (1765–71, 2:4). Elsewhere he claims to have given what is "almost a litteral translation from the *Chartah Bhade of Bramah*" (1765–71, 2:60).

our own bottom" in the last and boldest of his three volumes (1765–71, 3:1). All religions, he argues, whether of Europe, Asia, Africa, or America, have many points of doctrine in common however much they differ in the exterior modes of worship. These fundamental points of religion are the primitive truth, which indelibly impressed itself upon humankind at the period of its creation (1765–71, 3:4) and which it will never wholly be able to efface although it has deviated from it owing to the taint of original sin. But it is only in Hinduism that we find the primitive truths fully articulated, even though the Hindus have subsequently raised an idolatrous superstructure upon them. Moses's version of the creation and fall of man is "clogged with too many incomprehensible difficulties to gain our belief" (1765–71, 3:9), but it is made intelligible by the Hindu doctrine that mankind are fallen angels. As to the Egyptians, various proofs show that they and the Greeks received the doctrine of metempsychosis or transmigration—which is central to the full articulation of the primitive truth—from the Indians, among whom alone it is not a secret or sectarian truth but a belief widely held, and for whom therefore it must be original. The key to all scripture is found in Hinduism.

Thus Holwell's admiration is such that he is led to class the Hindu scriptures with the scriptures of Moses and of Christ, the Old and the New Testaments of the Bible, as the three divine scriptures, of which only the Hindu revelation expounds the full scheme of the angelic fall and human redemption, articulated by transmigration. Transmigration accounts for the problem of original sin in the scriptures of the Jews and the Christians: All mankind stands accused for the guilt and disobedience of one man and one woman, a detail that is unintelligible without an understanding of transmigration. In fact, says Holwell, the fall of man occurred in heaven long before Adam and Eve, who were fallen angels incarnate as are all humans and, indeed, the entire animal kingdom. This goes to show that the Bible is incomplete in itself and can be finally understood only in the light of the Hindu scriptures revealed by the new Orientalism. "The mission of *Moses* may without offense be considered as a very imperfect one, so designated by God himself; not only for that it was limited to one tribe of beings favoured of God, but also as it is totally silent upon all the *primitive truths* but one, viz., *the unity of the Godhead*" (1765–71, 3:108). In relation to contemporary Christian belief Holwell identifies himself as a Christian deist. Consistent with the transmigration doctrine and his enthusiasm for the primitive truth as found in Hinduism, he became a strong advocate of vegetarianism and opposed the Cartesian doctrine that animals are machines without souls.

By the end of his book Holwell has completely rewritten Christianity with the help of Hinduism or, at any rate, some rough approximation of it. The following articles summarize his newly found beliefs, "proved beyond the power of refutation," as he thought (1765–71, 3:206):

1. Original sin began in heaven and not with the transgressions of Adam and Eve.

2. Man and beast are animated by fallen angels, and their existence can only be accounted for by the (Hindu) doctrine of transmigration.

3. Animals were not made for the use or domination by man.

4. Man, by murdering and eating the brute animals, violates the commands of his creator and of his own original nature.

5. The taking of animal life and of "intoxicating potations" is the cause of all early evil, physical and moral, producing a second defection from God, which offers Satan an open field for his diabolical purposes against the human species.

6. Man has no chance of putting Satan at defiance, subduing the universal depravity of the species and restoring piety and morals, except by putting a total stop to the three primary vices: murder, the taking of animal life, and intoxication. But, "cut off the root, and the branches will necessarily perish" (the same); in doing so the primitive age would be restored, and the reform in morals "would probably restore also the globe to its pristine beauty and natural fertility" (the same).

7. It rests upon the clergy of all nations to begin the general reform.

The clergy did not respond, and the pristine beauty and natural fertility of the globe have not been restored.

Alexander Dow (as we saw in the last chapter) attacked Holwell's account of Hinduism and gave his own in the preface to his translation of Firishtah, under the titles "A dissertation concerning the customs, manners, language, religion and philosophy of the Hindoos" and "A catalogue of the Gods of the Hindoos" (Firishtah 1768:xxi–lxxvi). Here is a fair sample of his tendency to put Hinduism in the most favorable light, reading it as a species of monotheism, as did Holwell:

We find that the Brahmins, contrary to the ideas formed of them in the west, invariably believe in the unity, eternity, omniscience and omnipotence of God: that the polytheism of which they have been accused, is no more than a symbolical worship of the divine attributes, which they divide into three principle classes. Under the name of BRIMHA, they worship the wisdom and creative power of God; under the appellation of BISHEN, his providential and preserving quality; and under that of SHIBAH, that attribute which tends to destroy. (Firishtah 1768:lxvii)

Holwell and Dow quickly appeared in French translation, and Voltaire was "lavish in his praise" (Marshall 1970:8). These, together with Scrafton's *Reflections on the government . . . of Indostan* (1761) plus a curious French text from India called the *Ezour Vedam*, were the main Indian materials with which Voltaire constructed the case for a pre-Mosaic deism against the claims of the Church. This last, as the admirable study by Ludo Rocher shows (*Ezour Vedam* 1984), had been composed by Jesuits to prepare Indians to receive the truths of Christianity, thereby giving a deist pre-Christian teaching a Hindu form: a Upaniṣad-like dialogue between Biach (Vyāsa) and Chumantou (Sumantu). The tendency to minimize the differences separating Christianity and Hinduism operates here, too, but in another direction; instead of reading Hinduism through the lens of Christianity, a partial form of Christianity is read back to Hindus as Hindu scripture. It is ironic that it had the effect of giving Voltaire ammunition against Christianity.

Thus the first wave of the new Orientalism showed a tendency to test the limits of accepted opinion and proved of use to the critique of Christianity from the position of deism in both intramural (Holwell) and extramural (Voltaire) varieties.[3] We see these features also in the early Indian writings of Nathaniel Brassey Halhed, which drew fire from the orthodox. The topic of his transgression was Indian time.

3. P. J. Marshall (personal communication) has come upon a spectacular example of the unsettling effect of Hinduism upon Christian belief among the English in Calcutta in a notebook of Warren Hastings in the library of the University of Minnesota (Ames MS B.114). Marshall writes:

[Hastings] recognizes that in public he is taken to be Christian but then, he admits, in "hipocricy [*sic*]; . . . prudence or rather necessity imposed silence." But, "I am unable not unwilling to receive and understand. What my inability is founded on I cannot to a certainty determine." To me, though, it is very clear. He cannot see anything that distinguishes Christianity from the other religions about which he knows. "Is the incarnation of Christ more intelligible than . . . those of Bishen?" Europeans prevail over non-Europeans not because of the superiority of Christianity but for secular reasons: "a free government, cold climate and printing and navigation." Christianity does not make people "better." "Let those who know the lower uneducated class in England . . . say how much more rarely crimes are committed in England than in India."

All the major seventeenth- and eighteenth-century European writers had given some account of the Indian doctrine of the four *yugas* or world ages through which, in cycles of 4,320,000 years, the world passes repeatedly from a golden age through successive periods of decline and back to the starting point. Indian time, in the immensity of its ages and its cyclical form, functioned as the sign of the essentially Indian. It stood in opposition to Christian time as defined by St. Augustine, whose short span of some six thousand years was suspended as a bridge between two eternities, before the creation of the world and after its final dissolution.

Halhed was drawn to the claims of Indian time, proclaiming all the while his reliance upon the Mosaic chronology (as a cover, one feels): "The Hindoos as well as the Chinese have ever laid claim to an Antiquity infinitely more remote than is authorized by the Belief of the rest of Mankind"—authorized, that is, by the Bible (Halhed 1776:xxxvii). He finds the plausibility of Hindu accounts of remote ages and their complete confidence in the truth of them to be impressive. While, therefore, the Chinese and Indians furnish reasons to entertain the notion of a duration for history much longer than that of the Bible, science does so too. (Doubts about the Mosaic chronology are found in the Western world among the geological discussions of Giuseppe Recupero concerning Mount Etna, as reported in Brydone's *Tour through Sicily and Malta*, 1774.) Halhed argues that human reason can no more reconcile itself to the very long lives of the first patriarchs in the Bible than to the long human lifespan the Hindus attribute to the earlier world ages, but he points out that the Hindus allow for a human lifespan of a thousand years in the third world age; which corresponds nearly in length and chronology to that of the patriarchs in the opening chapters of Genesis. In the fourth world age, in which we now live, the lifespan contracts to a hundred years. This, in brief, is Halhed's argument, which concludes, after again professing an unshaken reliance upon Divine Revelation "before which every suspicion must subside," that "the World does not now contain Annals of more indisputable Antiquity than those delivered down by the ancient Bramins" (1776:xliii).

The whole intricate dance did not fool George Costard, clergyman and writer on the history of earliest times, who, although a family friend of Halhed, nevertheless blasted him in a pamphlet (see R. Rocher 1983:58–59, app. B). The drift of his critique is to show that Sanskrit and its literature are more recent than Moses and that only the Bible is a reliable guide to early history. (He also attacks Recupero's geological evidence for a long chronology.) Halhed's introduction and Costard's pamphlet stirred up a considerable controversy in the reviews in Britain and in France over the claims of great antiquity for Sanskrit literature, creating between them a situation in which the new Orientalism was allied to skepticism and against orthodox belief.

There is a certain symmetry to the career of Halhed, for at the end of it he embraced an unorthodoxy that mirrored his admiring fascination with Indian time at its beginning. Having returned from India and having become a member of Parliament, he took up the causes of Richard Brothers, a messiah who calculated that the millennium would arrive 4 May 1795, and the prophet Joanna Southcott, whom he regarded as "Christ incarnated in a woman" (see R. Rocher 1983:195). A man of education, intelligence, and position, Halhed destroyed his reputation and made himself a laughingstock because of this obsession. Many thought he had gone mad. His declining years were those of a recluse, "scribbling page after page of computations and interpretations" that combined Hindu cosmology and myth with Biblical revelation and Greco-Roman mythology in "an intensely personal and passionate search for the hidden truth, for the grand scheme which God ordained for the world" (R. Rocher 1983:194).

Seen against the backdrop of the writings of these participants in the first wave of the new Orientalism, which gave it a reputation for testing the limits of reason in the construction of a favorable reading of Hinduism, Sir William Jones's taking up of the Mosaic ethnology appears as nothing less than a project to make the new Orientalism safe for Anglicans. Jones in effect showed that Sanskrit literature was not an enemy but an ally of the Bible, supplying independent corroboration of the Bible's version of history after the flood. In this reading some parts of Hinduism's testimony was magnified—the flood narrative of the Purāṇas above all—but one part had to be rejected: the long cycles of Indian time, so impossible to reconcile with Biblical time. The promising linkage Halhed proposed between an emergent long geological time in the West with Indian time, to breach the narrow bounds of the conventional British dating of the beginning of history (4004 B.C.), came to nothing. Jones effectively guaranteed that the new admiration for Hinduism would reinforce Christianity and would not work for its overthrow. In doing so he broke the frame of the Halhed-Costard controversy. Now the great antiquity of Sanskrit literature could be accepted, even welcomed, by the orthodox, because the content of that literature supported the Bible against the skeptics upon their own, rationalist, terms.

One might have expected that dispensation to hold for a very long

time. It was widely admired, and it supplied material for a whole scholarly career to Thomas Maurice who was, with William Robertson, the
first of the non-India hands to write histories of ancient India without
the benefit of knowing Sanskrit. Maurice, an English cleric, was a thorough admirerer of Jones and paid him the compliment of foregoing
the pleasures of original research by helping himself liberally to that of
his hero. The result was impressive in extent if not quality. There is the
seven-volume *Indian antiquities* (1793–1800), and *The history of Hindostan; its arts, its sciences, as connected with the history of the other great
empires of Asia, during the most ancient periods of the world* (1795–98)
and *The modern history of Hindostan* (1802–03), in two volumes each.
The fourth and fifth volumes of the *Indian antiquities* proved popular
enough to reissue as a separate volume, *A dissertation on the Oriental
trinities* (1800). It showed that the Christian doctrine of the Trinity
had been revealed to mankind in earliest times, and after the fall from
grace polytheism erected itself on a muddled version of it, whence the
Hindu trinity of Brahmā, Viṣṇu, and Śiva. In addition, Maurice wrote
a number of pamphlets and the beginnings of his memoirs, which were
to have included "the history of the progress of Indian literature in
Britain, during a period of thirty years" (1819:t.p., 1820). The whole
structure and much of the substance of these works is from Jones, but
without his genius. Maurice accepts the antiquity of Hinduism and its
role as the key to ancient paganism and as independent proof of the
Biblical narrative, but attacks those parts of it, especially the doctrine
of the four ages of cyclical time, that conflict.

A kind of Protestant canonization of Jones's work followed his un-
timely death in India, scarcely ten years after his arrival, although (for
reasons that will become apparent in the next chapter) the process lost
its momentum and did not complete itself under the attacks of Indophobes. That lay in the future. For the moment, Thomas Maurice me-
morialized the sad occasion with *An elegaic and historical poem, sacred
to the memory and virtues of the honourable Sir William Jones* (Maurice
1795)—a poem, alas, whose beauties are known only to the few. Jones's
protégé in Orientalism, John Shore, Lord Teignmouth, on the other
hand, wrote a biography that was widely read and constituted a major
step in the canonization of Jones. Its highest purpose was to enroll Jones
in a catalog of the lay thinker-saints of British Protestantism in series
with Bacon, Locke, Milton, and Newton, those exemplary intellectuals whose lives, it was argued, showed that Protestantism had a special affinity with political liberty, literature, and science and whose work
showed that true science supported the Protestant truth while popery

Figure 4. Statue of Sir William Jones in St. Paul's Cathedral. (Photo courtesy The Conway Library, Courtauld Institute.)

suppressed it (Shore 1805; Jones 1807, vols. 1–2). This had some play, but did not last.

Perhaps the most striking sign of the canonization of Jones is one that may be seen to this day in St. Paul's Cathedral. It gives testimony to just how benevolent the British view of Hinduism could be under the Jonesean dispensation. A colossal statue of Jones, by John Bacon, was erected in his memory by the East India Company (figure 4); it is

Figure 5. Detail showing the translation of Manu's "Institutes." (Photo by R. H. Barnes).

hard to miss, because it is one of the four large statues under the corners of the dome. Jones, in a toga, rests his hand on a book, which is his translation of Manu's "Institutes," the name Manu is in Nagari script on the spine (figure 5).[4] One might have thought it surprising that a Dharmaśāstra text of the Hindu law should be on display in the basilica of the Anglican church—but there are even greater surprises. On the front of the pedestal on which he stands there is a complex scene. Two allegorical figures (History? the new Orientalism?) stand to either side, drawing back a drape to reveal a display of Indian mythology, one of

4. The spelling is actually "Menu," a peculiarity of Jones's scheme of transliterating Sanskrit, Persian, and Arabic in which Persian pronunciation of the first vowel influences the rendering into roman of all three languages. The matter is fully explained in Trautmann (n.d.), "The Lives of Sir William Jones."

Figure 6. Relief on the front of the pedestal. (Photo courtesy The Conway Library, Courtauld Institute.)

them illuminating it with a lamp, the other with a torch (figure 6). The display itself depicts, at the top, a section of the zodiac with the inscription above: "COURMA AVATAR," i.e., the tortoise (Kūrma) avatar of Viṣṇu. In the center a woman, dressed in a sari, holds in her right hand a tablet on which is carved a relief of the *devas* and *asuras* drawing on the snake to churn the milk ocean for its fourteen treasures, some of which are represented around the churning scene: the elephant of

Figure 7. Detail showing scene from Hindu scriptures. (Photo courtesy The Conway Library, Courtauld Institute.)

Indra, Airāvata; pots containing poison (*viṣa*) and ambrosia (*amṛta*); sun and moon; the horse that draws the chariot of the sun; the bull; and so forth. A four-armed figure of Viṣṇu sits atop the churn, and the bottom of it rests upon the carapace of a tortoise, his Kūrma avatar. In her left hand the central female figure holds a three-faced image (*trimūrti*) of God in his three aspects (figure 7). It is all quite astonishing to find this scene from Hindu scriptures, not to speak of graven images of Viṣṇu and other gods, in a Christian church; I venture to say that it is unique.

To understand how it got there we have to decipher its meaning, not to Hindus but to the Anglicans of Jones's day. We can find the guidance we need in the writings of Jones's admirer Thomas Maurice. The significance of this scene from the Purāṇas is alluded to in a contemporary pamphlet he wrote called *Sanscreet fragments, or interesting extracts from the sacred books of the Brahmins, on subjects important to the British Isles* (1797:20 ff.): The rainbow that figures in the Bible at the end of the great flood, as God's promise to Noah that he would never again destroy the earth in a deluge, figures in Indian mythology as one of the treasures churned up by the Kūrma or tortoise avatar of Viṣṇu, whence Christianity receives proofs of its truth from Hindu scriptures. The scene as a whole, therefore, is presented not under the aspect of a depiction of pagan idolatry but as a benign, independent record of the truth of the Biblical story of the universal flood. The three-headed figure represents another of Thomas Maurice's preoccupations, on which he wrote a considerable amount: the so-called Hindu Trinity as, again, a testimony to the truth of the Christian doctrine of the Trinity (1793–1800, 4–5: 1800). It is in this character as independent and scientifically elicited proof of the truth of Christianity that, for perhaps the first and the last time, figures of Hindu mythology were admitted to the sanctum of a Christian church. Such a depiction would have been unthinkable in an English church before Jones, and it became impossible later, as the nineteenth century progressed and Indophobia set in. It was Christian Indomania's brief moment.

## Lord Monboddo on Sanskrit

Information about Sanskrit and its similarity to Greek reached James Burnett, Lord Monboddo, from the Calcutta Orientalists while he was in the midst of a vast scholarly project, and it fit the direction of his work so very well that he absorbed the new learning eagerly.

Lord Monboddo was writing two six-volume works more or less simultaneously: *Of the origin and progress of language* (Burnett 1773–92) and *Antient metaphysics; or, the science of universals* (Burnett 1779–99), the first proving the divine origin of language and taking Greek as the

standard of linguistic perfection, the second promoting a Platonic, the-
istic position in criticism of the mechanical philosophy of Descartes
and of Newton. The third volume of the second book, titled "History
and philosophy of man," is a survey of the variety of the human species
that gives Lord Monboddo a certain place in the history of anthropology; the inquiry continues in volume four, "The history of man" (1795),
in which the new knowledge of Sanskrit appears. We will examine it
presently, but in order to see how Monboddo's project predisposed him
to a favorable reception of Sanskrit it will be useful to consider briefly
what views he held before the new Orientalism of Calcutta came into
his view. For this purpose we will examine chapter 12, "Of the antiquity of the Egyptians," of the first volume of the first book, published
in 1773.

Egypt plays a premier role in Lord Monboddo's system: "Egypt was
the parent-country, at least with respect to Europe and the western
parts of Asia, of language, as well as of other arts." The Pelasgi of
Greece got their language from Egypt; indeed they were Egyptian colonists, "Egyptian and Greek languages being originally the same." As
to India, when the Greeks reached it under Alexander, they found (so
says Strabo) monuments to Bacchus or Dionysus and Hercules. The Indians said that Bacchus came from the west and taught them agriculture, the use of wine, and other arts of civil and social life. This agrees
with the Egyptian story that their Bacchus (that is, Osiris) overran the
known world, civilizing men and teaching them the arts of life. In India, Osiris built cities such as Nysa and other monuments to himself
(according to Diodorus Siculus). The Indian veneration of the cow and
other customs are in common with those of the Egyptians. "And I am
disposed to believe," Lord Monboddo says, "that the arts and sciences,
of which it is certain the Indians have been in possession for many ages,
have risen from seeds sown there by the Egyptians," citing Père Pons
of the Jesuit *Lettres édifiantes* (Burnett 1773–92, 1:466–467).

The new Orientalism fell on the fertile soil of this argument about
the unity of Egyptian, Greek, and Indian language, arts, and sciences,
and germinated at once. In the 1795 text, the "History of man" section of *Antient metaphysics,* it bursts into flower. The "Shanscrit," Monboddo says, is the original language of India and all the other languages
of India are dialects that are more or less corrupt; it is "the most perfect
language that is, or, I believe, ever was, on this earth; for it is more
perfect than the Greek" (Burnett 1779–99, 4:322), citing Sir William
Jones. He discusses various features of Sanskrit from the description

given by Halhed in the introduction to the *Code of Gentoo laws*, which shows it to be a language of the greatest art (that is, civilized or polished rather than rude or barbaric) since it abounds in flexion, the greatest art of language.

Monboddo had made the acquaintance of Charles Wilkins after his return to Britain—Wilkins was of course the translator of the *Bhagavad Gītā* and the European who had the best knowledge of Sanskrit at that time—and had received from him more information. Wilkins, Monboddo announces, has proved the resemblance between Sanskrit and Greek. "They must, therefore, be dialects of the same language: And that language could be no other than the language of Egypt, brought into India by Osiris, of which undoubtedly the Greek was a dialect" (1779–99, 4:323). Languages of course are subject to change, so that the Greek and the Sanskrit are not identical; but it is the Greek that has changed, and not the Sanskrit, which was preserved against change by the extreme conservatism of the brahmin priests. Thus Sanskrit is the pure, unchanged language of ancient Egypt, taken there by Osiris and transmitted without change by the most conservative priesthood known to history. But there is more. In the opening volume of his *Origin and progress of language*, Monboddo was cautious about extending the paternity of the Egyptian language beyond Europe and Asia; now, in his enthusiasm for his new learning about Sanskrit and the doctrine of the *Monde primitif* of A. Court de Gebelin (vol. 2, 1775) that all languages of the world were descended from a single, primitive language, he puts caution aside and asserts that all languages, including those of America, are descendants of the ancient Egyptian—of which Sanskrit is the living relic.

Such a doctrine could not, of course, survive Champollion's decipherment of the Egyptian hieroglyphics, which lay several decades ahead. With it came the recognition that the language of ancient Egypt bore no close relation either to Greek or to Sanskrit. But it is worth making the point that Monboddo's doctrine shows again that, prior to the great decipherment, Indomania and Egyptomania generally reinforced each other and that they ran together (quite contrary to Bernal's thesis in *Black Athena*, 1987, according to which they are opposed). The effect of the decipherment was, as it were, to let the air out of the obsession with the supposed connection of India and Egypt in ancient times.

In the meantime, however, the sponsorship of Lord Monboddo itself perhaps told against the enthusiasm for Sanskrit in Britain. Not because of Monboddo's advocacy of vegetarian diet, or cold baths, or exposing one's naked body to the elements—these are eccentricities of which the British like to think they are tolerant. What made Lord Monboddo a laughingstock was an eccentricity that went too far: his belief in the existence of men with tails.

The evidence came from one Koeping, a Swedish sailor serving as lieutenant aboard a vessel of the Dutch East India Company a century previous, in 1647. In the Nicobar Islands of the Bay of Bengal, he relates, they saw "men with tails like those of cats, and which they moved in the same manner" (Burnett 1773–92, 1:234). These creatures came alongside in canoes and traded parrots for iron, thus showing by their knowledge of trade and the art of navigation, Monboddo believed, that they were indeed human—although perhaps they lacked language and were like those other speechless men, the Ouran Outangs (1773–92, 1:238). The encounter between the two varieties of man ended badly, however. The next day, after the Dutch sent a boat ashore with five men who did not return, a larger landing party was sent ashore. "When they landed, the men with the tails came about them in great numbers; but by firing their cannon they chased them away: but found only the bones of their companions, who had been devoured by the savages; and the boat in which they had landed they found taken to pieces, and the iron of it carried away" (1773–92, 1:235–236).

The story had good credentials. Monboddo came across a retelling of it in the sixth volume of Linnaeus's *Amoenitates academicae* (by one Hoppius, an associate), and, after corresponding with Linnaeus, he acquired a 1743 Stockholm reprint of Koeping's account, which a Swedish gentleman translated for him. Moreover,

The author who relates this is, I am well informed, an author of very good credit. He writes in a simple plain manner, not like a man who intended to impose a lie upon the world, merely for the silly pleasure of making people stare; and if it be a lie (for it cannot be a mistake), it is the only lie in his book; for everything else that he has related of animals and vegetables has been found to be true. (1773–92, 1:236–237)

Much of Monboddo's writing, the aspect of it that gives him a place in histories of anthropological thought, consists in passing in review evidence of variation within the human species, of the various marginal cases whose existence is problematical for any determination of the limits of the human; whence the fascination for him of Wild Peter of Hanover and the wild girl of Auvergne as empirical cases of feral humanity, and of the Ouran Outang of Angola which, although lacking language, was evidently human: "They are exactly of the human form; walking erect, not upon all-four, like the savages that have been found in Europe; they use sticks for weapons; they live in society; they make huts of branches of trees, and they carry off negroe girls, whom they make slaves of, and use both for work and pleasure" (1773–92, 1:174–175). He believed in the scale of being and the plenitude of natural forms, siding with Aristotle's maxim that "every thing which can exist does exist" (1779–99, 3:248). In short, his whole cast of mind disposed him to be receptive to reports of exotic forms of humanoids and to take them as varieties of a single species. He was convinced that we have not yet discovered all the variety of nature, not even in our own species. Monboddo's countrymen, however, were out of step. Such things could no longer be believed, no matter how trustworthy the empirical evidence was shown to be. In the end, Lord Monboddo's men with tails were done in by the gentlemen scholars of Calcutta. In 1792 the third volume of *Asiatic researches* published an account, "On the Nicobar Isles and the fruit of the mellori," by Nicolas Fontana, who made a point of determining the truth of Koeping's account:

Linnaeus seems to have been too credulous, in believing this man's story, for in all my examinations, I could discover no sort of projection whatever on the *os coccygis* of either sex. What has given rise to this supposed tail, may have been the stripe of cloth hanging down from their posteriors; which, when viewed at a distance, might probably have been mistaken for a tail. (Fontana 1799:151)

## John Playfair on Indian Astronomy

British enthusiasm for Indian astronomy began with a paper read by the mathematician John Playfair before the Royal Academy of Edinburgh on 2 March 1789, titled "Remarks on the astronomy of the brahmins" (1790).

The modernist sense of history, as a process of developmental and progressive change, depends greatly upon the history of science as a narrative of the cumulative growth of knowledge, and the narrative of the progress of astronomy forms its very core. To ask, therefore, what is the place of India in the history of astronomy (or astronomy and mathematics, the two being closely associated) is to ask about its place in the history of civilization.

In Playfair's view the history of astronomy is a unitary story of progress from the Chaldeans to the Greeks, culminating in the *Syntaxis* of Ptolemy, whose system, without opposition or improvement, dominated the astronomy of Egypt, Italy, and Greece for five hundred years. It passed to the Arabs and Persians and from them to Tartary, and from the Arabs to Spain and to the northern nations "where, after exercising the genius of Copernicus, of Kepler, and of Newton, it has become the most perfect of all the sciences." Because the systems of astronomy of all these nations show their interconnectedness clearly, says Playfair, the unitary character of the history of astronomy inclines us to believe that the development of observation of the heavens and reasoning about them "is an experiment on the human race, which has been made but once" (1790:136).

It is a matter of extreme curiosity, therefore, to find that the brahmins of India stand entirely outside this story. Their system of astronomical knowledge appears to be wholly separate from that unitary body of science "which has traversed, and enlightened the other countries of the earth" (the same). Indian astronomy is ancient and original, differing and therefore not derivable from that of the Greeks, the Arabs, the Persians, or the Tartars. The brahmins of today follow its rules without understanding its principles, Playfair says, and can give no account of its origin, "except that it lays claim to an antiquity far beyond the period, to which, with us, the history of the heroic ages is supposed to extend" (the same).

European enthusiasm for Indian astronomy was the creation not of the British but of the French, and Playfair was commenting as mathematician upon the Indian materials that they had published. Jean Dominique Cassini, director of the Paris observatory, had explicated astronomical tables from Siam (but based on a meridian near about Benares, and hence essentially part of the Indian system), which Simon de La Loubère had taken to England and presented in his *Description du royaume de Siam* (1691), subsequently reprinted in the memoirs of the Académie des Sciences. But it was G. Le Gentil and Jean-Sylvain Bailly, both of them leading astronomers, who were especially responsible for promoting the idea of the originality and antiquity of Indian astronomy. Le Gentil had gone to India in 1761 and 1769 to observe the transit of Venus, and came to know of Indian tables and rules of calculation from calendar makers in the vicinity of Pondichery. He published tables

given him by a learned brahmin of Tiruvalur in the memoirs of the
Académie des Sciences in 1772, giving further force to a growing enthusiasm for India that followed the publication of a French translation of Holwell's "Shaster" in 1768—which was much beloved of Voltaire—and Anquetil's translation of the *Zend-Avesta* in 1771. Bailly's
four-volume *Histoire de l'astronomie* (1775–82), opening with a chapter
on antediluvian astronomy, argued that the first recorded astronomical
observations of the ancient civilizations dated from around 3000 B.C.
and presupposed a period of development at least 1,500 years long. India
played a role in that history, but it is in the appendix volume, *Traité de
l'astronomie indienne et orientale* (1787), that Bailly exhibits his mastery
of the newly available Indian materials. Playfair's wonderfully clear exposition of the issue was wholly inspired by Le Gentil and Bailly and
rested upon Indian tables supplied by them and Indian methods of calculation explained in their writings.

The argument directs itself to the tables, of which there were four:
those of Siam and of Tiruvalur, mentioned above, and two others sent
by missionaries, Patouillet (thought to be of Narsapur) and du Champ
(of Krishnapuram). To establish the unity and identity of the Indian
system Playfair describes features common to these tables but different
from the Ptolemaic system and its successors. The nub of the argument has to do with the epoch of the tables, their observational starting point. To calculate the position of a celestial body one needs "the
position of the body in some past instant of time, ascertained by observation" (1790:142), called the epoch of the tables, the mean rate of
the body's motion, and the correction that adjusts for motion above or
below the mean. Three of the tables have epochs that are not especially
ancient—that of Siam (A.D. 638), that of Krishnapuram (A.D. 1491),
and that of Narsapur (A.D. 1569)—but the Tiruvalur tables are set out
from the beginning of the Kali *yuga*, in 3102 B.C. Is it real or fictitious?
That is, Playfair asks, has the position of the heavenly bodies it posits
for that epoch been determined by actual observation, or by calculation
from the modern epochs of the other tables? If it is an imposture, the
brahmins "have furnished us with means, almost infallible, of detect-
ing" it (1790:152). Only astronomy in its most perfected state is able to
go back forty-six centuries and ascertain by calculation the configuration of the heavenly bodies as a test of the supposed observation. Moreover, he adds, the calculations of modern European astronomy, with all
the accuracy that the science derives from the telescope and the pendu-
lum, "could not venture on so difficult a task, were it not assisted by

the theory of gravitation, and had not the integral calculus, after an hundred years of almost continual improvement, been able, at last, to determine the disturbances in our system, which arise from the action of the planets on one another" (the same).

Any system of astronomical tables, however accurate at the time of its making and however exactly it represents the position of the heavenly bodies at its epoch, Playfair continues, will become less accurate as one departs from the time of the epoch, both before and after that time, if the corrections for those gravitational effects are not taken into account, and the error will grow with time. Indeed, a cumulative error is inevitable, quite apart from the question of gravitational effects, from the inevitable small errors in determining the mean motions. These errors must accumulate with time and produce an effect that becomes larger with every day that one moves away from the instant of observation. For both reasons it is a general truth that, given a system of astronomical tables based on observations whose date is unknown, that date will be the time at which the tables "represent the celestial motions most exactly" (the same). Here, then, we have a method by which to judge the pretensions of Indian astronomy to so great an antiquity.

The burden of Playfair's argument is, then, to demonstrate that the positions of heavenly bodies at the commencement of the Kali *yuga* (i.e., 3102 B.C.) as given in the table are very accurate, by comparing them with modern computations whose accuracy has been refined by knowledge of the gravitational effects of such bodies on one another, which is necessarily more accurate than could be achieved by premodern means of computation, which rested on observation. This he proceeds to do, and stands astonished before the result:

That observations made in India, when all Europe was barbarous or uninhabited, and investigations into the most subtle effects of gravitation made in Europe, near five thousand years afterwards, should thus come in mutual support of one another, is perhaps the most striking example of the progress and vicissitudes of science, which the history of mankind has yet exhibited. (1790:160)

One example of the detail of the argument must suffice by way of illustration. At the commencement of the Kali *yuga* (3102 B.C.), the beginning of the zodiac is 54° before the vernal equinox according to the Indian astronomers, and the star Aldebaran, the first star of the constellation Taurus, is 53°20' after the beginning of the zodiac, hence 40' before the equinox. Modern observation, and the present rate of precession of the equinoxes (50 ⅓″, slightly less, it might be added, than the Indian value of 54″) would place Aldebaran 1°32′ before the equinox. But adding in the correction due to the variability of the precession discovered by La Grange and published only in 1782, in the amount of 1°45′22″, the longitude of Aldebaran is 13′ from the equinox at that time, agreeing, to within 53′, with the determination of the Indians. The brahmins could not have fixed the position of Aldebaran at the beginning of the Kali *yuga* by calculating backward from a modern observation, for they make the precession of the equinox too great by more than 3″ annually, so that they would have placed the fixed stars 4° or 5° further back at their ancient epoch than they in fact did (1790:153–154). This argument alone, Playfair believes, makes it highly probable that the Indian zodiac is as old as the Kali *yuga,* that is, that the tables of Tiruvalur are based on observations made in 3102 B.C. The multiplicity of examples he gives raises the probability of the proofs such that "their being false were much more wonderful than their being true" (1790:192).

The question of Indian astronomy occupied some of the best scientific minds of Europe and figured largely in the work of the Calcutta Sanskritists. Jones corresponded with Playfair, and he wrote a few articles on astronomical matters himself. In "On the chronology of the Hindus" (1807, 4:1–46) he fended off the Hindu *yuga*-cycle of 4,320,000 years and fitted the events of Puranic history into the frame of the shorter Mosaic chronology; "On the antiquity of the Indian zodiack" (1807, 4:71–92) showed (rightly) that the Greek and Indian zodiacs were the same and argued (wrongly) that the Greek was derived from the Indian; and "The lunar year of the Hindus" (1807, 4:126–165) expounded the doctrine of lunar asterisms (*nakṣatras*). In astronomy Jones was no more than an amateur, and far better writings on the astronomy of the Indians were soon being produced by Samuel Davis and H. T. Colebrooke in the *Asiatic researches.* The enthusiasm of the pioneers was then checked by the skepticism of John Bentley, and controversy raged until the extremes of each gave way to soberer assessments.[5]

Indian astronomy continued for a time to be a central issue for British-Indian relations in ways that are still little explored, and which we cannot follow here even if we were able. It is important to be clear that, as in Playfair's argument, the question was never whether Indian as-

---

5. See Sen c.1985 for discussion and references.

tronomy had something new to offer Europe, but was, instead, an investigation into the antiquity of Indian astronomy using the modern astronomy of Europe as the standard and means of investigation. This continued to be the stance of the Calcutta Sanskritists as they delved deeper into the Sanskrit sources, and they shared it (as we shall see in the next chapter) with their later critics, the Indophobes. But, for the Orientalists, that by no means rendered the content of Indian astronomy a merely antiquarian issue. If Newtonian astronomy was to take root in Indian civilization, the Orientalist educational theory ran, it would have to be grafted on a native rootstock of the existing astronomical science of the Hindus. Hence the study of Sanskrit texts of astronomy had a larger purpose within the project of modernism.[6]

The early enthusiasm for Indian astronomy could not be sustained at its original level. The Marquis de Laplace wrote India out of the place Bailly had given it in the history of astronomy, and Maurice could cite Laplace in proof that the famous tables of Tiruvalur were utterly impossible and that the supposed conjunction of the planets in 3102 B.C. differed too greatly from modern tables to have been established by observation (Maurice 1812:7; Laplace 1809, 2:250).

## Francis Wilford on Puranic Geography

Francis Wilford, officer in the army of the East India Company, devoted his leisure to the study of the geographical sections of the Purāṇas, looking for evidence of Indian knowledge of Egypt and other civilizations in ancient times. He had been born in Hanover and went, as lieutenant, with the Hanoverian troops sent by the British government to India in 1781. Following the Treaty of Mangalore (1784) he devoted himself to Indian antiquities. He became a member of the

6. Sen c.1985 is a fine summary of the scientific issues. For the larger cultural issues see Chris Bayly's article, "Colonial Star Wars" (n.d.), which is a suggestive probing of territory that is still largely unknown. One would like to know a good deal more about works written by British-Indian educators and by missionaries to graft Newtonian astronomy upon the base of Indian astronomy (in keeping with Orientalist educational policy) or, contrarily, to refute Indian astronomy by means of Newtonian astronomy. Two interesting relics of these colonial star wars that I have come across are James Ballantyne's *A synopsis of science, in Sanskrit and English, reconciled with the truths to be found in the Nyáya philosophy* (1856) and H. R. Hoisington's *The Oriental astronomer* (1848), in Tamil and English. These are examples of a largely lost literature of Orientalist modernization.

Asiatic Society and was regarded as one of its best Sanskritists, along with Wilkins and Colebrooke (Klaproth c.1865).

Wilford published many articles in the *Asiatic researches,* the most important of which are the longest ones, "On Egypt and other countries adjacent to the Cálí River, or Nile of Ethiopia, from the ancient books of the Hindus," in the third volume (1792), and "An essay on the sacred isles in the west" in volumes 8, 9, and 10 (1805). These writings attracted considerable attention, for the first gave a proof not only of a close and continuing intercourse between India and Egypt in ancient times but also of the substantial identity of their mythologies and that of ancient Greece—the unity-of-paganism theme upheld—and promised more to come. The second purported to show the wider range of geographical reference in the Purāṇas, including reference to Britain under the name Śvetadvīpa, "white island" (i.e., "Albion"), among the "sacred isles of the west" of the title. It was all quite astounding.

The argument of these writings depends on a series of identifications between Sanskrit place-names and those in other languages, very like the way in which Bryant's argument is built up, and it is equally difficult to convey a sense of the text in this short space. Let me leave it at this: According to Wilford, the Purāṇas speak of Egypt under the name Āgupta or Guptasthān (Gr. "Ægyptos") or Miśrasthāna (Biblical "Misraim," Arabic "Misr") and Ethiopia under the name Kuśasthāna, "land of Kuśa," that is, the Biblical Cush. One can see why Sir William Jones was ambivalent about Wilkins's work: On the one hand the argument was built entirely of etymologies, many of the loosest kind, for which he had lampooned Bryant; on the other, it gave new evidence for the exact etymologies that he had identified in the third anniversary discourse connecting Sanskrit *miśra* and *kuśa* with Egypt and the Cushites. He asked to see Wilkins's sources. In a note appended to Wilkins's article on Egypt in the third volume, Jones says that, having read the original Puranic and other Sanskrit passages, both alone and with a pandit, "I am happy in bearing testimony to his perfect good faith and general accuracy both in his extracts and in the translation of them" (Jones, in Wilford 1792:464), and adds two literal translations of supporting sources. One of these is a *Skanda Purāṇa* passage in praise of the Nīla River, supposedly the Nile of Egypt, which, Jones adds, all the brahmins allow to be in Kuśadvīpa, that is, the Biblical Cush. The second, from the *Padma Purāṇa,* is truly amazing, for in nine Sanskrit verses it reprises the story of Noah, his three sons, and the curse of Ham. The passage says that to Satyavarman (whom Jones had elsewhere identified with Noah) were born three sons, Śarma, Kharma, and Jyāpati (i.e.,

Shem, Ham or Cham, and Japhet), upon whom their father, the sovereign of the whole earth, devolved the kingship so that he could retire to a life of meditation. Jones's translation of the passage continues:

One day by the act of destiny, the king, having drunk mead, became senseless, and lay asleep naked: then was he seen by Kharma, and by him were his two brothers called, to whom he said: "What has now befallen? In what state is this our fire?" By those two was he hidden with clothes and called to his senses again and again. Having recovered his intellect, and perfectly knowing what had passed, he cursed Kharma, saying: "Thou shalt be the servant of servants; and since thou wast a laugher in their presence, from laughter shalt though acquire a name." Then he gave to Sharma the wide domain on the south of the snowy mountain, and to Jyapati he gave all on the north of the snowy mountain; but he, by power of religious contemplation, attained supreme bliss. (Jones, in Wilford 1792:466; spelling and punctuation modernized).

The passage most clearly proves, Jones says, that Satyavrata or Satyavarman of the Purāṇas was Noah—an identification he had been the first to propose—which fixes the utmost limit of the Hindu chronology. And it gives no support to the view (of Voltaire) that Moses borrowed any part of his work from the Egyptians, but shows to the contrary that he wrote what he knew to be truth itself from the traditional remembrance of his people.

Some years after Jones's death, Wilford, now Captain Wilford, delivered himself of "On the sacred isles of the west" (1805), an even longer and more densely referenced treatise purporting to show that the White Island (śveta-dvīpa) of the Puranic geographies is England and the sacred isles of which it is one refer to Britain. It is more misplaced learning in the manner of Bryant. However, the story lies not in the content of the article but in its introduction.

Wilford says that in preparing his essay for publication he compared his notes of Puranic passages with the originals, and soon found that wherever the word śvetam or śvetadvīpa occurred the writing was somewhat different and the paper of a different color, as if stained:

Surprised at this strange appearance, I held the page to the light, and perceived immediately that there was an erasure, and that some size had been applied. Even the former word was not so much defaced, but that I could sometimes make it out plainly. I was thunderstruck. . . . When I reflected, that the discovery might have been made by others, either before or after my death, that in one case my situation would have been truly distressful; and that in the other my name would have passed with infamy to posterity, and increased the calendar of imposture, it brought on such paroxisms as threatened the most serious consequences, in my then infirm state of health. (Wilford 1805:248)

When he began to study Sanskrit, Captain Wilford tells us, he quickly found that the geographical information he sought was inter-mixed with masses of mythological and historical information in ex-ceedingly lengthy Purāṇas. So he made his pandit into what we would call a research assistant and directed him to read through the Purāṇas and make extracts of the information he sought. He gave him money to hire assistants and scribes and directed him to engage another pandit, giving him for his further encouragement a place in the college at Benares. Naturally Wilkins had to brief his pandit on what kind of in-formation he wanted him to look for, and he further amused him-self, he said, "with unfolding to him our ancient mythology, history and geography. This was absolutely necessary as a clue to guide him through so immense an undertaking, and I had full confidence in him" (1805:249–250).

You have guessed the rest. Having discovered the erasures, Wilford asked his pandit to supply more of the originals from which he had made extracts, and there followed a period during which, as we must imagine, the pandit worked night and day to supply his patron with what he wanted to see. He had to work, moreover, all alone, for he had pocketed the money for hiring assistants and scribes. One cannot but be impressed by the accomplishment of this obliging pandit, for Wil-ford states he composed no less than 12,000 brand new Puranic *ślokas*—about half the length of the *Rāmāyaṇa!*—and inserted them into manuscripts of the *Skanda* and *Brahmāṇḍa* Purāṇas, not to mention other phony verses he put into the *Padma Purāṇa*. Wilford says that be-cause many chapters of these works are lost they are called "the Puranas of thieves or impostors." His mortification deepened when he found that he was the unwitting instrument, in his earlier article on Egypt, of an imposture perpetrated on the late Sir William, and that the verses on Śarma, Kharma, and Jyāpati were nowhere to be found in the *Padma Purāṇa*.

Did the discovery that his pandit had been somewhat too helpful lead him to abandon the White Island thesis? Not at all. Wilford announced his relief at finding that the frauds were not so extensive as to vitiate his present or earlier work. Deeply committed to the Mosaic ethnology and to the natural religion frame of comparative analysis, he continued to make wide-ranging identifications of the features of Egyptian, Greek, and Indian mythology, religion, and history on the basis of the Puranic geographies. Even more telling is the fact that the Asiatic Society published his work, and the French translated it into their own language (Wilford c.1846). Like any mastering framework, Mosaic ethnology provided both aids to new discoveries, and resistance to its own demise. It would take the decipherments of Champollion to kill off the Egypt-India theory and contain the European Indomania within bounds of reason. But the fraud of Wilford's pandit became a celebrated case and (as we shall see in the next chapter) it was a first-rate club with which its critics could beat the new Orientalism.

## Charles Vallancey: Celtomania and Indomania

Charles Vallancey was an English military engineer (rising to the rank of general in 1803) who became interested in the language and antiquities of Ireland while he was posted there. He was a prolific writer of books and pamphlets on those subjects, not to speak of his works on fortification, stonecutting, inland navigation, and the tanning and currying of leather. The effect of his writing on Irish antiquities was considerable but perhaps not entirely salutary; indeed, the judgment of his memorialist in the *Dictionary of national biography* is severe: "Vallancey may be regarded as the founder of a school of writers who theorise on Irish history, language, and literature, without having read the original chronicles, acquired the language, or studied the literature, and who have had some influence in retarding real studies, but have added nothing to knowledge" (Moore 1899:82). For our purposes he is important for showing a connection between Celtomania and Indomania and the shaping influence of the Mosaic ethnology.

The two parts of Vallancey's Irish interests, namely language and antiquities, are bound together into a unified whole by the Mosaic ethnology, and the Mosaic ethnology is the governing paradigm of his writings even before the first results of the new Orientalism came his way and were eagerly absorbed into his project. Prior to the appearance in England of the first volumes of *Asiatic researches,* he had already published a great deal on Ireland: four of the six volumes of his *Collectanea de rebus hibernicis* (1770–1804); the *Essay on the antiquity of the Irish language* (1772), dedicated to Jacob Bryant; *A grammar of the Iberno-Celtic, or Irish language* (1773); and *A vindication of the ancient history of Ireland* (1786). In this body of work it is his purpose to recuperate the reputation of the medieval manuscript histories of Ireland, showing that they are not monkish forgeries of the ninth and tenth centuries but genuine records of Ireland's most ancient history, according to which the Irish people descend in two lines from Magog of the Genesis narrative (Vallancey 1786:i–ii, 1). He wishes, further, to show that the Irish language is the language of an ancient civilized people, being "free from the anomalies, sterility, and heteroclite redundancies, which mark the dialects of barbarous nations" and that, being rich and melodious, precise and copious, it "affords those elegant conversations which no other than a thinking and lettered people can use or require"; thus it is large of vocabulary and regular of grammar (Vallancey 1773:ii). More particularly, the Irish language is an amalgam of the Celtic and the Punic, Ireland having been colonized by Phoenicians, come hither to trade for the tin of Britain, at an early date. As against Sir William Temple, who argued that the Irish language was used nowhere else in the world but Ireland, the Scottish highlands, and the Isle of Man, Vallancey wishes to show that it is older than and ancestral to all the languages of Europe by virtue of its dual heritage, both Celtic and Phoenician being dialects of the Hebrew, the first language of mankind. Phoenician is the source of Greek and Latin, in Vallancey's view, and every nation in Europe looks to the Celtic as their mother tongue (Vallancey 1773:xii–xiv). There is also a Scythian element in the formation of the Irish language, hailing from Iran and Central Asia.

Indeed, the similarities Vallancey sees between Irish and other languages seem boundless, and as we read on we lose our sense of surprise and shock long before we encounter word lists comparing Irish with Japanese and Chinese. Judging, then, from the affinity of the Celtic language with almost every language of the known world, he says, "we might conclude with *Boullet,* that it was the primaeval language. There is not only a great affinity between the Iberno-Celtic and the Hebrew, Persian, and the other oriental dialects; but what is more remarkable, there is a surprising affinity also, between the old Iberno-Celtic, or *bearla feni,* with the dialects spoken on the vast continent of North America" (1773:iv–v). Of American Indian languages he specifies the Algonquin, as reported in the book of Baron Lahontan, who says they are the most ancient and noble tribe on the continent, as indeed their name in Irish indicates: *cine algan* or *algan cine,* the noble tribe. All this strengthens Vallancey's belief in the peopling of North American by Phoenicians. In the end the Celtic language covers the globe.

With a proclivity to see connections on the basis of the slightest similarities it is only to be expected that Vallancey would eagerly ingest
whatever results of the new Orientalism might seem to be of service to
the vindication of the Irish language and the antiquity of its people.
Jones, whose earlier work in Persian Vallancey knew well, offered a
crumb in the sixth anniversary discourse: a parallel between the ancient
Irish writing called Ogham and the Sanskrit texts called Āgamas, which
Vallancey seized upon and proceeded to overinterpret (Jones 1807, 3:
125–126). But it was Wilford whose researches provided the crucial material that resulted in Vallancey's pamphlet, *The ancient history of Ireland, proved from the Sanscrit books of the Bramins of India* (1797).

The gist of this new material is as follows. In the Purāṇas the British
Isles appear (according to Wilford) under the name Trikūṭācala, "the
mountain with three peaks": "for the Pauranies consider all islands as
so many mountains the lower parts of which are covered by the sea"
(1797:9). The three peaks are the golden peak (Suvarṇakūṭa), silver peak
(Rajatakūṭa), and iron peak (Ayakūṭa); alternatively they are also called
*dvīpas* or islands. The Silver Island is more commonly called Śvetadvīpa
or White Island, that is, Albion or England. The Golden Island (Suvar-
ṇadvīpa) or Peak (Suvarṇakūṭa) is synonymous with Sukuta or S'kuta,
that is, Scotia or Scotland; other derivatives (Suvarṇeya or Svarṇeya) are
the origin of Juvernia and Jvernia (Hibernia). This Suvarṇeya was regarded as the abode of the ancestors, Pitṛsthāna or Pitṛikasthāna, Pitṛka
being Patricius, the Apostle of Ireland (St. Patrick!). This is only the
beginning of Vallancey's lucubrations on the amazing findings of Wilford, for in a passage from the *Brahmānda Purāṇa* supplied by Wilford
through another gentleman, Mr. Gore Ousley, then at Benares, Vallancey finds a proof that the Phoenicians colonized Ireland, a proof the
details of which we will leave it to interested readers to find for themselves in the pages of this curious pamphlet. He also shows with reference to the *Indian antiquities* of Thomas Maurice that the superstitions
of the druids of Britain contain many vestiges of the pure theology of
the Biblical patriarchs, blended with the corruptions of Sabian idolatry
and, more particularly, that various designations of the Buddha, who
is equivalent to the Egyptian Hermes and the Mercury of the West,
are represented in druid religion and "in many relics of their festivals
and sports, still practised in Britain" (1797:28–29). Wilford's Puranic
researches figure largely in Vallancey's subsequent writings: the remaining volumes of the *Collectanea*, the *Prospectus of a dictionary of the language of the Aire Coti, or, ancient Irish* (1802), and *An essay on the primi-*

*tive inhabitants of Great Britain and Ireland* (1807), which today are
the hardest and most unprofitable of reading matter.

But for all its learned foolishness, the conjuncture of Celtomania and
Indomania in Vallancey's later writings rests on one item of fact beneath all the fancy, for Sanskrit and Irish *are* near kin as members of
the Indo-European language family. It is not surprising therefore that
Jones's relations with Vallancey were as ambivalent as were his relations with Bryant, whose conclusions he embraced and the looseness of
whose methods he made sport of. Here are Jones's comments on Vallancey, appearing in letters he wrote on two consecutive days. On 11
September 1787 he wrote to Joseph Walker,

When you see Colonel Vallancy, whose learned work I have read through
twice with great pleasure, I request you to present him with my best remembrance. We shall soon I hope see faithful translations of Irish histories and poems. I shall be happy in comparing them with the Sanscrit,
with which the ancient language of Ireland had certainly an affinity. (Jones
1970:770–771)

Just the previous day, however, he had written to his friend and former
pupil the second Earl Spencer a much more candid appraisal:

Have you met with a book lately published with the title of *a Vindication
of the Ancient History of Ireland?* It was written by a friend of mine, Colonel
Vallancey; but a word in your ear—it is very stupid. . . . *Vallancey* begins
with stating a fact (which is the only curious part of the book) that the
*Irish* have histories of their country, from the first population of it, *in their
own language;* one of which histories he is translating. Then he insists with
great warmth, that those histories could not be invented by modern priests:
perhaps not; but what is his reason? Because those priests did not understand *Persian,* (which he calls *Southern Scythian*) and the ancient Irish were
*Persians,* who having emigrated from the Caspian settled in *Ierne* or *Iran,*
and brought with them the *old Persian* history, which *he* finds in the *Irish*
manuscripts. I conceive this to be visionary; & am certain, that his derivations from the Persian, Arabic, & Sanscrit languages, are erroneous. (Jones
1970:768–769)

He concludes: "Do you wish to laugh? Skim the book over. Do you
wish to sleep? Read it regularly" (1970:769).

There is however one more word to be said. Besides providing another sorry chapter in the history of error, it seems to me that this
examination of the Vindicator of Irish History suggests that Celtomania and Indomania run together at a rather profound level. For British
ethnologies from General Vallancey onward seem to show that an open-

ness to the one tends to go with an openness toward the other, and that, contrarily, anti-Irish feeling on the part of the English and the Scots tends to go with hostility toward the Indians and, as well, toward the claims of language to show a relationship among them.

In sum, British Indomania was not a shapeless enthusiasm for things Indian, but a phenomenon with a structure, which is to say both an internal organization and boundaries. It was an enthusiasm for the Hindus or "native" Indians as distinct from, and even as opposed to, the Muslim "conquerors." It was an enthusiasm for the ancient writings in Sanskrit, conceived as repositories of the primitive experiences and religion of the human race and, as such, confirmatory of the truth of Christian scripture. It was an enthusiasm for ancient wisdom as distinct from future wisdom; it had, so to say, a Masonic character. And it was an enthusiasm for those Sanskrit writings as the key to the universal ethnological narrative.

British enthusiasts of India included Orientalists of great talent and genius, such as Jones and Colebrooke, and amateurs, such as Vallancey and Maurice, who knew no Indian languages. The discourse of Indomania, accordingly, was a mixture of pearls and dung. No sharp divide created by professional self-definition and closure yet separated "scientists" from "amateurs," or fostered the possibility of a scientific interest in India that was not also impelled by some strain of Indomania; that parting of ways would come much later. For the moment the better qualified and the less qualified were part of the same overall phenomenon.

But the case of Wilford shows that it was more than a question of discriminating the qualified from the unqualified, because Wilford was a very able Sanskritist. The judgment of the Sanskritist Julius von Klaproth, writing over a half-century later, shows how Orientalism itself divided over Wilford: "One cannot but deeply regret that the perfect knowledge of Sanskrit and other Indian languages that Wilford had acquired, the assiduous reading of the ancient books of the brahmins and his many laborious researches, should not only have been without benefit for the literary world but that they should in fact have rendered a disservice to the study of antiquities and mythology in Europe" (Klaproth c.1865:609). In spite of Wilford's obvious shortcomings the comparative mythologists of Germany still accept his supposed discoveries, Klaproth complains, and even improve upon the dreams of their compatriot. It is evident that the scandal of Wilford troubled Orientalists

for a very long time. It was a central issue for the internal politics of
Orientalist knowledge, and it provided ammunition for those, such as
Klaproth, who sought the exclusion of enthusiasm from Orientalist research in the interest of making it scientific. And it was a gift to the
critics of Orientalism from without.

CHAPTER 4

# British Indophobia

British Indomania did not die of natural causes; it was killed off. The Indophobia that became the norm in early-nineteenth-century Britain was constructed by Evangelicalism and Utilitarianism, and its chief architects were Charles Grant and James Mill. The key texts are two: Grant's "Observations on the state of society among the Asiatic subjects of Great Britain, particularly with respect to morals; and the means of improving it" (1797), and Mill's *History of British India* (1817). They require our close attention. But first, to get a sense of the changing spirit of the period, it will be useful to take a brief look at John Shore's biography of Sir William Jones.

## John Shore's Life of Jones

That the public mood in Britain, which nurtured Indo-mania in the eighteenth century, had decisively changed as the century came to a close is evident in the biography of Sir William Jones written by John Shore, Lord Teignmouth, and published in 1805. By then, aspects of Jones's character had begun to lose the glamour they had in his lifetime. Shore's biography shows the points at which he felt that Jones's reputation was in need of the attentions of what we have come to call a spin doctor, providing clues to the new mood. Shore focused principally on Jones's religious beliefs and politics.

Shore, Orientalist and protégé of Jones in Calcutta, had become a member of the Clapaham Sect of Evangelicals after returning to England. To the increasingly popular Evangelical movement, Jones's religious views now seemed excessively rationalistic and, although filled with references to God, were by the measure of the new standard of religiosity noticeably lacking in references to Christ. Shore devotes several pages to quotations from the publications and letters of Jones, but it is apparent that he finds only just enough to make a favorable case: As a young man, wanting to satisfy his doubts about scripture, Jones had read the Old and New Testaments in the original and developed a rational proof that the former prophesied the coming of Jesus as the Messiah in the latter (Shore 1805:65–67). His professed willingness to accept the results of a purely rational examination of the truths of the Mosaic account of man's primitive condition regardless of whether they proved favorable to Scripture could now seem dangerously akin to the skepticism of Voltaire, the very thing Jones had argued against. This acceptance of secular reason was of course the basis of the anniversary discourses, and it now needed defending from the very religion that Jones had championed in the discourses. In the culmination of his treatment of the issue Shore did his best to place Jones on the honor roll of Protestant scholar-heros with Bacon and Newton and Locke, as innovators in science who had tested scripture with reason and found it sound, to their great praise "and we may hope to their eternal happiness" (1805:331). The note of defensiveness is new and unmistakable.

As to political views, Jones had been a radical Whig who proposed a greatly enlarged franchise and was sympathetic to the cause of the American Revolution, views that got him in a certain amount of trouble in his lifetime.[1] Shore is at pains to show that Jones "was not tainted with the wild theories of licentiousness, miscalled liberty, which have

---

1. Three political pamphlets of Jones were controversial. *An inquiry into the legal mode of suppressing riots, with a constitutional plan of future defense* (1780, reprinted four times) opposed the use of the army as a means of suppressing disturbances such as the Gordon riots and argued instead for the use of local militias under the form of the *posse comitatus*. *The principles of government* (1782c, reprinted seven times), "written by a member of the Society for Constitutional Information," aimed to show, through a dialogue between a scholar and a peasant, that principles of good government could be inculcated in the unlettered and that, therefore, the franchise should be enlarged (sevenfold, as Jones estimates) to include all adult males excluding only paupers. This was the object of a famous libel case leading to Fox's Libel Act of 1792 (Cannon 1990:185–186). *A speech of William Jones, Esq. to the assembled inhabitants of the Counties of Middlesex and Surry, the Cities of London and Westminster, and the Borough of Southwark* (1782d) also advocated a very substantial increase of the franchise and the limiting of royal power.

been propagated with unusual industry since the revolution in France" (1805:400), and he asserts that Jones would have moderated his views had he lived to see the doleful outcome of that event.

On the other hand, aspects of the Orientalist self-image are muted in Shore's *Life;* there are only truncated examples of the obligatory references to the signs of Orientalist knowledge leading to love: friendship with Indian scholars, and the tears of the pandits at Jones's death (1805:411). Meantime, the scandal of Wilford's fraudulent pandit came to Shore's knowledge only after the body of his biography had been set in type, and he was obliged to acknowledge it in his preface and to defend Jones's reputation against the anticipated charge of gullibility. Overall one has the sense of a turning tide and the feeling that Shore was hard put to reconfigure the image of Jones so that it would catch the new religious and political mood, which was shaped by Evangelicalism and the darkened assessment of the French Revolution in the age of Napoleon. The new mood was not favorable to Orientalism, and ultimately it turned to Indophobia. The texts of Charles Grant and James Mill were its most eloquent expressions.

## Charles Grant's "Observations"

Charles Grant was a Scotsman, an India hand, and an Evangelical who, after returning to Britain, became very influential in the councils of the East India Company. The "Observations on the . . . Asiatic subjects of Great Britain" (1796) is a very long policy paper that makes the case for an aggressively Anglicizing and Christianizing stance toward India and its culture, in opposition to the prevailing Orientalist policy of respect for Indian laws, religion, and custom that had been set in motion by Warren Hastings. It is above all a direct attack on Hinduism and Indian civilization and on the Indomania of Grant's contemporaries and fellow servants of the Company (Embree 1962:148). Its influence was immense. It invented the reform agenda for British India and in doing so created a justification for British rule. It would be difficult to overestimate its importance since some form of Grant's view, secularized into a notion of progress, dominated the apparatus of British rule until 1947 (Embree 1962:157). Accordingly I will consider its argument in some detail. I will, however, abstract it from the masses of proof texts that Grant assembled from travelers, Orientalists, and translations of Indian works, by which he gave it the weight and gravity that is the sign of a well-informed review of the question.

Grant tells us that it was "chiefly written in 1792," and it is well to keep the time horizon in mind. On the one hand the first volume of the *Asiatic researches* had been published only four years earlier. The prior texts for Grant were mostly pre-Jonesean, such as François Bernier's *Travels in the Mogul empire* (1656–68), Halhed's translation of the *Code of Gentoo laws* (1776), and, on Hindu religion, passages from Abu'l Fazl's *Āʾīn-i Akbarī*, translated by Francis Gladwin (1783–86), and Charles Wilkins's translation of the *Bhagavad Gītā* (1785). He did not cite Jones himself except in footnotes that appear to have been added later.[2] The proof texts, therefore, belong largely to the first phase of the new Orientalism before or at the time of the formation of the Asiatic Society. On the other hand the feel of the piece is very post-Jonesean, and it represents the beginnings of a turning tide. The new sensibility is found in the Evangelicalism of its religious stance, which was to be a growing force in British life, and also in its alarm at the course of the French Revolution. One seems to see, in the passage about to be cited, a feeling that at the bottom of the deepening crisis of France lay the irreligion propagated by Voltaire, which, in Grant's view, was in some way connected with the favorable portrait of Hindu society and religion purveyed by the English Orientalists Voltaire so admired, Dow and Holwell. Not terribly successful at first, the "Observations" was a foretaste of things to come. It was trotted out in 1813, with the backing of Wilberforce and the Evangelicals, who were demanding that Company-ruled territories be opened up to missionaries, and again in 1833, when the East India Company charter was up for renewal before Parliament and when Company policy was subjected to parliamentary scrutiny and debate. Grant's text seemed to gather power with each appearance.

After tracing the history of the East India Company in India Grant comes to the "State of society and manners among the people of Hindostan," and he comes straight to the point of his polemic, the attack upon Indomania.

It has suited the views of some philosophers to represent that people as amiable and respectable; and a few late travellers have chosen rather to place some softer traits of their characters in an engaging light, than to give a just delineation of the whole. The generality, however, of those who have writ-

---

2. Charles Grant was elected to membership of the Asiatic Society shortly after its founding, but his record of attendance shows that his interest was casual at best (eight meetings in all), and he gave no papers, according to the *Proceedings* (Asiatic Society 1980). The citations and narrative of the "Observations" show no evidence that he knew Sanskrit.

ten concerning Hindostan, appear to have concurred in affirming what foreign residents there have as generally thought, nay, what the natives themselves freely acknowledge of each other, that they are a people exceedingly
depraved. (1796:20)

This uncompromising judgment falls especially upon those Indians who
are under British rule, the Bengalis, and among them especially the
Hindus, and the content of their moral depravity (which Grant descants
upon at length) is that they are lacking in truth, honesty, and good faith
to a degree not found in European society. Grant is blunt in the interest
not of condemning the Indians but of determining "their true place
in the moral scale," an expression I ask readers to remember because it
will become of considerable theoretical importance later in the chapter.
What he insists upon is the universality of this great depravity in Hindu
society, giving it a general moral hue, "between which and the European moral complexion there is a difference analogous to the difference
of the natural colour of the two races" (1796:25). But the purpose is
neither condemnation for its own sake nor to assert the permanent in-
feriority of another race. Although Grant's description of the Indians
is unfavorable in the extreme, "his wish is not to excite detestation, but
to engage compassion, and to make it apparent, that what speculation
may have ascribed to physical and unchangeable causes, springs from
moral sources capable of correction" (1796:31).

Passing to the moral sources of this depravity, Grant considers in
turn the influence of climate, of government and laws, and of religion.
He largely dismisses the first. The climate of India is undoubtedly less
favorable to the human constitution than that of Europe, but as a cause
of the Hindu character too much has been imputed to climate. It is not
to nature but to human institutions, namely to government, laws, and
religion, that he looks for the formative causes.

## GOVERNMENT

Grant's argument relies heavily upon the trope of Oriental despotism. This idea, by which Aristotle had contrasted the unfree-
dom of the Persians with the liberty of the Greeks, had been revived
since the Renaissance and applied to the Ottoman Empire to contrast
it with Europe, and then generalized to other Eastern regimes, especially that of Mughal India.

Despotism, the mode of government generally prevailing in the
East, appears to have existed at all times among the Hindus, Grant says,
and has greatly influenced the formation of their character. When an

individual is dependent on the will and caprice of another he becomes degraded in thought and action. All regard for what is valuable in life is reduced to personal interest and all thought for the public good and the future is lost in the precariousness of the present hour. Fear is the main principle of action, leading to distrust; as arbitrary power does not lead one to expect truth and justice in government officers, it does not produce integrity and veracity in its subjects.

The character of the Hindus must have been debased in several respects by their oppression by numerous invaders—in this much Grant agrees with the tenets of Indomania, which inclined to attribute the shortcomings of contemporary Hindu society to the burden of Muslim rule, from which it would be enfranchised by British rule on Orientalist lines. But Grant opposes this by arguing that the government of Hindus, too, has always had a despotic character, since long before the invasions of Muslim adventurers. The Hindus "did not receive the despotic form of government from the Tarters, nor were they degraded only when they became subject to Mahomedan conquerors."

They have had among themselves a complete despotism from the remotest antiquity; a despotism, the most remarkable for its power and duration that the world has ever seen. It has pervaded their government, their religions, and their laws. It has formed by its various ramifications the essentials of the character which they have always had, as far as the light of history goes, and which they still posess; that character, which has made them a prey to every invader, indifferent to all their rulers, and easy in the change of them; as a people, void of public spirit, honour, attachment; and in society, base, dishonest, and faithless. (1796:32)

Although the ancient Hindu form of government scarcely exists any longer, except in Nepal, their laws and religion remain. Grant develops his proof of the debasing effects of Oriental despotism upon the Hindu character through a long series of damning quotations regarding Hindu law and the Hindu religion.

### LAW

The whole fabric of Hindu law is "the work of a crafty and imperious priesthood, who feigned a divine revelation and appointment, to invest their own order, in perpetuity, with the most absolute empire over the civil state of the Hindoos, as well as over their minds" (1796:35). The priestcraft theme, a distinctly Protestant motif, was by no means Grant's invention; it was a critique of Catholicism turned to new purposes in India. The laws themselves, taken from Halhed's translation of the *Code of Gentoo laws,* are quoted at length under five heads: laws giving the privileges and duties of the ruler; laws establishing the privileges of the superior castes; laws that give a direct sanction to immoralities; laws that promote oppression and injustice; and laws that show a spirit of cruelty (1796:36ff.). The rubrics suffice to convey the drift.

## RELIGION

As to religion, the proof of its contribution to the general moral depravity of the Hindus is again rendered under five heads: ceremonial and pecuniary atonements (showing that sin can be repaired by ritual, without true repentance); doctrines relating to transmigration (which promotes, Grant alleges, a sense of fatalism about one's condition rather than a sense of personal responsibility); the characters of Hindu deities (largely to do with sexuality—their "abandoned licentiousness" and the worship of the *lingam*); modes of worship (including hook-swinging and the institution of temple prostitutes); and superstitious opinions affecting daily life (largely rites of prognostication and healing) (1796:46ff.). Besides Gladwin's translation of Abu'l Fazl's *Āʾīn* and Wilkins's translation of the *Gītā,* Grant appeals to the authority of a number of (Protestant) missionaries and travelers going back to Roger, Baldeus, Bernier, and a number of the older authorities. It is clear that this bill of particulars in the condemnation of Hinduism is not here drawn up for the first time, but builds upon a (largely missionary) tradition of condemnation.

But if indeed abject slavery and unparalleled depravity are the characteristics of the Hindus, and if such are the consequences of Hindu government and religion, "how has Hindostan flourished under that system, as it is said to have done in ancient times?" (1796:58). The "ancient splendour of India" that has been a foundational truth for Indomania is a decided obstacle to his argument, and Grant meets it by returning to climate, which is now cast in a benevolent role. India certainly possesses advantages, but they are derived from nature—genial climate, fertile soil—not government. Political institutions had cramped its natural powers, produced general corruption, and failed to defend the country against foreign invasion.

But again, the ancient splendor of India as recorded by Greek and Latin authors and recently revisited in the Rev. William Robertson's

*Historical disquisition concerning the knowledge which the ancients had of India* of 1791 (which makes claims for the refinement of ancient Indian civilization and the happiness resulting from government policy) would not just go away, and Grant returns to the subject in a long footnote in which he attacks Robertson for painting a picture that is "far more beautiful than the original." Robertson falls in with the view, advanced by the writers of the Scottish Enlightenment, of a progressive development of society starting from the savage state and conceives the original inhabitants of Hindustan to have advanced from such a state "through a long series of internal improvements, to the highest stages of refinement, unaided even by the accession of extraneous lights" (Grant 1796:58n.). Grant opposes Robertson's position with an argument upon the facts of the Tower of Babel narrative: So far from beginning in a state of savagery, he says, it appears more probable that mankind already had the habits of civilized life at the time of its dispersal from the plains of Shinar, and humans would, "without sinking into barbarism, soon spread into the luxuriant regions of India, where the rich abundance of the soil would speedily lead them to the arrangments of a regular society." The profile of early Indian history is not a rise from savagery to civilization, but from an initial civilized life to greater refinement under the rich abundance of its soil. Savagery is not the initial condition of the human race but a fall from an initial state of civilization. Moreover India's civilization derived from outside India. It is here for the first time, in a footnote attacking Robertson's progressivist, social-evolutionary interpretation of Indian history, that Grant makes contact at last with the premier Orientalist of his age, making common cause with Jones's Mosaic ethnology. Jones's "Discourse on the Hindus" is pressed into service in support of the argument that, in respect of the brahmin system of religion, law, and science, of which Robertson makes so much in developing proofs of the progressive view of Indian civilization, they did not spring up in India but from a source nearer the original seat of the human race after the flood of Noah. And in any case, learning was monopolized and concealed by the brahmins, and it "spread little light among the great body of the people" (1796:59n.). As to the wealth of India, it was the result of nature's special bounty in the warmer zones, but it was largely monopolized by princes, brahmins, and chief persons of the other castes.

Robertson constructed the "ancient splendor" interpretation largely upon the accounts of India in Greek and Latin, especially that of the Seleucid ambassador Megasthenes, who was sent to the court of Candragupta Maurya in the fourth century B.C. Against the very favorable picture of India given in Megasthenes and other ancient writers, Grant asserts the claims of a different, far more negative reading, in which the splendor of ancient India becomes a sign for the cruelty of its polity. In this reading, large armies, abundance of jewels and "effeminate" finery, richly endowed temples of fine workmanship and great cost, large bodies of priests, and so forth, would appear striking to the eye of a foreign ambassador living in the capital, but there is no reason to think this wealth was spread widely among the population. Indeed, there is no reason to believe that the common people ever lived upon anything but rice or coarse grains, ever wore anything but a loincloth or a half covering of ordinary cotton, ever lived in anything better than huts of mud brick with straw roofs. "Such is the present style, and such in all probability it ever has been, not because the people preferred this, but because they had no choice" (the same).

Thus Grant's diagnosis: The general depravity of Hindus results from government, laws, and religion—in short, from moral causes. The cure must be of the same kind.

The true cure of darkness, is the introduction of light. The Hindoos err, because they are ignorant; and their errors have never fairly been laid before them. The communication of our light and knowledge to them, would prove the best remedy for their disorders; and this remedy is proposed, from a full conviction that if judiciously and patiently applied, it would have great and happy effects upon them, effects honourable and advantageous for us. (1796:60)

In a word, the cure Grant proposes is education in the arts, philosophy, and religion of the English, and the best way of communicating British light and knowledge is through education conducted in the English language. It is perfectly in Britain's power, Grant argues, to teach the Hindus English and, through simple writings in that medium, gradually and progressively to educate them in the elements of British arts, philosophy, and religion; they will "silently undermine, and at length subvert, the fabric of error" (the same). English is a key that will open to the Hindus a world of new ideas.

It is not warrantable to infer, Grant argues, that because the Hindus are at present in a low state, they must remain so forever. The history of nations that have risen from rudeness to refinement shows the contrary, otherwise the Britons "ought still to be going naked, to be feeding on acorns, and sacrificing human victims in the Druidical groves."

In fact, his policy proposal goes to the further civilization of a people who had already made considerable progress in the ancient past but who, owing to the fraud and imposition of the brahmins, "were rendered first stationary, then retrograde" (1796:63).

But is there not, in the era of the French Revolution, a serious flaw in the reasoning? Will not the people learn to desire English liberty, a share in the government of their country and commissions in the army, and finally throw off English rule and assert their independence? Will not the communication of the Gospel and of European light lead to popular government and the assertion of independence? Grant considers these objections carefully and concludes that the influence of climate will prevail over love of liberty. Indolence, pusillanimity, and insensibility will be partially amended by moral improvement, but the tropical sun will still be oppressive. There is, then, no rational ground for apprehending that the Indians will become turbulent for English liberty. The spirit of English liberty is a growth of ages, and is not to be caught from a written description of it, especially by distant and feeble Asiatics.

What, finally, are the best means of perpetuating Britain's empire in India, in Grant's view? It is here, as we come to the nub of the thing, that Grant insists on the distance between the two peoples.

At present, we are every way different from the people whom we hold in subjection; different in country, in language, in manners, in customs, in sentiments, and in religion; their interest also, for the reasons mentioned in the early part of this memoir, they must conceive to be different from ours. What then can be a healing principle with regard to all these points, but a principle of *assimilation,* a *common-bond,* which shall give to both parties the reality and the conviction of mutual benefit from the connection? Without an uniting principle, a conjoining tie of this nature, we can suppose the country to be, in fact, retained only by mere power; but in the same degree than an identity of sentiments and principles would be established, we should exhibit a sight new in the region of Hindostan, a people actively attached, cordially affected to their government, and thus augmenting its strength. (1796:82)

We thus arrive at the grand question: How shall the British make the Indians love them? It had been the aim of Alexander, Grant says, to establish his authority in the affection of the nations he had subdued—so Robertson's *Disquisition* had recently recalled—by abolishing all distinctions between the victors and the vanquished; thus his European and Asiatic subjects were incorporated and became one people, by obeying the same laws and by adopting the same manners, institutions, and discipline. In short, they were assimilated. Britons should apply this principle; however they should not follow Alexander's policy fully. It would suit neither the British nor the Indians "that the distinctions between the two races should be lost" by intermarriage (the same), nor should the British impose upon India laws framed for their own country. They should rather attach their subjects to themselves by affection and interest, by winning them to their religion and sentiments, and in doing so add to the happiness of the Indians and render British authority permanent and secure.

Thus Grant constructs the case, giving a new reading to Orientalist productions, that the Indians are "every way different" from the British. It was nothing new to say the two were different; what told against the tide of Indomania, which had been running toward a sympathetic understanding and tendency to emphasize the common humanity of Europeans and Indians, was the new insistence that the Indians were different in "every way."[3] The materials that Grant used were the ones produced by the Orientalists themselves; what differed was the reading. It cannot be an accident that, in constructing the case for difference "every way," Grant entirely suppressed mention of the Jonesean doctrine of a kinship between European languages and Sanskrit, and hence between Europeans and Indians, even while citing the very third anniversary discourse in which the connection is made plain.

## Grant and Macaulay on Education

What Grant's new version of the policy of love amounts to is this: The Indians should assimilate to the ways of the British, but the British should take care not to assimilate to the ways of the Indi-

---

3. The following passage from Percival Spear, I would argue, is in direct lineal descent from Grant's "Observations":

The contact of two races so dissimilar in character, in culture and in institutions as the English and the Indian raises the problem of the contact of cultures in its most acute form. Mutual influence is easiest when two cultures are basically the same; radical difference tends either to mutual repulsion, or to absorption of one by the other. (Spear 1963:126)

This point of view could not be more different from the Orientalist view of Hamilton, cited earlier, about how indifference gives way to empathy through the mastery of language.

ans—and the two races should remain distinct. Alexander had his men take Asian wives as a part of the assimilation policy; Grant wanted to omit that part. East India Company servants, who often took Indian wives or concubines in the eighteenth century, were now to observe racial endogamy and promote the cultural assimilation of Indians to England without themselves succumbing to "the disease of indianization" (Farrington 1976:6). We might call this policy one-way asexual assimilation. It became the official creed of nineteenth-century British India.

The change it brought to the sexual politics of empire was immense. The British rulers of Bengal in the eighteenth century were men who, except for an elite few like Sir William Jones who brought his wife with him, had little or no prospect of finding European wives and who, many of them, took Indian ones; in the nineteenth century the new creed of endogamy made English domesticity in India normative and brought British women to India in large numbers. The signs of the old dispensation are those eighteenth-century portraits of Englishmen dressed as Indian gentlemen smoking hookahs or watching Indian dance performances; the sign of the new dispensation are the handbooks of British-Indian domesticity, such as F. A. Steel and G. Gardiner's *Complete Indian housekeeper and cook* (1909).[4]

A change so momentous inevitably had effects upon the learning of Indian languages, in ways that are only partly known. Several of the new Orientalists, such as Alexander Hamilton and Sir John Shore, had Indian wives, and it cannot but have helped them develop a fluency, if not in Sanskrit and Persian, at least in Hindustani and other modern languages. Richard Burton said that the Indian wife was a walking dictionary of Hindustani (Burton 1893, 1:135). Halfway through the nineteenth century George Smith considers the effects of the change in sexual relations on language learning in a highly ambivalent backward glance charged with alternating feelings of repulsion and regret. Smith looks at the eighteenth-century British rulers of Bengal from the vantage of the sexual dispensation we have come to call Victorian:

Cut off from European society, separated, by correspondence, from England by a distance in time of nearly two years, they were driven to find in

---

4. Kenneth Ballhatchet's *Race, sex and class under the Raj* (1980) was the first systematic study of the sexual politics of British India, concentrating on the military and the regulation of prostitution. The changing sexual mores of the British rulers of India, of course, had British origins. Lawrence Stone (n.d.) dates the onset in England of the sexual morality we call "Victorian" at about the beginning of the nineteenth century or a bit before, that is, just about the time of Grant's memorandum on education.

native society what we now have in all the luxuries and amenities of English civilization. Never since these have been so largely introduced overland, and added at once to the comforts and inefficiency of both branches of the Service, have they known the natives so well, or been so much beloved by them. At the same time, this state of things was accompanied by evils of the very worst character, dissipation and debauchery of all kinds, and concubinage of a thoroughly oriental character. The absence of a middle Anglicised class of natives, who might save the trouble of personally attending to the details of duty, put many of our countrymen in positions, where, as we know, the tendency was to become so enamoured of native life, and so well acquainted with the native language, as to forget the dignity and nationality of the Briton, the responsibility and duty of the Christian. Hence all the linguistic likings and power of the British were diverted into a vernacular and utilitarian channel, and a facility acquired in it which we shall look for in vain now. With the vices and follies of our early rule of India, have we not also given up much of the manliness and common sense? Do not passing events teach us that Clive was wiser than his modern successors, that his policy of ruling Asiatics on oriental principles, was wiser than that of white-washing them with semi-Anglicism? (Smith 1857:251)

But much the largest effect Grant had upon India, and upon the British study of Indian languages, had to do with his role in the formation of educational policy, leading to the "white-washing" of Anglicism of which Smith was to complain. In a word, the educational effects of the impulse to promote one-way assimilation were two: to promote the teaching of English to Indians, and, paradoxically, to institutionalize in England the teaching of Indian languages to prospective civil servants.

Grant's Anglicist policy as it applied to the education of Indians was fostered by Charles Trevelyan and given memorable expression by Thomas Babington Macaulay (scion of a famous Evangelical family) in his well-known *Minute on Indian education* of 1835. It aimed, in Macaulay's words, through English-medium instruction in the arts and sciences of Europe, to form an elite class that was "Indian in blood and colour, but English in taste, in opinions, in morals, and in intellect" (Macaulay 1835:249), what Smith in the passage given above called the "middle Anglicised class" of Indians. The government of India, unable to educate the mass of Indians directly, would do so indirectly through this class; by a process of "filtration" or interpretation, European learning would be conveyed to the Indian masses by their Anglicized betters (Macaulay 1835:249; Clive 1973:chap. 12). English not only is the language of India's rulers but has become a repository of the best of European thought. By contrast the literatures of Arabic and Sanskrit contain "medical doctrines which would disgrace an English Farrier—Astronomy, which would move laughter in girls at an English boarding school—History, abounding with kings thirty feet high, and reigns thirty thousand years long—and Geography, made up of seas of treacle and seas of butter" (Macaulay 1835:242–243).

Macaulay's *Minute* is a masterpiece of English polemic prose, making brilliant use of satire to oppose the Orientalist establishment, and in doing so it has been more successful than it deserves to be in casting the anti-Anglicist position of the Orientalists as a stand-pat conservatism. It is important not to take Macaulay's polemic characterization of the opposing position for the simple truth, as it so often is. In fact, the Orientalist position with which H. H. Wilson and other luminaries of the Asiatic Society were identified did not argue against the modernizing and Europeanizing objective of the Anglicist policy, but it held that science would not take root in Indian society unless it was taught through the Indian languages and through the modernization of their literatures. Opposing the "filtration" metaphor of the Anglicists with the metaphor of "engrafting" European learning upon the rootstock of Indian civilization, advocates of the Orientalist policy for education wished to develop the powers of the Indian vernaculars to become effective vessels of the new learning so that European knowledge should become domesticated to the Indian scene. In doing this they treated Sanskrit, Persian, and Arabic as the equivalent of the Latin and Greek through whose literatures English and the other modern languages of Europe had been developed and had become repositories of the highest civilization. Thus Newtonian astronomy, for example, was to be grafted upon the astronomical knowledge of India contained in the Sanskrit texts of Jyotiṣa, through which European science would be seen to be a further, more perfect development of the Indian astronomical science. In a very real sense the clash of the Anglicist and Orientalist educational policies was an argument within the paradigm of modernization, not a clash of progressives and conservatives.

In their struggle against the Orientalist establishment, entrenched in its authority over matters of cultural policy since the times of Hastings and the first formation of the Asiatic Society, the Anglicists propounded a countertheory to that of the Oriental renaissance. It was not, now, the study of Sanskrit and Indian antiquities that would bring a second renaissance to the West, as the study of Greek learning had been the foundation of the first Renaissance. Rather, as Macaulay argued in his famous *Minute*, it had been the diligence of the English in studying Greek and Latin literatures during the Renaissance, when almost everything worth reading was contained in the writings of the ancient Greeks and Romans, that had put English literature ahead of the Greek, the Latin, and the Sanskrit:

Had our ancestors acted as the Committee of Public Instruction has hitherto acted [in supporting Arabic and Sankrit scholarship]; had they neglected the language of Cicero and Tacitus; had they confined their attention to the old dialects of our own island; had they printed nothing and taught nothing at the universities but Chronicles in Anglo-Saxon and Romances in Norman-French, would England have been what she now is? What the Greek and Latin were to the contemporaries of More and Ascham, our tongue is to the people of India. The literature of England is now more valuable than that of classical antiquity. I doubt whether the Sanscrit literature be as valuable as that of our Saxon and Norman progenitors. In some departments—in History, for example—I am certain that it is much less so. (1835:243)

Thus the renaissance idea became contested territory, in which the Orientalists, having identified Sanskrit as the Greek or Latin of India, were now answered by Macaulay, who believed English to be to India as Greek and Latin had been to England, and who regarded Sanskrit and Arabic as no better than repositories of a completely outmoded knowledge, although he had studied neither, as he freely admitted. Insofar as the Anglicist position tended to prevail over the Orientalist one (without entirely overcoming it), Evangelical influence drove British policy down a path that tended to minimize and denigrate the accomplishments of Indian civilization and to position itself as the negation of the British Indomania that was nourished by belief in Indian wisdom.[5]

The other side of the education question that divided the Orientalists and the Anglicists concerned the training of the Company's British personnel.

Until the end of the eighteenth century British lads as young as fifteen years old were sent to India to become "Writers" in the East India Company service. The administrative responsibilities the Company acquired with the conquest of Bengal and the defeat of the French in South India created a need for better training of its servants, and in 1800, Marquess Wellesley, the governor-general, founded his "University of the East," the College of Fort William at Calcutta, where all

5. Gauri Viswanathan's *Masks of Conquest* (1989) explores this territory more fully than I can here.

Writers were to follow a three-year course before proceeding to their posts in Bengal, Madras, or Bombay. The course included what were regarded as the three classical languages of India (Arabic, Persian, and Sanskrit), six modern languages (Hindustani, Bengali, Telugu, Marathi, Tamil, and Kannada), and Indian law. Wellesley turned to the membership of the Asiatic Society for professors of the college, H. T. Colebrooke becoming in this way the first European to hold a professorship of Sanskrit. Indians were appointed as assistants for language teaching. The formation of the College of Fort William completed the triangle of overlapping institutions—the governing council, the Asiatic Society, and the College of Fort William—through which Orientalists circulated in the formation of their particular conjuncture of power and knowledge, and the teaching of Indian languages, which heretofore had rested on the private arrangements individuals made with pandits and munshis, was now institutionalized under British auspices. Moreover, the College of Fort William, as David Kopf's admirable study (1969) shows, became an important public space in which, through the juxtaposition of British Orientalists and Indian teachers, British Orientalism contributed to the profound restructuring of Bengali upper-class culture. A few years after its founding, the court of directors made provision for similar schools in Madras and Bombay, although the original plan was that all recruits were first to be educated at Calcutta, and secondarily at Madras and Bombay if, at the determination of Calcutta, they were to be assigned outside of Bengal (see also Farrington 1976:3–7).

Nevertheless, the formation of the College of Fort William, which Wellesley had undertaken without consultation and on his own authority, did not sit well with the Company grandees in London. For one thing, there was the question of patronage. Members of the court of directors were used to controlling appointments to writerships and collecting large fees for doing so. What would become of that arrangement if Calcutta could decide who passed into the service and where they were to be sent? There was also the question, dear to the Evangelical cause, of the bad effects of early exposure to India on British youth. It was not long before the court of directors decided to set up the East India College in England, which it did in February of 1806, first in Hertford Castle, which it had leased for the purpose, and then in Haileybury, its permanent location, which it occupied until its dissolution in 1858. Haileybury did not eliminate the College of Fort William; a compromise was reached whereby the first two years of training would be passed at the East India College, followed by further training in the

College of Fort William—or at Madras or Bombay, after the strangle-hold of Calcutta was relaxed a few years later.

Charles Grant played a critical role in this development, and the re-port of the 1804 committee on the question of the formation of the East India College, whose recommendation carried the day, was largely his work (East India Company 1804; Farrington 1976:7). A principal motive was to make sure that British boys were not exposed to the dan-gers of Indian culture too soon and to give them a fortifying inocula-tion of European culture before shipping them out.

Nor ought it to be the only object of such a system to form good servants for the Company; the system should Aim also at making them good sub-jects, and enlightened Patriots. They are to leave their Native Country at an early Age, to pass many years of Life among People every way dissimilar to their own; their sphere of action is placed at a remote distance from the Parent State; they are to manage interests of the highest value to that state; and our vast acquisitions there with the continually increasing number of Europeans in those territories, tend to strengthen their Attachment to that Quarter. It is therefore of importance that the Young Men, before their departure, should be imbued with reverence and love for the Religion, the Constitution, and the Laws of their own Country; and hence the plan of their studies should comprehend some elementary instruction in those most essential branches of knowledge. Those branches will also be best learnt before the Young Men have launched out into the World, which without such instruction they would go unfortified against erroneous and danger-ous Opinions. (East India Company 1804:15)

We see here the signature idea of Grant: The Indians are a people "every way dissimilar," and British lads are not to assimilate to them.

While, then, the East India College would insure that its servants did not become too attached to India, it had nonetheless to include in its course of study the rudimentary instruction in Indian languages that the candidates would continue in India, whether at the College of Fort William or in Madras or Bombay. Thus the same impulse that founded the East India College as a means of cultural inoculation made it also the means by which the teaching of Indian languages (both "classical" and "vernacular") was institutionalized on European soil. Alexander Hamilton, member of the Asiatic Society and retired officer of the East India Company's army, became, by virtue of his appointment to the East India College, the first Sanskritist to hold a professorship in an institution of higher learning in Europe.

The Company aimed high, hoping to create a college that was the equivalent of those of the established universities. Offering high salaries and a university-like status, it largely succeeded in attracting a distinguished staff, as Farrington notes. Initial appointments included

Bewick Bridge, mathematician and Fellow of Peterhouse, Cambridge, Edward Christian, Downing Professor of Law at Cambridge, William Dealtry, mathematician and Fellow of Trinity College, Cambridge, Thomas Malthus, political economist, Alexander Hamilton, the Sanskrit scholar, and Charles Stewart, former Assistant Professor of Persian at the College of Fort William. These six alone published some thirty-seven books during their careers at the College. (Farrington 1976:8)

The Company's 1804 report is particularly revealing on the condition of the study of Indian languages and literatures in Britain. It is a reproach to our country, the report argues, that in spite of our vast connection with the East no steps have been taken to make provision at home for the learning of Oriental languages. Retired Company servants are indeed capable of teaching them in England, but having passed through the service they are not willing to stoop to the condition of private teachers of languages. Thus the knowledge of languages acquired in India dies with them in Britain, and, notwithstanding the large numbers of Oriental scholars retiring to their native soil, no store of Oriental learning is formed at home (1804:18). Britons learned Indian languages in India, and since their knowledge did not reproduce itself, Orientalism relied on a perpetual recourse to the pandits and munshis in India itself.

The report goes on to say that political reasons argue for the formation of seminaries in Britain to promote the study of the most important languages of India and Asia. The French were doing so much better in this matter and had set a high value upon institutions of this kind. The French government encourages the study of Oriental literature, the report says, and it is pursued with ardor; Paris so abounds in persons proficient in Persian, Arabic, Turkish, and even "Shanscrit" that a scholar of our own (Alexander Hamilton) has written that he "conversed among them more frequently in Persian than in French, and that he daily witnessed among them conversations in Persian, Arabic and Turkish." It seems inexpedient "that whilst France flourished in Oriental learning, Britain should possess little productive stock of that kind within itself, and tho' rich in it abroad, where its riches are more exposed, continue still poor at home" (1804:18). Rivalry with the French, it would seem, was the best argument one could make to the court of directors for the establishment of professorships in Indian languages in Britain. Indomania and the wisdom of the Indians was not all what Charles Grant and the other members of the Company's committee had in mind; quite the contrary. Ironically, it was Indophobia that created the professorship of Sanskrit at the East India College, which Alexander Hamilton was the first to enjoy.

## James Mill's *History*

James Mill's highly influential *History of British India* (1817)—most particularly the long essay "Of the Hindus," comprising ten chapters—is the single most important source of British Indophobia and hostility to Orientalism. It is convergent with Grant's "Observations" in a number of ways; indeed one is tempted to see it as a kind of secularized version of the latter. Mill, a Scotsman like Grant, was educated for the ministry and licensed to preach by the Presbyterian Church, but he lost his faith and exchanged it for the Utilitarianism of Jeremy Bentham (of which Mill became the mouthpiece and chief publicist), with its faith in progress and in the principle of the greatest good of the greatest number. Accordingly Mill's prescription for the Indians is not conversion to Christianity, but modernization, and while Grant's "Observations" rode the broad stream of a popular movement (Evangelicalism), Mill's work, belonging to a sect of philosophical radicalism that was anything but popular, made its way by influencing a section of the elite. In addition to developing what can be read as a secularized version of Grant, Mill gave the whole project a theoretical base drawn from the social evolutionism of the Scottish Enlightenment authors— the very social evolutionism that Grant had opposed in his critique of Robertson—elaborating it in an all-out attack upon the British Sanskritists in the person of Sir William Jones.

The *History of British India* was a great success, both publicly (going into its fifth edition by 1858) and for its author personally. Mill had worked on it for many years while raising a large family on his earnings as a journalist. He educated his children himself, and the education of his son John Stuart Mill was based largely on the materials of the *History*. John Stuart served as research assistant to his father while the *History* was being written. (Thomas 1985.) Publication of the *History* established James Mill's credentials as an expert on India, in recognition of which he was given a position in the East India Company offices in London, which solved his financial problems; he remained in Company service for the rest of his life, conducting a strenuous second career of writing and reviewing in the Utilitarian interest after hours. His book was a prescribed text at Haileybury for students preparing for the Indian Civil Service, and through it Bentham's Utilitarian philosophy acquired a considerable influence in the administration of India (Stokes 1959).

Mill's assessment of Indian civilization was cordially disliked by the distinguished Sanskritist H. H. Wilson, who was long the secretary of the Asiatic Society, the first Boden Professor of Sanskrit at Oxford, and the leading Orientalist in the generation after Colebrooke. He said, bluntly, of its contemptuous treatment of India's claims to civilization, "its tendency is evil" (Wilson 1858:xii). It is startling to find this phrase in Wilson's preface to the fifth edition of Mill—or rather, it is surprising that Wilson agreed to edit and continue Mill's history at all, since he was so fundamentally opposed to Mill's assessment of Hindu civilization. Perhaps he believed that by editorial corrections and replies in the footnotes to the errors and distortions of Mill's text he could minimize the damage of a work that would continue to exercise a great effect upon the British whether he liked it or not. In any case, the fifth edition comprises a text by Mill that is hostile to Indian civilization and editorial comments in the footnotes by Wilson that are hostile to the point of view of the text. Wilson's Orientalism is the veritable object of attack in Mill's analysis of Hindu civilization. It is rather as if the prey were trying to embrace the boa constrictor, and with about as much effect.

Mill's attack upon Orientalism begins with the question of authority, the issue of greatest vulnerability for him. As we have seen, Orientalist claims to authority rested on knowledge of languages as a means of access to the mind, and Orientalists such as Holwell used it to advance the claims of the new Orientalism against the (merely) eyewitness authority of the traveler and the missionary. Grant had been very supportive of the study of Oriental languages, although what he emphasizes in his attack upon what he considered the more superficial travelers (such as Megasthenes) is not language mastery but the authority of Europeans, such as merchants, who had long and intimate association with Indians—people, indeed, such as himself. In short, Grant's is the authority of the India hand, the one who asserts that he "understands the natives" because of long working relations with them. Mill had a considerable problem for his book in respect to these authority claims because he knew no Indian languages and had never been to India. In the preface he addresses the issue by boldly attacking the authority of the India hand and Orientalist, turning a weakness into a strength by a bit of word magic.

The meat of the thing is the demonstration of a proposition that has been framed to minimize the content of the India hand's expertise in favor of that of the metropolitan stay-at-home, the proposition that one who brings to the writing of a history of India only those qualifications that can be acquired in Europe is better fitted "in an almost infinite degree" than one who brings to the task only those qualifications that can be acquired in India. Mill purports to show that the India hand's expertise is limited to the gathering of facts presented to his senses in the colony, while the higher-level mental functions are associated with the metropole: "the powers of combination, discrimination, classification, judgement, comparison, weighing, inferring, inducting, philosophizing in short: which are the powers of most importance for extracting the precious ore from a great mine of rude historical materials" (Mill 1858, 1:xxiii). That these are more likely acquired in Europe than in India, Mill judges, will not admit of much dispute. The India hand's gathering of facts recorded in native books that have not been translated and from conversations with natives, facts not yet recorded in writing, remains at the level of sense impression; moreover, once they are put in writing they become available to all. But any one individual can supply from personal observation only a fraction of the mass of facts upon which a full account of India must be based, so that the person best qualified for writing the history of India is not the observer of facts but one who can sift and weigh evidence skillfully. "As soon as every thing of importance is expressed in writing, a man who is duly qualified may obtain more knowledge of India in one year in his closet in England, than he could obtain during the course of the longest life, by the use of his eyes and ears in India" (the same). Thus the Orientalist and India hand are turned into mere eyewitnesses, and their authority is a wasting asset that perishes by the very act of publishing the results of their researches.

The situation of the India hand and Orientalist is even worse than that, for the testimony of a witness is inescapably partial, and only the judge who hears all the testimony is in a position to reach the truth. The very vividness of sense impressions compared with the effect of another person's description is liable to "hang a bias on the mind" (1858, 1:xxiv) and render the conception of a complex scene erroneous. The

India hand who wishes to write a history of India is caught in a fatal dilemma, Mill argues: either to examine a part of India's history minutely, or to take an overall view that is fated to be a cursory one. If the latter, it is a law of human nature that the effect of the cursory view is to strengthen the prejudices and confirm the prepossessions or false notions held by the observer. In the cursory survey the mind attends to those objects that fall in with the current of its own thoughts and confirm its previous ideas, by the principle of association of ideas. In contrast, the writer of a history of India who has never been a percipient witness in India (Mill, for example!) is placed in the position of a judge piecing together the fragmentary and interested testimony of witnesses: "Is it not understood, that in such a case as this, where the sum of the testimony is abundant, the judge, who has seen no part of the transaction has yet, by his investigation, obtained a more perfect conception of it, than is almost ever possessed by any of the individuals from whom he has derived his information?" (1858, 1:xxvi).

This is the burden of the case. Construing Orientalist knowledge as mere fact gathering, it consigns it to the level of description and reserves for activities of the kind Mill claims to exercise the superior dignity of philosophizing or, in our own terms, of theory; then as now in the contest of description versus theory, description must always be the loser. By showing the two kinds of activity to be mutually exclusive he preempts the claim that his work must have less authority than that of someone who, like Jones, may be said to be well prepared both for the descriptive and for the theorizing part of the formation of a critical history of broad scope. But it is also a claim for the authority of the metropole over the colony, of the British philosopher over the India hand, and one, moreover, that is saturated with imagery of seeing: It asserts that one gets from the distance and great height of Britain a superior sight of India, more complete and balanced than one can get in India itself.

We turn now to Mill's theoretical frame for the study of Hindu civilization, which he announces in the following words: "To ascertain the true state of the Hindus in the scale of civilization, is not only an object of curiosity in the history of human nature; but to the people of Great Britain, charged as they are with the government of that great portion of the human species, it is an object of the highest practical importance" (1858, 2:107). Nothing would be gained from reciting the dismal details of Mill's assessment of the state of India's civilization in his long essay "Of the Hindus" (1858, 1:107–376, vol. 2:1–164), whose intent to

minimize the Indian accomplishment and to subvert the expertise of
the Orientalist is evident on every page. It is a sorry showing for the
claim that, untainted by direct knowledge of India and its languages,
the critical historian is an impartial judge; it demonstrates, to the contrary, that theory offers inlets for prejudice the equal, at least, of impressions of sense. But it is worth clarifying further its relation to the
Orientalists and to their ethnological paradigm.

As we have seen, Grant completely suppressed Jones's argument for
a kinship between Europeans and Indians, even though he read and
cited Jones's discourse "On the Hindus" and said nothing of the similarity of Sanskrit to Latin and Greek, which was its foundation. Grant
was otherwise in sympathy with Jones's Biblical orientation and, indeed, he makes use of those aspects of Jones's version of the Mosaic
ethnology to combat the progressive social evolutionism of Robertson's
theory of India's ancient splendor. Mill, too, had read the anniversary
discourses and was if anything much better read in the new Orientalism
than was Grant; Mill, also, maintains a telling silence over the Jonesean
doctrine and makes no mention of the similarity of Sanskrit, Latin, and
Greek. The argument from silence was once regarded as a weak argument, to be used sparingly and with care, but for some time now authors have become responsible for the infinity of what they do *not* say,
and they are liable to be charged with erasures, elisions, suppressions,
guilty silences, and significant omissions. The argument from silence is
made more easily today, but even by the higher standard of the past,
the complete silence of Grant and Mill on the core argument of Jones
is surely significant of a tendency to stress the difference "every way"
of the Indians and the British.

Grant does not offer an alternative ethnological paradigm, beyond
passing use of the phrase "moral scale" or "scale of humanity." In Mill
the idea of the "scale of civilization" becomes the explicit theoretical
foundation of his review of Hindu (and Muslim) civilization. By this
he intends the idea of a staircase or progressive series of stages of development from rudeness, savagery or barbarism, and ignorance to order, regularity, knowledge and civilization. It is deployed as a framework
within which India is judged to be very deficient and the Orientalists
to have been lacking in judgment. Mill ignores the segmentary Mosaic
ethnology of Jones and asserts the claims of an ethnology based on the
scale of civilization and the idea that human history is a story of development in a series of stages from rude beginnings. In doing so he develops ideas that have exercised some of the best minds of the Scottish

Enlightenment, especially John Millar of Glasgow, whose *The origin of the distinction of ranks* (1806; first ed., 1771), he particularly notes as containing the earliest elucidations of the subject, although of course the ideal of developmental stages (hunting, herding, agriculture, commerce) was characteristic of several of earlier Scottish luminaries, among whom one would certainly include Adam Smith and Adam Ferguson. It is from this tradition that Mill draws his fundamental theoretical position in opposition to the radiating structure of the Mosaic ethnology.[6]

The direct confrontation with the Orientalists is found in the "General reflections" chapter with which the essay "On the Hindus" in the *History of British India* concludes:

It was unfortunate that a mind so pure, so warm in the pursuit of truth, and so devoted to oriental learning, as that of Sir William Jones, should have adopted the hypothesis of a high state of civilization in the principal countries of Asia. This he supported with all the advantages of an imposing manner, and a brilliant reputation; and gained for it so great a credit, that for a time it would have been very difficult to obtain a hearing against it. (1858, 2:109)

But "the fancy magnifies the importance of a favourite pursuit." Jones was also motivated to exalt the Hindus in the eyes of the European masters so as to ameliorate the temper of their government. But his greatest weakness was that he held vague and indeterminate notions as to the signs of civilization, to which term, as with most men, he attached "no fixed and definite assemblage of ideas" (1858, 2:109–110).

Mill's attack upon Jones continues with a showing that Jones is promiscuous with his use of the term "civilization," applying it, for example, to the Arab poets of the Muʿallaqāt prior to he advent of Islam. "If courtesy and urbanity, a love of poetry and eloquence, and the practice of exalted virtues be a juster measure of perfect society, we have

6. Jane Rendall (1982) gives a very detailed showing of how the "philosophical history" of the Scottish Enlightenment informed the writings of the Scottish Orientalists, including Alexander Hamilton, James Mackintosh, William Erskine, John Leyden, Alexander Murray, Monstuart Elphinstone, John Crawfurd, and Vans Kennedy, as well as the writings on ancient Indian civilization of those who were not India hands, William Robertson and James Mill. Rendall shows that the stages of social evolutionism that one finds in Adam Smith and other writers was a strong form of philosophical history. This kind of historical writing was taught in Edinburgh by Dugald Stuart and in Glasgow by John Millar (author of *The origin of the distinction of ranks,* 1806, a leading text of this approach). James Mill, however, developed the stage theory into an attack upon Orientalism, in which Dugald Stewart concurred.

certain proof, that the people of *Arabia,* both on plains and in cities, in republican and monarchical states, were eminently civilized for many ages before their conquest of *Persia*" (Jones 1807, 3:50)—which state Mill, *per contra,* characterizes as "the wild, comfortless, predatory, and ferocious state of the wandering Arabs." "We need not wonder," he continues, "if the man, who wrote and delivered this, found the Hindus arrived at the highest civilization" (1858, 2:110).

Here again there is little profit in prolonging the exposition of an argument whose point has been made. It is worth adding, however, that civilization is not a simple, homogeneous, readily measurable thing or quality. Mill shows once more how adept he is at making a virtue out of a difficulty:

It is not easy to describe the characteristics of the different stages of social progress. It is not from one feature, or from two, that a just conclusion can be drawn. In these it sometimes happens that nations resemble each other which are placed at stages considerably remote. It is from a joint view of all the great circumstances taken together, that their progress can be ascertained; and it is from an accurate comparison, grounded on these general views, that a scale of civilization can be formed, on which the relative positions of nations may be accurately marked. (the same)

The effect of the complex and composite character of the components of "civilization" is that its content eludes definition, which gives the analyst—Mill himself—degrees of freedom to shift his ground at need. Nowhere is this more clear, perhaps, than in Mill's long discussion of the astronomy-and-mathematics issue that remained in his day a matter of continued discussion and that he evidently considered a capital point to settle in fixing the place of India in the scale of civilization. Taking comfort from Bentley in his criticism of the high antiquity attributed to Indian astronomy by Playfair and Bailly, Mill comes up against Colebrooke's masterly assessment of Indian algebra. The complexity of achievement of ancient Indian astronomy and mathematics cannot be entirely set aside, and he concludes by shifting assessment from its accomplishments to its purposes:

Exactly in proportion as *Utility* is the object of every pursuit, may we regard a nation as civilized. Exactly in proportion as its ingenuity is wasted on contemptible and mischievous objects, though it may be, in itself, an ingenuity of no ordinary kind, the nation may safely be denominated barbarous.

According to this rule, the astronomical and mathematical sciences afford conclusive evidence against the Hindus. They have been cultivated exclusively for the purposes of astrology; one of the most irrational of all imaginable pursuits; one of those which most infallibly denote a nation barbarous; and one of those which it is the most sure to renounce, in proportion as knowledge and civilization are attained. (1858, 2:105–106)

## Dugald Stewart: Sanskrit a Hoax

In the atmosphere of increasing hostility to the new Orientalism's claims for India's civilization, it was perhaps to be expected that resistance to the Indo-European concept should not stop at passing it over in silence or minimizing it, but should take the form of an outright rejection. The extreme of this rejectionism was realized in the counterclaim that the Sanskrit language was a fabrication of artful priests. The one who elected to make an ass of himself by declaring Sanskrit a fake was no less a personage than the leading Scottish philosopher of his generation, Dugald Stewart.

Stewart's conjecture, briefly put, was that the brahmins, coming into contact with the Greek language through the conquests of Alexander, which reached into the Panjab, invented a new language in which the words of their native dialect were joined with terminations and syntax taken from Greek. The brahmins quickly brought "to a systematic perfection an artificial language of their own, having for their guide the richest and most regular tongue that was ever spoken on earth;—a tongue, too, abounding in whatever abstract and technical words their vernacular speech was incompetant to furnish" (Stewart 1827:110). The very closeness of the correspondence between Sanskrit and Greek was turned to the advantage of this theory—it was closer, he argued, than could be accounted for by common descent—and some ways in which Sanskrit appeared closer to Latin were attributed to subsequent intercourse with Rome. In brief, the reason Sanskrit resembles Greek is not because the two are historically related through a common ancestral language as Jones had proposed, but because Sanskrit *is* Greek, in Indian dress; its antiquity goes no farther back than the time of Alexander. Stewart offers as an analogy the "kitchen Latin" of the monasteries of Roman Catholicism, spoken by half-educated friars who wish to conceal their conversations from the servants. Sanskrit, he proposes in so many words, is "kitchen Greek," by which the brahmins keep their conversations from the ears of the profane. The whole argument is carried out under the distinctly Protestant trope of priestcraft, applied alike to Catholic clergy and the brahmins.

This ludicrous notion, as extreme in the other direction as the over-
heated imaginings of Wilford, has much to tell us of the deeper foundations of British resistance to the Indo-European concept. Indeed, examining the lead-up to this argument, one is struck by the confidence
with which Stewart digs the pit into which he proceeds to fall.

The argument appears in the third volume of Stewart's *Elements of
the philosophy of the human mind,* which appeared in 1827. His section
on "Conjectures concerning the origin of the Sanskrit" is the culmination of a long disquisition on etymology, "considered as a guide to
our conclusions concerning the origin and migrations of the various
tribes of our species" (1827:80); it concludes with two appendices—altogether some seventy pages devoted to the critique of the new Orientalism. Stewart's error is the more interesting because it was so very well
informed. He cites many of the Calcutta Orientalists including Dow,
Halhed, Jones, Wilkins, and Colebrooke and unsigned articles in the
*Edinburgh review* by Alexander Hamilton, whose identity he seems to
know, referring to him as "a gentleman who authority is deservedly
high in all matters connected with Indian literature" (1827:125–126). He
is also familiar with some of the missionary literature outside the new
Orientalism, Lord Monboddo, James Mill, and several of the writers
on the astronomy question. He is, in short, well read in the literature
of the new Orientalism and in other relevant writings, but he does not
know Sanskrit. What emboldens him to take up so extreme a position
against the experts?

It should be said in Stewart's favor that the problem he addresses is
a real one and is central to the whole project of comparative philology:
that of determining whether similarity of features between two languages is due to common descent of both languages from a common
ancestral language or to the borrowing of those features by one language from the other. In the comparisons of vocabularies, the sifting
of true cognate words from later borrowings is one of the major problems of method, and the criteria for such decisions were only gradually
worked out in the course of the nineteenth century. Much the same,
*mutatis mutandis,* can be said about the question of the relation of Indian astronomy to the Greek. Similarities between the two could be
interpreted either by appeal to the idea of common descent or by borrowing in one direction or the other, and the means of deciding among
these alternatives emerged only gradually.

It is quite natural therefore that when Europeans came upon similarities of Sanskrit to Greek or of Indian astronomy to Greek astronomy, some of them should have become advocates of the theory that

Indians had borrowed from Greeks. And, indeed, Stewart found such advocates. Edward Gibbon, in his history, had remarked, "I have long harboured a suspicion that some, perhaps much, of the Indian science was derived from the Greeks of Bactriana" (Gibbon 1776–88, 7:294). "To this hint, however," Stewart says, "I paid but little attention, till I found the same opinion stated with considerable confidence by the very learned *Meiners* in his *Historia de vero Deo;* who refers, in support of it, to the proofs alleged by *Bayer* in his *Historia regni Graecorum Bactriani*" (Stewart 1827:104). In fact, Stewart was appealing to the older writers whose works had been swept aside by the new Orientalism: Christoph Meiners's book was published in 1780, before the founding of the Asiatic Society; Gottlieb Siegfried Bayer's was published even earlier, in 1738. Hamilton, whose high standing in the opinion of Stewart we have already seen, attacked the older view in the *Edinburgh review* on two occasions. Reviewing Wilkins's *Sanskrit grammar* in 1809 he said, "To adopt the hypothesis of the learned Bayer, we must suppose the inhabitants of Hindustan to have waited till Alexander the Great conquered Bactria, in order to obtain appellations for the most endearing ties of nature, and to enable them to express the venerable relations of father and mother" (Hamilton 1809:372–373).[7] In his 1820 review of Bopp's *Conjugationssystem* (1816), he takes the position that Bopp's analysis has decided the issue in favor of codescent, and observes, as if he were speaking for the benefit of Dugald Stewart directly, "If there be any who can still think that such coincidences might arise from the casual intercourse of commercial relations, or from the Greek kingdom of Bactria, during the brief period of the reign of the Seleucides in that country, we cannot help thinking that these gentlemen should be prepared to show, that the much nearer vicinity and longer domination of the Macedonian and Greek empire, had produced similar effects on the languages derived from the Hebraic stem" (1820:435). Stewart read Hamilton's reviews but nevertheless defended Bayer against him—in effect embracing an indefensible position, then nearly a century old, at a time when Bopp was laying the foundation of Indo-European comparative philology upon the opposite view of the question.

That a chill British wind was blowing, cooling the ardor for the

---

7. Père Coeurdoux had made the same argument as early as 1768: "De plus, les Indiens avoient-ils manqué jusque-là de terms pour appeler leurs pères, leurs mères, leurs frères, et pour désigner leur pieds, leur nez, leur dents?" (Coeurdoux c.1768:661). Coeurdoux's manuscript was first published in 1808 by Anquetil; possibly Hamilton read the passage there.

new Orientalism, is apparent in the way Stewart introduces his conjecture:

Of late years, a perfectly new subject of speculation has been opened to philologers in the Sanscrit, or sacred language of the Indian Bramins; which, in the systematical regularity of its structure, as well as in its *unfathomable antiquity,* would appear to form an exception to every other tongue known in the history of the human race. At first, it strongly excited the curiosity of learned and inquisitive men, from the hope held out by some distinguished members of the Asiatic Society, that the knowledge of it would furnish a key to immense stores of wisdom and of fancy locked up in the repositories of the Bramins. But as this hope has not hitherto been realized, a suspicion has, of late, gained ground, that these artful priests have little or nothing to communicate which is likely either to enlarge the boundaries of science, or to add to the classical treasures of imagination already in our possession. (1827:100)

The fraud of Wilford's pandit, to the recitation of which Stewart devoted a whole appendix to his section on Sanskrit, was the chief exhibit supporting the bill of indictment. It was owing to this case that Stewart authorized himself to entertain his suspicion of the productions of the artful priests of India and, by extension, of the British Orientalism that studied those productions and in his view magnified their worth.

But there is a noticeable Celtic element to the discussion as well. Stewart is very critical of the Irish researches of Charles Vallancey and his enthusiasm for the supposed primitive Gaelic poetry of Ossian. General Vallancey's researches had been encouraged by Jones and Wilford, and this attention "contributed much to procure to the dreams of the learned Irishman, the very general attention which they once drew in this island" (1827:89–90n.). Enthusiasm for a connection between Celtic and Indian antiquities had once been such that Henry Flood, Irish parliamentarian, left a bequest valued at £5,000 a year to Trinity College, Dublin, "to promote the elucidation of these problematical and interesting facts" (1827:90). But the Flood bequest was without effect, according to Stewart, who called General Vallancey's writings "a philological misadventure"—a good characterization for his own conjecture (1827:92). As to Sanskrit, he wondered aloud whether its excellencies may have been somewhat overrated by Sir William Jones from the same bias that led him to overrate so immensely the merits of those ancient compositions of the Arabs, for which he had been so harshly criticized by Mill. Stewart could recollect a time when it was as fashionable to extoll the poems of Ossian—later shown to be the fab-

rications of James Macpherson, who purported to be their translator—
as it has since become to deride them. "Macpherson's translation they
allowed to be as good as an English version could be; but they insisted
(and who could contradict them?) that there was a richness and force
in the original to which no known language but the Greek could do
justice" (1827:126–127n.).

Some years ago Hans Aarsleff wrote a fascinating book, *The study of
language in England, 1780–1860* (1967), which posed the question of
why, given the head start British scholars had in the comparative study
of Indo-European languages through their access to Sanskrit, the study
of language in England followed other paths less productive for knowledge while the Germans dominated the development of Indo-European philology. The answer he gave had to do with the dominance in
Britain of Horne Tooke's system of etymology and its connections with
the British tradition of associationist psychology, which was resistant
to the system of Bopp, upon which the comparative philology of Indo-
European languages was constructed. There is certainly something in
this argument (Stewart himself cites Horne Tooke approvingly), and
Aarsleff's book brings this British linguistic tradition, connected especially to early-nineteenth-century studies of Anglo-Saxon, out of the
shade into which it was cast by the success of comparative philology.
But the exemplary tale of Dugald Stewart's conjecture, equal in futility
and opposite in direction to the conjectures of Wilford, seems to say
that the study of Sanskrit by Britons was stultified by forces that lay
outside the study of language itself and had rather to do with the
emerging culture of Indophobia. Indeed, as Wilson and other returned
Orientalists were to find, English universities did not foster the study
of Sanskrit.

For James Mill, the writings of Sir William Jones were emblematic of
all that separated Orientalism from his own position, Utilitarianism,
and accordingly he held Jones up before the world as a negative example. It has been of inestimable benefit to the reputation of Jones in
the present day to have been attacked by so unsympathetic a figure as
James Mill. But an effect of the attack has been to obscure the common
ground between them. Neither Jones nor any of the British Orientalists
had any doubt as to the present superiority of European civilization to
that of India, and Asia generally, in every respect except perhaps in poetry, where the higher development of the imaginative powers in Asia
could be a source for the reinvigoration of the poetry of the West. For

Jones, Europe was a sovereign princess of transcendent majesty and Asia a handmaiden, possessing a beauty of her own, although a lesser one (Jones 1807, 3:12). The mathematics and astronomy of India or indeed any other part of Asia had nothing new to teach the Europe of Newton. On this Jones and Mill were agreed. Both were trying to find India's place within a developing idea of modernism. What divided them was the valuation of the past achievements of India.

But having said that, it is possible to misapprehend the relation between the two in the other direction, as a difference of mere detail upon a common ground. For what profoundly separated Jones and Mill, and the Oriental renaissance from British Indophobia, was the power of the idea of ancient wisdom in the one, and of progress or future wisdom in the other. The Oriental renaissance depended upon the conviction that a numinous truth was captured in the Veda, that this wisdom was mankind's original religion and the source of civilization. As opposed to that, it was the formation of an idea of progress unqualified by the idea of ancient wisdom that sustained Mill and gave him the theoretical grounding for an aggressive policy of modernization. With the idea that the primitive condition of humankind was rude, ignorant, and barbarous, Mill quashed the ancient wisdom idea and forced new, harsh readings of India's past upon the scholarly product of Orientalism.

Hitherto the British empire in India had no higher purpose than to yield profits to the shareholders of the East India Company. Grant put forward a nobler purpose, the moral uplift of the Indians; Mill promoted the civilizing project of liberating the Indians from their own past, to use the language of Majeed's recent study of Mill (Majeed 1992). The appeal of such justifications of empire was irresistible. The price of having thus provided the Indian empire with a moral basis, however, was the systematic denigration of Indians and Indian civilization. Love of the English language and the arts and sciences of which it was the repository was made into the negation of Indian civilization. The price, in short, was Indophobia.

Indomania did not die out completely in Britain but became, so to say, recessive, finding a place under the aspect of eccentricity. Unitarianism, spiritualism, Theosophy, vegetarianism, pacifism . . . there remained, and remain, aspects of British culture, marginal to be sure but nevertheless indelibly British, through which Indomania was reproduced in some fashion. It is not an accident that the young Gandhi, trying to find some point of attachment in England, where he had gone to study law, found the vegetarians congenial and discovered his voice in their meetings, and it was in Britain that he came to appreciate the *Bhagavad Gītā* of his own country, in the mirror, as it were, of British Indomania. Had he lived in the twentieth century, J. Z. Holwell would certainly have been one of Gandhi's British followers.

It is worth saying again: Indophobia did not spring up naturally from the soil of Britain, it was deliberately built. India was very different from Britain, to be sure, but Britons did not believe they were "every way different" from the Indians until Grant taught them to think so.

# CHAPTER 5

# Philology and Ethnology

"Comparative philology" and "ethnology" were names that gained currency in English more or less at the same time, in the early nineteenth century. In that period philology and ethnology were generally thought of as closely related to each other, and they were often twinned. Both the British and the American Association for the Advancement of Science, for example, had a section on "Philology and Ethnology" before the two split apart in the era of Darwin (when, moreover, "ethnology" gave way to "anthropology," for reasons explained in Stocking 1971). The twinning of comparative philology and ethnology before mid-century and their separation in, roughly, the 1870s is an important datum for our inquiry, since ways in which the ethnology of India was conducted greatly changed after the parting of ways, as the two kinds of knowledge congealed into separate specialist disciplines. But India was not only affected by the changing relation between the two; it had a crucial role in the development of each, through the European study of Sanskrit.

The European "discovery" of Sanskrit (that is, the discovery of its similarity to Latin and Greek) was fundamental to the formation of comparative philology, and we may almost say (simplifying greatly) that the one led directly to the other. This is a well-known theme of the histories of linguistics, for which the famous passage from Jones's third anniversary discourse (cited in chapter 2) has become the obligatory proof text. The new science of comparative philology was the elucidation of historical relations among languages and their classification into families on the basis of the radiating, segmentary family tree model taken over from the Mosaic ethnology. Its core was the analysis of the Indo-European language family, in which the study of Sanskrit was joined to the traditional study of Greek and Latin, and this novel conjuncture threw an utterly new and different light upon the study of the languages and the peoples of both Europe and India. For Europeans, India became "family," and Greek civilization, which (as Bernal 1987 nicely shows) had hitherto been agreed to have taken its first lessons from Egyptians and Phoenicians, now had a shared ancestry, rather, with the Persians and Indians. The histories of linguistics usually date the commencement of comparative philology to the year 1816, when Franz Bopp published his pioneering study of the system of conjugation in Indo-European languages, *Conjugationssystem der Sanskrit*. It came to maturity between then and the publication, in 1833, of his *Vergleichende Grammatik des Sanskrit* (English translation, 1845–53). The Dane Rasmus Rask generally gets double billing with Bopp as a founder of the science, and all the European nationalities contributed to its advancement, but it was the German scholars, on the whole, who led the development of Indo-Europeanist comparative philology upon foundations that had been laid by the new Orientalism of British India, and it is their view of the origins of comparative philology that prevails in the histories of linguistics.[1]

The role that the study of Sanskrit played in the formation of comparative philology, then, is well known and needs no elaboration. Its role in the formation of ethnology, on the other hand, is scarcely remembered at all, largely because of the subsequent split and disciplinary formation of ethnology and linguistics. This process of separation (not quite complete in American anthropology, which considers linguistic anthropology one of its four constituent fields) had the effect of constituting separate foundational histories for philology and ethnology such that the ethnological content of philology's history and the linguistic content of ethnology's history was downplayed or lost. I will try in this chapter and the next to recover the lost connection between the two in respect of the role of Sanskrit and the British Sanskritists in the construction of British ethnologies of India.

The name ethnology was invented in eighteenth-century Germany and was naturalized in Britain by James Cowles Prichard in his *Natural*

---

1. See Aarsleff 1982, introduction.

*history of man* (1843).[2] As we shall see in the next chapter, Prichardian ethnology, which was *the* ethnological paradigm of the British metropole in the first half of the nineteenth century, was essentially a classification of peoples based upon the classification of languages by the methods of comparative philology, which resulted in the twinning of philology and ethnology in the scientific division of labor of the time. In this ethnology the study of physical features was actively pursued, but it was subordinated to the results of linguistic study and was assumed to tend in the same direction. In this conception language and physique tell the same story, but language comparison was believed to be the superior method by which to uncover the story, and the study of bodily features and structures was distinctly subsidiary. Prichardian ethnology was strongly influenced by the Jonesean Mosaic ethnology and regarded the methods and results of comparative philology as a fundamental part of its science.

Sanskrit came into this ethnology in two ways. At the global level it entered into ethnological thinking through its effect upon the formation and content of Indo-Europeanist comparative philology, serving to fix the place of Indians in the ethnological big picture as kin of Europeans and founders of civilization. At the level of the internal ethnology of India Sanskrit again played a capital role, for it was largely a question of the relation of the existing languages of India to Sanskrit. The ethnology of India in this second sense was in the charge of a specific sector of India hands—the British Sanskritists whether they were administrators or missionaries—interacting with their Indian teachers and assistants in India itself. It was mainly a British matter, or rather a British-Indian matter, in that it was based upon interactions between Britons and Indians in India under British rule.

Thus both in British India and, under Prichard's leadership, in the metropole, ethnology, as an inquiry into the relations of nations, stocks, or races, was principally a project of classification, conceptually identical with the classification of languages by philologists. Accordingly its leading method in this period was the collection and comparison of vocabularies; physical and social traits, although they were assiduously

2. The *Oxford English dictionary*, s.v. *ethnology*, gives Prichard as the author of its first occurrence in English. Vermeulen 1992 traces its essentially eighteenth-century German origins. Earlier reflexes of Greek *ethnos* in English have a distinctly religious semantic orbit: e.g., *ethnic* means "heathen," "pagan," "non-Christian," and "non-Jewish" (*OED* s.v., citing examples from the fifteenth century), as does *nation* in the King James Bible ("Why do the nations so furiously rage together?" Psalms 2:1).

recorded and added bulk and complexity to ethnological systems, played a secondary role, distinctly subordinate to the comparison of lists of words. At bottom that configuration rested upon a belief that languages and peoples coincided; at bottom it rested upon the story of the Tower of Babel.

It is important to insist upon the point and to oppose it to the narratives that comprise the common sense of anthropology. Hindsight is the advantage we have over the dead; we know how the story came out. But hindsight can also be misleading. For example, it is common to render the story of the rise of physical or biological anthropology as a linear progression starting from Johann Friedrich Blumenbach's classification of races by physical types, *De generis humani varietate nativa* (On the natural variety of mankind, 1776), to the genetics-based anthropology of today. But to do so, focusing on the study of physical features and representing it as a story of the cumulative improvement of knowledge, misses the fact that the classification of physical features in early-nineteenth-century British anthropology submitted to the greater authority of language classification. Again, much of what might be called the beginnings of social anthropology in British India may seem to have emerged from the scholar-administrator in the field, especially in rural administration and revenue matters, but as we have already seen in Hamilton's critique of Buchanan (in chapter 2), there was a considerable ideological and methodological divide between the Orientalist and the rural administrator gathering information of a kind that was coming to be called "statistics," descriptive and tabular material for regional and local gazeteers. I hope to show in this chapter that we need to focus upon the critical role of the British Sanskritists in supplying the principles of classification and interpretation at the highest level of generalization, which gave a degree of overall organization and intelligibility to the vast masses of ethnographic materials the personnel of the British Indian administration generated.

I will take up the Sanskritist-led ethnology of early-nineteenth-century British India in this chapter, and the language-led ethnology of the British metropole in the next. I begin with a sketch of the interaction of the British Sanskritists and their Indian teachers and interlocutors in this process and the process by which the new Orientalism, at first virtually a monopoly of the Asiatic Society in Calcutta, spread and institutionalized itself elsewhere in India and in Europe.

# The New Orientalism in Calcutta and
# Its Introduction to Europe

For a couple of decades after the founding of the Asiatic Society nearly all the small but growing number of Europeans who knew Sanskrit were British (Fra Paulinus, mentioned before, being the obvious exception) and were India hands who had learned Sanskrit in India, from Indians. The new Orientalism rested upon a collaboration, of a colonial and unequal kind, between European Orientalists and their Indian teachers. As long as it continued to take Sanskrit instruction from the pandits, the new Orientalism remained a virtual monopoly of British India and, more especially, of the Asiatic Society. Eugene Irschick, in his recent book *Dialogue and history* (1994), has argued that the formation of knowledge in colonial India was a dialogic process involving interactions of both rulers and ruled and the attachment, in this process, of multiple meanings to the common constructs. This is surely right, and it is a valuable corrective to the Saidian conception of Orientalism as the construction of Europeans alone, imposed upon a weak and effectively passive Orient (Irschick 1994:8). It was indeed the dialogic character of this knowledge making that gave the Asiatic Society its monopoly, and made it, for a while, unable to reproduce itself in Europe. The authority of the Society was enhanced with the formation of the College of Fort William in 1800, which centralized the training of Company servants in Calcutta and put their instruction in Indian languages under the supervision of members of the Society and their Indian assistants. David Kopf (1969) shows that the Asiatic Society and the College of Fort William taken together constituted the means by which British and Indian scholars were brought together and mobilized for the production of Orientalism and the means of teaching it to British lads.

This relation, of British Sanskritists and their Indian teachers and assistants, is of fundamental importance and deserves further study than I am able to give it in this book. The main point, however, needs making: Under the spell of the Orientalist authority claim, that language mastery leads to understanding and liking, nothing is easier than to romanticize that relation. But, as Rosane Rocher shows, British relations with their pandits were in fact fraught with ambivalence, in that the more benevolent and friendly aspects that conformed better to the

Orientalist self-image were offset by increasing worries about the corruption and unreliability of pandits serving the courts as experts on Hindu law and a felt need to end British reliance on the expertise of the pandits by achieving a direct knowledge of that law (R. Rocher 1993; see also Mukerji 1985; and R. Rocher 1989). The scandal of Wilford's pandit could only have encouraged the search for direct control of the sources of Orientalist knowledge generally.

Turning to substance, the collaboration of Britons with pandits in pursuing the ethnological question of India's place had a number of effects. The British Sanskritists brought from Europe a strong disposition to solve ethnological questions by means of language comparisons. As it happened, the pandits were the keepers of the most advanced linguistic science to that time, the science of (Sanskrit) grammar or Vyākaraṇa. In this way a number of brahminical ideas entered into the formation of British-Indian ethnology, increasingly so as British knowledge of Vyākaraṇa deepened through the remarkable mastery of its literature achieved by H. T. Colebrooke.[3] Thus Indian linguistic tradition strongly reinforced the European association of language and ethnology.

Two specific elements of Indian grammatical science came to dominate the ethnology of British India in the early nineteenth century, and they are central to the argument of this chapter. The first of these is the Vyākaraṇa doctrine of the unity of all languages as corruptions of the eternal and incorruptible Sanskrit language. This the British Sanskritists adopted and reinterpreted as a local truth—the truth of the descent of all the major modern Indian languages from Sanskrit, within the larger paradigm of the Mosaic ethnology. I will refer to this composite formation as the doctrine of the linguistic unity of India; I want to stress that it is not simply a British creation, as it is usually taken to be, but an emergent formation growing out of the conjuncture of British Sanskritists and their pandits under colonial conditions. This position was strongly associated with the Calcutta Orientalist establishment.

The second bit of Indian grammatical science is more technical: the analysis of the vocabularies of the modern languages of India into words of Sanskrit, foreign, and local (*deśya*) origin. In the hands of the British Sanskritists of Madras, Bombay, and elsewhere, this analytic of the Vyākaraṇa tradition became a tool for the exploration of the notion

3. The landmark works of Colebrooke in this regard are his article on the relation of the modern languages of India to Sanskrit (1801) and his Sanskrit dictionary (1805), which are discussed later in this chapter. Both rest on a knowledge of the Vyākaraṇa literature that is quite astonishing in its range and depth.

of an "aboriginal" Indian population prior to the coming of the Sanskrit-speaking Aryans, and again the Indian component of this emergent knowledge formation needs to be restored to the historical record. As we shall see, not only was the Indian origin of this analytic perfectly explicit in early British accounts, it was pointed to as a warrant of proof. The discussion in question undermined and attacked the linguistic unity of India doctrine and advanced the claims of the newer Orientalist establishments of Madras and Bombay against those of Calcutta, as I will show in this chapter. But I am getting ahead of the story.

The intellectual achievements of the Asiatic Society were very considerable, as we may see from O. P. Kejariwal's fine survey of the first fifty years, when the Asiatic Society was under the successive leadership of four distinguished scholars: Sir William Jones, Henry T. Colebrooke, Horace Hayman Wilson, and James Prinsep (Kejariwal 1988). In effect, the Asiatic Society was the site in which Indian history was constructed, yielding a view of its past that was entirely new both for Europeans and for Indians. Moreover, the history of India was brought into relation to the history of Europe and the Near East. The crowning achievement of these efforts was the decipherment of the Brahmi inscriptions of Aśoka, whose vast empire had covered most of India and Pakistan in the third century B.C., but whose edicts, inscribed on rock faces and stone pillars, had been a closed book for perhaps a millennium. The credit goes to Prinsep, who used the bilingual coins issued by Greek kingdoms of the Panjab in the aftermath of Alexander's expedition as his Rosetta Stone, but the accomplishment presupposed the built-up mass of Orientalist knowledge formed by the many Britons and Indians whose work had been motivated and directed toward this goal by the Asiatic Society. It is an accomplishment that is not well known but deserves to be reckoned with the decipherments in that age of the Egyptian hieroglyphics and the cuneiform of Darius's Behistun Inscription. Their effect taken together was to create a unified public space in which all the national histories thus revealed were simultaneously present rather than being, so to say, hidden from one another in separate rooms as private possessions. The juxtaposition of national histories in the nineteenth century occasioned by the Orientalists' decipherments bore a resemblance to the intellectual consequences of an older imperialism through which, in the Hellenistic period, the Greek language became a medium through which the national histories of Egyptians (Manetho), Babylonians (Berossus), Jews (Josephus), and Greeks could address one another and argue among themselves. Here, too, the public space was an outcome of conquest, and it is one in which the Indians were teachers but the finalities were British. It is striking that, although Sir William Jones raised the question of membership for Indians at the inaugural meeting and published the writings of Indians in early issues of *Asiatic researches*, it was only in 1829 that Indians were admitted to the Asiatic Society as members (Kejariwal 1988:152) and added their voices to the debates about Indian civilization within the utterly novel historical frame in which it had been brought into relation to the history of Europe and Islam.

The monopoly of the Asiatic Society was fleeting, and Orientalist institutions were soon established elsewhere in India and transplanted to Europe. The monopoly was inherently unstable for a number of reasons. The Society's British personnel retired to Britain after their service in India, and although Orientalism initially tended not to reproduce itself at the metropole since the retired Company servants did not teach the languages they had acquired from Indian teachers, the work of the Asiatic Society, including that at the College of Fort William, served to facilitate the formation of new centers of Orientalism by producing English-medium materials for the study of Sanskrit and other Indian languages in the absence of Indian teachers. In addition, the success of the Asiatic Society prompted emulation in other parts of British India and in Europe. Finally, the politics of the education question resulted in the ending of the monopoly held by the College of Fort William over the training of civil servants, which promoted the formation of centers of learning in Madras and Bombay and led to the creation of the East India College in England. For a time—indeed for the better part of a half-century from its founding in 1784—the Asiatic Society remained preeminent, presiding over a widening circle of the new Orientalism, but in the end some of the new centers challenged that preeminence. Emblematic of this process was the formation, in London, of the Royal Asiatic Society in 1824 under the leadership of Colebrooke after his retirement from India. Other colonial centers of Orientalism were invited to become branches of the new Royal Asiatic Society, and branches were formed at Madras and Bombay. Calcutta demurred, preferring to keep its separate and originary identity. But it was, inescapably, something less than it once was—no longer *the* Asiatic Society, but one among many. It was inevitable that it should come to be called the Asiatic Society *of Bengal*.

Alexander Hamilton, the first Sanskrit professor in Britain (at the East India College), became the conduit by which knowledge of Sanskrit passed from Calcutta to Paris and thence to Germany. Hamilton, who had served as an officer in the army of the East India Company, learned Sanskrit in Calcutta and became a member of the Asiatic Society; in 1790 he had petitioned the government for facilities to study Sanskrit. He resigned his commission and returned to Britain in 1796, where he lived off the proceeds of journalism, writing for the *Monthly review* for a time, and then for the *Edinburgh review*, of which he was one of the founders. By the Peace of Amiens (25 March 1802), hostilities between Britain and Napoleonic France were suspended, and Hamilton, like many other Britons, took the opportunity to travel to France, only to become a prisoner of war by the decree of 23 May 1803, when war resumed. Hamilton was however treated most liberally by the French authorities, being allowed to live wherever he liked in Paris and to move about freely. He spent the time in the company of Orientalists, especially Louis Mathieu Langlès, with whom he collaborated in cataloging the Indian manuscripts in the Bibliothèque Nationale, which service was probably the reason of his liberty. He also taught Sanskrit to a few students, of whom the most notable was Friedrich Schlegel, whose *Über die Sprache und Weisheit der Indier* (On the language and wisdom of the Indians, 1808) had a vast effect in fomenting German Indomania and Sanskrit study. Schlegel's brother August Wilhelm Schlegel later repaired to Paris to study Sanskrit, going on to become the first professor of Sanskrit in Germany (1818), and his student Franz Bopp also went to Paris for Sanskrit study, as did Friedrich Max Müller somewhat later.[4]

Paris had indeed become the European hub of the new Orientalism. Antoine-Léonard de Chézy was appointed the first chair of Sanskrit outside Britain, at the Collège de France, in 1815, a position filled by a succession of notable scholars including Eugène Bournouf and Sylvain Lévi. The Société Asiatique was formed a year before the Royal Asiatic Society, in 1822. Brian Houghton Hodgson (whom we shall meet shortly) divided his large collection of Indian manuscripts between Paris and London, and it provided a basic resource for Orientalist study of India in Europe. As we have seen, after his return to Britain, Hamilton remarked on the greater enthusiasm to be found in Paris for Oriental learning generally and for Sanskrit in particular, and said that he conversed among the Orientalists more frequently in Persian than in

---

4. For the information in this paragraph I rely on Rosane Rocher's biography (1968) and article (1970) on Hamilton, and on Jane Rendall's work on the Scottish Enlightenment (1982).

French.[5] That enthusiasm, however, remained centralized in Paris. The political fragmentation of Germany promoted its multiplication there, for chairs of Sanskrit were established in the universities of nearly every German statelet in their efforts to acquire the best experts in the prestigious new field of study.

Hamilton's pivotal role in the transmission of the knowledge of Sanskrit to the Continent has long been known, but little was known of Hamilton's scholarship until Rosane Rocher identified his unsigned articles in the *Monthly review,* the *Asiatic annual register,* and the *Edinburgh review;* her attributions of the latter were subsequently confirmed by the *Wellesley index.* She has recovered a hidden continent of scholarship whose authorship may have been apparent to contemporaries—Dugald Stewart was certainly in the know, for example—but which in any case was lost to view for later generations. Since Hamilton was a very accomplished Orientalist but one who published very little under his own name, the identification of his unsigned articles is a little like bringing the dead back to life. The articles are in the form of reviews, including reviews of the volumes of *Asiatic researches,* and they contain a great deal of original research based on a good knowledge of Latin, Persian, Arabic, and Sanskrit. This body of work taken as a whole is very impressive indeed, in two ways: for the very high quality of its Orientalist knowledge, and for the fact that general-purpose reviews of

5. See Grant, writing in the East India Company's *Report* (1804:18) and Hamilton, in his *Edinburgh review* articles (1802, 1806, 1807, 1808, 1809, 1820).

Notwithstanding the superior advantages which the English orientalists derive from our establishments in the centre of Asia, it may be doubted, whether the zeal and abilities of our [European] neighbours, devoted to the cultivation of eastern learning, will not compensate that disadvantage; and whether we may not in time have more to learn than to communicate. (Hamilton 1806:93)

Similarly,

From the first establishment of European settlements in India, the attention of missionaries, and of all individuals in any degree tinged with literature, had been directed towards a language [i.e., Sanskrit] whose wonderful structure recommended it to investigation, as much as the interesting monuments of high antiquity, which it was said to contain. This curiosity has been transmitted to England, and imported in much larger quantities to the Continent of Europe. It has been usually shipped, however, as an article of private trade; and by no means formed a part of the East India Company's regular investment. Their patronage has only been recently extended to literary researches. The eminent persons who now direct that establishment, have not imitated the apathy of their predecessors. (Hamilton 1809:366)

Thus the most strategically placed of the new Orientalists, the one most responsible for the transmission of Sanskrit learning from Calcutta to Paris, remarks on the British paradox (the greater enthusiasm for Indian studies on the Continent despite Britain's imperial connection) at a moment when Calcutta's quasi-monopoly still held.

the highest standing found it desirable to have Orientalism represented
in their offerings. Knowledge of these writings helps to fill out the picture of the connection between the Calcutta Sanskritists and the comparative philology of Franz Bopp. Hamilton was extremely well qualified and well placed to read the situation of the new Orientalism in
Europe, and his assessment of the current publications of the field constitute a valuable record of its progress there.

The single most important of Hamilton's writings for our purposes
is his 1809 review of Charles Wilkins's *Grammar of the Sanskrita language* (1808). From it we can establish three important points about
the state of play at that date. First, as Hamilton remarks, no fewer than
three Sanskrit grammars appeared in that year, written by Wilkins,
Colebrooke and the Baptist missionary and scholar William Carey (all
of them of the Asiatic Society); a fourth appeared a bit later, that of
H. P. Forster (1810). "England, at least, has been amply supplied with
information in that particular" (Hamilton 1809:366).[6] Earlier, in 1804,
Carey had published the first Sanskrit book printed in Nagari characters, the *Hitopadeśa,* as a textbook for students in the College of Fort
William. Thus the means of learning Sanskrit in Europe had been put
into print, and its study was no longer tied to India and the pandits. The
kind of Indianist career exemplified later by Max Müller, who never vis-
ited India, was now a possibility. Second, in his discussion of the relation
of Sanskrit to the "vernacular dialects"—that is, the whole question of
the internal ethnology of India—Hamilton reviews Colebrooke's important article on the subject and shows that at this early point in the
nineteenth century it was still possible to believe in the linguistic and
ethnological unity of India, that is, that all its languages descended
from Sanskrit and that its people were a single nation, although subject
to the invasions of various peoples since its original settlement. (This
is a point to which I shall return.) Third, the article concludes with a
discussion of the relation of Sanskrit to other languages, more particularly to Jones's Indo-European thesis. Hamilton gives tables of words
in Sanskrit, Latin, Persian, German, and English that illustrate cognate
nouns, pronouns, and verbs, and he concludes with remarks on com-

6. William Carey was professor of Bengali and Sanskrit at the College of Fort William,
and his *Grammar of the Sungscrit language* (1804) was specifically designed for use in the
college. Wilkins's Sanskrit grammar came out in 1808. That of Colebrooke was published
in 1805 (rather, the first and only volume) and was based on a scholarly knowledge of
Vyākaraṇa that was far greater than that of the other two. A fourth British grammar of
Sanskrit was published within a year of Hamilton's review, that of the merchant-Orientalist
H. P. Forster (1810).

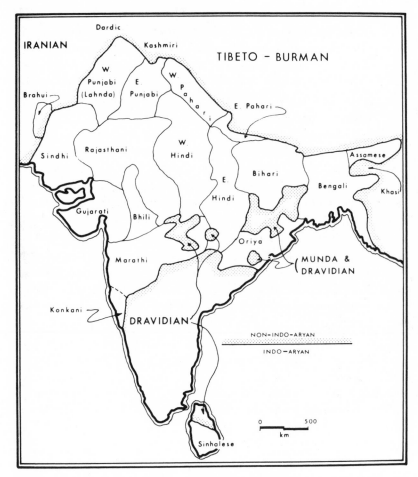

Figure 8.  Map of the Indo-Aryan languages. (From Trautmann 1981:7.)

parative grammar and morphology in these languages. Much material of the same kind appears in Friedrich Schlegel's celebrated book published in the same year as Hamilton's review; Rosane Rocher has shown that Schlegel had learned it from Hamilton in Paris (R. Rocher 1968). In a sense Hamilton's article supplies the word lists and analysis of morphology that we expect but do not find in Jones's third anniversary discourse, that appear in Schlegel, that are refined in Bopp's *Conjugationssystem* (1816), and that are thickened and solidified in his *Vergleichende Grammatik* (1833). Hamilton is, so to say, the connective tissue between the Orientalism of Calcutta and the comparative philology of Bopp.

# The Ethnological Composition
# of the Indian People

I turn now to the ethnology of British India and the question of the internal composition of the Indian nation. Let us begin with the linguistic map of South Asia as it appears today, according to the historical linguists (figs. 8 and 9).

The Indian subcontinent contains three major language families. The first is the Indo-Aryan, consisting of the descendants of Sanskrit, occupying most of the north, a good bit of the western coast, and much of Sri Lanka (i.e., the Sinhalese language). Second is the Dravidian family, dominating South India, having considerable representation in Central India and Sri Lanka (Tamil), with small remnants in North India (Maler) and Pakistan (Brahui). Third is the Munda or Austroasiatic family, represented in parts of east Central India and the northeastern regions of India and Bangladesh. (In nineteenth-century writings the Munda family is usually called Kol or Kolarian.) The connections of the Munda languages lie to eastward, with Khmer and other languages of Indo-China and of the larger Austro-Asiatic family. How the Dravidian family may be related to languages outside South Asia is uncertain (many think that it belongs to the Finno-Ugric family), although there is a general consensus that it entered India from the direction of Iran. Both Dravidian and Munda language families were established in the Subcontinent before the arrival, in about 1400 B.C. and from the direction of Iran, of Sanskrit, and neither is closely related to Sanskrit and the Indo-Aryan family or the encompassing Indo-European family. The cultural boundaries of Indian civilization are marked, more or less, by the Iranian languages in the northwest and the Sino-Tibetan languages of the Himalayas and the northeastern marches.[7]

---

7. The foregoing attempts to summarize the consensus within the guild, but of course there are dissenting views. The archaeolgist Colin Renfrew (1987) has wished to reinterpret the spread of the Indo-European languages to Europe by connecting it with the spread of agriculture, making it a very slow process that, therefore, must begin many centuries earlier than was hitherto thought. His treatment of India and Sanskrit (1987:chap. 8) is rather an afterthought, and he does not decide between two hypotheses, namely that Sanskrit was the language of the earlier Indus Civilization, or that it was (unlike Europe) brought by nomad conquest. (About the same time, in 1989, another archaeologist, J. P. Mallory, published a synthetic account of linguistic and archaeological evidence on the spread of Indo-European speaking populations, which sustains the mainstream view.) One of the last publications of the eminent anthropologist Edmund Leach is a skeptical piece called "The Aryan invasion over four millennia" (1990); it is typically engaging and over-

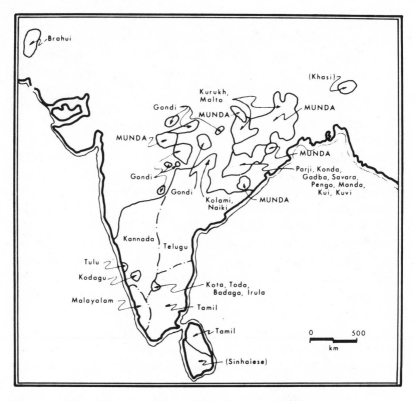

Figure 9. Map of the Dravidian and Munda languages. (From Trautmann 1981:10.)

The picture I have just given, which amounts to a macronarrative of Indian history, was constructed by the British-India hands in the first half of the nineteenth century, and it constituted a revolutionary new vision that neither the British nor the Indians had previously imagined. How did this view come about? When I first began looking into the

---

stated. Jim Shaffer (1984) is one of the Western archaeologists specializing on South Asia who oppose the idea that Sanskrit entered India through conquest.

In India there has always been a sector of learned opinion that believes that Sanskrit was indigenous, and S. R. Rao (1982) is notable among archaeologists who hold to the view that Sanskrit is the language of the Indus Civilization; recently Talageri (1993) argues that the Indo-European languages originated in India and spread to their present locations. Thus at the moment there is to a great extent an unlooked-for convergence of views that are critical of the prevailing consensus (although, of course, considerable differences exist among them) and tend in the direction of an earlier chronological horizon for Sanskrit in India.

matter I was aware that the crucial text is Bishop Robert Caldwell's *Comparative grammar of the Dravidian or South-Indian family of languages* (1856), one of the truly great works of British Orientalism in which the existence of the Dravidian language family is demonstrated and the relations among the Dravidian languages are traced in great detail. Moreover, Caldwell is clear about the three language families of India and clearly refutes the identity of Dravidian and Munda that some had proposed. To all intents and purposes, the modern consensus on this question was established by Caldwell. But Caldwell's first edition appeared as late as 1856, seventy years after Jones's pronouncement on Sanskrit. What, I wondered, filled the dead interval between?

The success of Caldwell's book—still in print over a century later—has been such that it has tended to blot out the record of what went before. Caldwell himself briefly identifies his predecessors and, although his criticisms of them are quite correct, he does them less than justice in the brevity with which he dismisses their accomplishments. I discovered that the dead period was in fact very lively, animated by the work of H. T. Colebrooke, Francis Whyte Ellis, the Rev. John Stevenson, and Brian Houghton Hodgson on the question of the linguistic and ethnic unity of India and the identity of the first inhabitants of India, the Indian aborigines. Caldwell's masterpiece is the culmination of three generations of the new Orientalism.

We may take as our starting point Colebrooke's 1801 article, "On the Sanscrit and Pracrit languages," in the seventh volume of the *Asiatic researches*, which holds that all the modern languages of India were descended from Sanskrit—the doctrine, in short, of the linguistic unity of India. Colebrooke's doctrine bears the strong impress of the brahminical teaching that all languages—all the languages in the world—are corruptions of the changeless, eternal Sanskrit language, although, as mentioned before, the British reading of this doctrine was to confine it to India: Only the languages of India were Sanskrit's daughters. Subsequent to Colebrooke's essay, and as the ethnological and linguistic terrain of India was explored further by scholar-administrators and scholar-missionaries, interpretations depart from the unity-of-origin doctrine and lead toward the three-language-family doctrine in distinct steps that we may characterize as follows:

1. By 1816, as Bopp and Rask were laying the foundations of comparative philology in Europe, Ellis published a demonstration that the languages of the Dravidian family are not descendants

of Sanskrit, overthrowing the unity-of-origin position and establishing the existence of the Dravidian language family long before Caldwell.

2. In the 1840s, Stevenson and Hodgson were propounding the theory of a unitary aboriginal language and people (including the Dravidian and Munda families), prior to the arrival into India of Sanskrit.

3. In his *Comparative grammar* (1856), Caldwell clearly established that there is a third ethnolinguistic entity (i.e., Munda), distinct from the Aryan and the Dravidian.

In something over fifty years from the commencement of the nineteenth century the master narrative of Indian history was entirely rewritten by the British Sanskritists and their Indian teachers, and it came to rest upon the three ethnolinguistic entities, the Indo-Aryan, Dravidian, and "Kolarian" or Munda language families. In respect of traditional brahmin learning, according to which all languages are the descendants, more or less corrupt, of Sanskrit, which informs Colebrooke's view, it was a revolutionary change. The steps that led away from the doctrine of linguistic unity, however, also used the conceptual tools of brahminical linguistic analysis and cited brahminical authorities for the departures. In the course of these developments new centers of learning asserted their authority against that of the Asiatic Society.

## The Linguistic-Ethnological Unity of India

Many regard Henry Thomas Colebrooke (1765–1836) as the greatest of the British Sanskritists. During thirty-two years of service in India and, thereafter, in England he wrote a number of works of fundamental importance on many difficult, disparate topics including mathematics and astronomy, law and the Veda. Colebrooke's 1801 essay on Sanskrit and Prakrit is a piece of major importance in that it gives an account of Pāṇini and other ancient Indian grammarians, followed by an overview of the genetic relations among the languages of India that is based on a reading of the ancient Indian treatises of Vyākaraṇa. Colebrooke is the first to discuss in a European language the Prakrits or (as he called them) the vernaculars of ancient India and to depict them as descendants of Sanskrit and precursors of the modern written languages of India or, rather, as the modern languages themselves. He thus derives all the major Indian languages from Sanskrit, excepting only those known to have come from the invasions of foreigners. This was explicitly an ethnological as well as a linguistic argument.

I must specify Colebrooke's view of linguistic-ethnic unity a bit more exactly. Ten "polished dialects formerly prevailed in as many different civilized nations, who occupied all the fertile provinces of Hindustan and the Dacshin," that is, India north and south (Colebrooke 1801:219). Colebrooke relied here on the ten traditional divisions of the brahmin caste by region, grouped into the five Gauḍas or North Indian divisions and the five Drāviḍas or South Indian divisions (I modernize his spellings):

The five Gauḍas:

1. The Sārasvata of the Panjab, speaking a Prakrit bearing their name, now extinct.

2. The Kanyākubjas of Kanauj, whose Prakrit was the language now called Hindi.

3. Gauḍa proper, or the Bengal nation, their Prakrit being the modern Bengali.

4. Maithila, the inhabitants of Tirhut, whose dialect differs slightly from that of Bengal.

5. Utkala or modern Orissa, its dialect being Oriya.

The five Drāviḍas:

6. Drāviḍa, the Tamil country, its dialect being Tamil.

7. The Māharāṣṭra or Mahratta. Its language "contains much pure Sanscrit, and more corruptions of that language, intermixed with words borrowed from Persian and Arabic, and with others derived from an unknown source" (1801:226).

8. Karṇāta (modern Karṇāṭaka), and the Kannada language.

9. Teliṅga (modern Andhra Pradesh), its dialect being Telugu.

10. Gurjara (modern Gujarat), of which the Prakrit (i.e., Gujarati) slightly varies from the Hindi—or perhaps, says Colebrooke, they should be reckoned as the fifth northern nation and Utkala as the fifth southern nation.

The Prakrits, then, are "the written dialects now used in the intercourse of civil life, and cultivated by learned men" (1801:219), dialects, that is, of Sanskrit. Other of the vernaculars, such as Panjabi, are also brought into relation to Sanskrit through another of the ancient grammarians' categories, that of Apabhraṃśa, "fallen" or corrupted dialects.

The unity-of-origin doctrine, however, had to be contended for against none other than Sir William Jones, in the latter's treatment of Hindi. Jones had said that nine-tenths of the Hindi language may be traced back to Sanskrit, but the remaining tenth, which could not, was perhaps the basis of the language, and he inclined to identify it with nomads from Central Asia (his Tartar nation, descendants of Japhet) and to think that this pure Hindi was primeval in North India, that is, prior to the arrival of Sanskrit (Jones 1807, 3:33–34). Thus Jones himself was the source of the idea of an aboriginal population whose language, which has been mixed with Sanskrit, can still be identified: This notion came to be called a "substratum" theory. Colebrooke did not wish to directly controvert Jones, but he suggested that the non-Sanskrit component of Hindi might represent modern refinements rather than primitive features. Both Colebrooke and, following him, Hamilton pulled back from Jones's position in favor of unity-of-origin, and it seems clear that in doing so Colebrooke was heavily influenced by his pandits and the ancient grammarians of Sanskrit and Prakrit that he was reading. In this respect the new Orientalism drew, for a moment, closer to the doctrine of its Indian sources as it came to know them more deeply.

Hamilton embraced Colebrooke's unity-of-origin theory and deployed it in his *Edinburgh review* pieces, and he joined Colebrooke in his skepticism about Jones's treatment of the origin of Hindi. He believed it not improbable that the brahmins entered India as conquerors, but thought it "a very gratuitous supposition" that "the words existing in the Hindi language, which can neither be traced to Sanscrit, Persic, or Arabic, must necessarily be the remains of the aboriginal tongue," since they could have come from one of the invaders subsequent to the brahmins, such as the Śakas, or from a Turkish element in the speech of Muslim invaders. He thought however that the Paiśāci or demons' languages spoken of by the ancient Indian grammarians was totally distinct from the Sanskrit in its origin, and he conjectured that it was that of the "mountaineers," "by some writers regarded as the aborigines of that country" (Hamilton 1807:293). Of these mountaineers he says, in another article,

Whether we are to consider the wild but harmless inhabitants of the mountains as a distinct race from the Hindus, must be determined by investigations not hitherto undertaken. It is also a matter of very curious inquiry, whether all these tribes of mountaineers throughout Hindustan, speak one language, and bear an affinity to each other in their configuration and customs,—authorizing the inference, that one great nation formerly peopled Hindustan, and were driven, by invaders, to the recesses of those hilly countries which they still occupy. (Hamilton 1808:93)

Jones, in his eighth discourse, had spoken of the Indian mountaineers as "many races of wild people with more or less of that pristine ferocity, which induced their ancestors to secede from the civilized inhabitants of the plains and valleys." He thought they sprang from the old Indian stem, although some of them soon intermixed "with the first ramblers from *Tartary,* whose language seems to have been the basis of that now spoken by the *Moguls*" (Jones 1807, 3:172–173). Hamilton's proposal of the unitary language and aboriginal character of all the "mountaineers" goes considerably further than this. But taken altogether, the testimony of Jones, Colebrooke, and Hamilton is that British belief in the ethnological and linguistic unity of India was never complete. Even in Colebrooke it applies only to the "polished" languages, that is, those that are written and have literatures. And these, in accordance with a common eighteenth-century notion that linked cultivation of the soil with civilization, are identified with the "fertile provinces" of India, implicitly leaving the question of the mountaineers an open one. Thus the identity and unity of the Indian aborigines was well established as an issue by the beginning of the nineteenth century.

## Dravidian

The unity of the *polished* languages, then, referred to the written languages of both North and South India and attributed to all of them a Sanskrit origin. Nowadays we recognize that the languages of North India, those we call New Indo-Aryan, are descendants of the Sanskrit, but those of the south fall into a nonrelated family called Dravidian. The discovery of the Dravidian family, although commonly thought to belong to Caldwell, was actually the accomplishment of Ellis, and we can date its public appearance to 1816, the year of Bopp's *Conjugationssystem—anno mirabilis* of the history of linguistics.

Ellis, I have come to think in the course of the research for this book, is one of the unknown greats of British Orientalism. He is well known to the historians of the British Indian land revenue system of South

India, having served in a number of roles connected with the revenue and having written the *Treatises on Mirasi right* (1818), a classic exposition of the pre-British regime of land tenure. But his contributions to Orientalism are little remembered, partly because his central achievement was eclipsed by Caldwell's work, largely because of an unfortunate set of events. After arriving in India in 1796 he joined the civil service of Madras, which he served until he died, prematurely and under mysterious circumstances, in 1819. He had distinguished himself as a Sanskrit and Tamil scholar, but, as one memorial has it, "he had resolved to dedicate his life to investigation until the age of forty, and, before that time, to prepare nothing for communication to the world" (Literary Society of Madras 1827:v), which was about his age at his death. Thus his Orientalist publications, which would have been abundant, are few. What is more, his papers were scattered and lost when he died; it was said that they were used by the cook of the collector of Madura, with whom he had been staying at the time, to light his fires and to singe chickens (Elliot 1875:220). Several pieces of his work were recovered and published after his death; Walter Elliot rescued one from among "some refuse papers" at the College of Fort St. George in Madras (1875:221). Much the most interesting to us are three "dissertations" on Tamil, Telugu, and Malayalam, printed for the use of the students of the college. The second of these, which I will examine closely, was published in Alexander D. Campbell's *Grammar of the Teloogoo language* (1816) as a long "note to the introduction"; it is of exceptional importance as the first proof of the Dravidian language family. The third was published long after by Elliot; the first has long since disappeared.

But however much one may feel that Ellis's individual accomplishment deserves greater recognition than it has received, the way in which the discovery of the Dravidian language family presents itself to the world in the pages of Campbell's *Grammar of the Teloogoo language* makes it very clear that it rests upon collective effort. Indeed the whole situation lends itself naturally to a Foucault-like story of how theoretical knowledge emerges from the concrete dispositions of practice. The three-cornered institutional base for Orientalism in Calcutta was reproduced in Madras: the seat of government, the Literary Society of Madras, and the College of Fort St. George, where young Britons were instructed in the languages of South India. Ellis was a leading player in all three; indeed, he was first chairman of the board of superintendence of the college. Campbell was a member of the board. The

College of Fort St. George brought together the young writers in need of instruction, the supervising India hands who had learned the languages by private arrangement with pandits and munshis, and the Indian language instructors. Campbell's Telugu instructor was Woodiagherry Vencatanarrain Ayah,

a young bramin of superior intelligence and remarkable acquirements, who, by his own merits alone, subsequently rose to the situation of Head English master at the College of Fort St. George, and lately to the more honorable office of Interpreter to the Supreme Court of Judicature at the Presidency. He generally sat by me while I wrote the notes from which this Grammar has been compiled, and I may therefore be said to have availed myself of his aid and advice throughout the work (1816:xxv).

The help of Patabhirama Sastri, head Sanskrit and Telugu master at the college is acknowledged by both Campbell and Ellis, and Ellis also mentions without naming him the head Tamil master at the college. The college, therefore, brought together British Orientalists, Indian scholars, and British students for pedagogy in Tamil, Telugu, Kannada, and other languages of the south. It served as a kind of marshaling yard in which the materials for the construction of the Dravidian concept were brought together—the major Dravidian languages and their scholars were juxtaposed in adjoining classrooms, as it were, under Orientalist direction.

Campbell's *Grammar of the Teloogoo language* was published by the College of Fort St. George and printed at the College Press. The advertisement for the book states that he wrote it out of "notes on the native grammars of the language, which he had taken to assist his own studies" in view of "the disadvantage under which the Teloogoo Students [of the college] laboured from the want of a work on the elements of that language." It was the existence of the college that stimulated Campbell to put what he had learned of Telugu in a form that would reproduce itself in subsequent generations of British servants of the Company.

A Telugu grammar had been published just two years previous by the scholar-missionary Carey, who taught at the College of Fort William in Calcutta, as part of the series of grammars upon which the Serampore missionaries were engaged (Carey 1814), and, as we have seen, he had earlier done a Sanskrit grammar (Carey 1804). The publication of Campbell's Telugu grammar was of itself a declaration of independence from the Orientalist establishment of Calcutta, and an assertion of superior command over the languages of South India. In his introduction, Campbell takes issue with Carey, who had expressed the prevailing view of linguistic unity, saying that the languages of the south, namely Telugu, Kannada, Tamil, Malayalam, and Sinhalese, "have the same origin with those of the North" (i.e., Sanskrit) although they "differ greatly from them in other respects: and especially in having a large proportion of words the origin of which is unascertained" (Carey, cited in Campbell 1816:xviii). Campbell's disproof of the theory of linguistic unity proceeds by demonstrating that Telugu does not have a Sanskritic origin and by publishing in the introduction the long note from Ellis previously mentioned (i.e., his "dissertation" on Telugu, printed for students of the college), which gives a comparison of Telugu, Kannada, and Tamil, showing them to be fundamentally similar and not derived from Sanskrit. In the latter piece Ellis too identifies the unity-of-origin thesis with the Calcutta Sanskritists generally, citing Wilkins's Sanskrit grammar and Colebrooke's essay on the Sanskrit and Prakrit languages. Thus the Madras Dravidianists are intensely aware that in this issue it is a question of schools, of Bengal versus Madras, of the College of Fort William versus the College of Fort St. George, and that they are advancing for the first time the claims of Madras to greater Orientalist authority over the South Indian languages. In doing so they invoke the authority of the pandits.

The groundwork of the argument of both Campbell and Ellis is provided by the older grammars of Telugu, of which Ellis particularly mentions the *Andhradīpaka* of Mamidi Venkaya. Both Campbell and Ellis conduct their analyses in terms of the Indian grammatical categories into which the lexicon of a language may be analyzed: *tatsama* or Sanskrit words unmodified except for word endings in the borrowing language, in this case Telugu; *tadbhava* or words derived from Sanskrit, via the various Prakrit languages, which have been altered in the transmission and therefore resemble their Sanskrit originals imperfectly; *deśya* or non-Sanskritic words proper to one of the regions of India, in this instance the Telugu country; and *grāmya* or (non-Sanskritic) words of purely local (village) scope. Campbell in his brief demonstration says that some of the native grammarians maintain that before king Andhraraiyadu established his residence on the banks of the Godavari the only Telugu was the *deśya* portion of the language, "which they consider coeval with the people," created by Brahmā. "This would imply that the nation still retain some faint remembrance of those times, in which their language existed independent of the Sanscrit; and it is certain that every Teloogoo Grammarian, from the days of Nunnia Bhutt to the present period, considered the two languages as derived from sources entirely distinct" (Campbell 1816:xxi).

Ellis's more elaborate comparative treatment of Telugu, Kannada, and Tamil follows similar lines, that is, identifying the Sanskritic and the *deśya* portions of the vocabularies in each. He then goes a step further—and this is the critical interpretive move, which at a stroke creates the conception of the Dravidian language family—by showing that the *deśya* words of any of the three have counterparts, or "cognates" as we now call them, in one or both of the other languages. Thus he shows not only that each of these languages is distinct from Sanskrit but also that the three of them form a unity that is accounted for by a common origin—the conception, in short, of the Dravidian family of languages. The demonstration consists of lists of words arranged under various heads and a paraphrase of the *Andhradīpaka* text, which concludes with this statement:

The author, supported by due authority, teaches, that, rejecting direct and indirect derivatives from the Sanscrit, and words borrowed from foreign languages, what remains is the *pure native language of the land:* this constitutes the great body of the tongue and is capable of expressing every mental and bodily operation, every possible relation and existent thing; for, with the exception of some religious and technical terms, no word of Sanscrit derivation is *necessary* to the Telugu. This pure native language of the land, allowing for dialectic differences and variations of termination, is, with the Telugu, common to the Tamil, Cannadi, and the other dialects of southern India: this may be demonstrated by comparing the Désyam terms contained in the list taken by Vencaya from the Appacaváyam, with the terms expressive of the same ideas in Tamil and Canadi. It has been already shewn that the radicals of these languages, *mutatis mutandis,* are the same, and this comparison will shew that the native terms in general use in each, also, correspond. (Ellis 1816:19)

Ellis did not live to put this important work on the comparative philology of Dravidian into a finished form, but of the high quality of his scholarship his few published pieces leave us in no doubt. The work draws upon the analytic means that had been devised ages earlier by the highly developed linguistic science of India to distinguish Sanskritic words from non-Sanskritic ones; it was first deployed in the ancient grammars of the Prakrit languages. This analysis, when applied to the Dravidian languages, serves to discriminate the borrowed Sanskritic words from the inherited Dravidian ones. Ellis adds to this method the comparison of word lists from the different South Indian languages and thus lays out very neatly the methodology and logic of the comparative method that Rask and Bopp were applying to the Indo-European languages.

Campbell and Ellis referred to the learned linguists of South India themselves as authority for their view of the non-Sanskritic origin of Telugu, as if to counter the authority of the Calcutta Orientalists by citing their pandits in opposition to those of Bengal. It is not clear that they were entirely correct in doing so, for although the non-Sanskritic origin of words identified as *deśya* is certainly a tenet of the Indian grammatical tradition, it does not follow, and does not appear to be the case, that the non-Sanskritic origin of particular languages was a conceptual possibility within that tradition. The whole analytic rests not so much on a conception of language history as on a conception of a calculus of value, whose two poles are the universal (Sanskrit) and the provincial (*deśya, grāmya*).[8] Similarly the brahminical notion of the five Drāviḍas invoked by Colebrooke largely has to do with identifying provincial groupings, within but not beyond which local custom (*deśa-dharma*) is authoritative, and it is not meant to assert the linguistic-ethnological multiplicity of India. In a way, the Dravidian conception has a long lineage in Indian conceptions, but in truth it is a new conception, dialogically formed by the new readings British Orientalists gave to the doctrines of Indian linguistic science.

What the larger frame for that reading was can be seen in manuscripts of Ellis (n.d.) preserved in Oxford. One of these—could it be a preliminary version of the lost "dissertation"?—consists of a long discussion of the history and ethnology of the Tamil language. One section undertakes the ethnological question under the rubric, "On the Natives by whom the Tamil language is spoken." Ellis opens the section by saying, "The Tamil is radically connected with that family of languages of which the Hebrew is probably the most ancient and the Arabic certainly the most polished" (n.d.: 2), that is, what is now called the Semitic family, although he admits that the connection is "not intimate" and difficult to establish. He gives a number of proposed cognates of Tamil words in Hebrew, Chaldaic, and Arabic—employing the usual method of word lists.

Although Ellis was wrong to classify Tamil (and the Dravidian lan-

---

8. This idea of the universal/provincial polarity in ancient Indian scientific discussion of language comes from Deshpande's fine book (1993).

guage family generally) with the Semitic family, the logic of looking to do so is perfectly clear in relation to the Mosaic or Biblical character of the then-prevailing ethnological model of Sir William Jones. If Sanskrit and other of what came to be called the Indo-European languages were spoken by the descendants of Ham, son of Noah, as Jones and Bryant had it, or if they were the languages of the descendants of Japhet, as others claimed, the logical place to look for the Biblical ancestors of the Dravidians of South India, once it is believed that they are non-Sanskritic, would be in the remaining line, that of Shem. Here again we see the ghostly trace of the Mosaic ethnology with its segmentary structure, prefiguring ways of conceiving the relations of Tamil, Telugu, and Kannada to one another to form the conception of the Dravidian family of languages as it had that of the Indo-European language family before; now it also framed the coordination and opposition of the two families to each other.

## The Linguistic-Ethnological Unity of the Aborigines

Ellis had shown that Telugu and its congeners were non-Sanskritic by showing that the *deśya* portion of the vocabulary was the large central core of the language; following the Indian grammarians of Telugu (so he said), he identified this core as the pure native language of the land. As such the Dravidian languages were aboriginal languages of India, existing there prior to the arrival of Sanskrit. This finding brought to the fore a new agenda: the comparative study of the aboriginal languages or the aboriginal element within the modern languages. The unity of the aboriginal languages of India was the leading doctrine of the 1840s and early 1850s, and its leading proponents were Brian Houghton Hodgson and the Rev. John Stevenson.

In 1823 Stevenson was sent by the Scottish Missionary Society to their Bombay mission, and he had a long Indian residence before retiring to Scotland in 1854. During this time he became an accomplished Sanskritist, editing for publication a number of Vedic texts, and a grammarian of the Marathi language. He became president of the Royal Asiatic Society, Bombay Branch. His intervention in the ethnological discussion marks the coming of age of the Orientalism of the Bombay region, and it was a strategic intervention because the Marathi language marks the border between the Indo-Aryan and the Dravidian languages. More important than the question of assigning the Marathi language to a family (it is Indo-Aryan) was the question of the linguistic and ethnological source of the *deśya* or non-Sanskritic portion of its lexicon.

Stevenson, then, carried the Campbell-Ellis methodology to the Maratha country in his 1843 article "Observations on the Maráthí language." He is not explicit about his debt, however, and we have to restore the Indian names of the analytic categories that Campbell and Ellis employ and which Stevenson renders only in English (Stevenson 1841–44a). Of 50,000 words taken from twelve random pages of Molesworth's dictionary, he says, 10,000 may be reckoned "primitives" (i.e., roots), the rest being derivatives of these, which may be set aside. Of the 10,000 primitives, he calculates, about one-half are Sanskrit more or less pure (i.e., the *tatsama* of the Campbell-Ellis argument); of the 5,000 remaining, about 2,000 are Sanskrit considerably corrupted (i.e., *tadbhava*), 1,000 are Persian and Arabic (*antardeśya*), and 2,000, or one-fifth of the whole, are unconnected with any of these but belong to "what I conceive to have been the language of the aborigines of India" (the *deśya* vocabulary). Belief in the unity of this aboriginal language is supported by the claim that many of the words of the latter class agree with (the Dravidian languages) Telugu, Kannada, and Tamil and are also traceable in (the Indo-Aryan languages) Hindi and Gujarati, words showing "not the slightest connection with the Sanskrit" (Stevenson 1841–44a:85). This very ambitious argument finds a single common language behind not only the Dravidian languages of South India but also the *deśya* elements of the Indo-Aryan languages of North India as well.

In this paper Stevenson demonstrates several Dravidian elements in Marathi and the unity of the Dravidian languages with Gujarati and Hindi in respect of several features. He points, for example, to the widespread use of auxiliary verbs, found in Gujarati, Hindi, and Marathi, found also in Telugu according to Campbell "though by the laws of euphony it is somewhat disguised," but missing in Sanskrit, Greek, and Latin. "There must, therefore, in India, have been some element, like the Gothic and other Germanic tongues in Europe, to produce this modification of languages, the greater part of whose vocables are Sanskrit; but where will either history or tradition allow us to look for any such modifying cause, except in an aboriginal language, following a different course in this respect from the Sanskrit?" (1841–44a:88).

This is Stevenson's big idea, and he runs with it through a series of articles published between 1841 and 1853 in the journals of the Royal Asiatic Society and of its Bombay branch, exploring elements that the modern languages of India, north and south, have in common. In "An essay on the language of the aboriginal Hindus" he proposes a list of forty primitive words, "all expressive of such ideas as men must use in the infancy of society, or in the first stages of civilization, and which retain their places in a language from daily use, more firmly than any others" (Stevenson 1841–44b:111). In another very long article, "Observations on the grammatical structure of the vernacular languages of India," he turns to comparative grammar. He summarizes the prevailing consensus under five heads:

1. The languages of the north have a strong family resemblance and all draw largely from Sanskrit.

2. The languages of the south have also a strong family likeness, but the prevailing ingredient in their structure is not Sanskrit.

3. To express ideas connected with religion, law, and the arts and sciences of civilized life, the languages of the south as well as the north draw almost exclusively from the Sanskrit.

4. Muslim rule has introduced Arabic and Persian words that are distinct from the original words of the Indian languages.

5. "It is usually taken also for granted that between the non-Sanscrit parts of the Northern and Southern families of languages, there is no bond of union, and that the only connecting link between the two is their Sanscrit element" (Stevenson 1849–51:72).

It is to this last proposition that Stevenson demurs, devoting many pages and much ink to the *deśya* element in the languages of North and South India in an attempt to show their original unity. He specifies his historical scenario thusly:

The theory which has suggested itself to the writer as the most probable is, that on the entrance of the tribes which now form the highest castes, those of the Brahmans, Kshatriyas, and Waisyas, into India, they found a rude aboriginal population, speaking a different language, having a different religion, and different customs and manners; that by arms and policy the aboriginal inhabitants were all subdued, and in great numbers expelled from the Northern regions, those that remained mixing with the new population, and being first their slaves, and then forming the Sudra caste. The language of these aborigines is supposed to have belonged to the Southern family of language, the most perfect remaining type of which family is the Tamil. (1849–51:73–74)

This amounts to saying that there is one and only one pre-Sanskritic ancestral language of India, and that it is Dravidian.

The other great proponent of a unitary aboriginal language was Brian Houghton Hodgson, and he, too, spoke from the margins of the world over which the Asiatic Society presided, namely from Darjeeling, in the eastern Himalayas. Hodgson was the first of the scholars I have been discussing to have gotten his language training at Haileybury, where he specialized in Persian, before shipping out (in 1818) for Calcutta and further study at the College of Fort William. His career was largely passed in the Himalayas, in Kumaon and, for twenty-three years, in Kathmandu, where he rose to the rank of resident. During this time he established the basis of Orientalist study of Mahāyāna Buddhism, and he collected hundreds of Sanskrit and Tibetan manuscripts, which he gave to libraries in Calcutta, London, and Paris (the latter were the sources upon which Eugène Bournouf worked). After he resigned the service in 1843 he passed thirteen years in Darjeeling, devoting himself to his researches, chiefly ethnological, which were published in the *Journal of the Asiatic Society*, successor at Calcutta to the *Asiatic researches*.

The vision Hodgson followed was at bottom the same as Stevenson's, that of a unitary aboriginal language and people, but he did so from a Himalayan starting point. He resolved to provide readers of the *Journal* "a general comparison of all the Aborigines from Cape Cormorin to the snows" (1848b:544) by means of comparative vocabulary lists, which were the signature method of the language-dominated ethnology of the period. He published a series of articles reporting vocabularies of languages of the supposed aborigines against a uniform list of English words, chosen, like the vocabularies of Stevenson's articles, to elicit the most primitive and unchangeable core of the lexicon.[9] The governing conception was that, just as the Hindus, Persians, Germans, English, Irish, and Russians are members of one family (which he calls

---

9. Hodgson's ethnological writings begin with a piece in 1833, "Origin and classification of the military tribes of Nepal," but the block of writings published in the late 1840s constituted a single project of a comparison of languages that spanned the Subcontinent, seeking to identify the aboriginal element in the Indian population: "On the aborigines of the sub-Himalayas" (1847), "Addenda et corrigenda" (1848a), "Ethnography and geography of the sub-Himalayas" (1848b), "The aborigines of Central India" (1848c), "Tibetan type of mankind" (1848d), "On the Che'pa'ng and Ku'su'nda tribes of Ne'pa'l" (1848e), and "Aborigines of Southern India" (1849).

the Iranian), so the "Tamulians" or Tamils, Tibetans, Indo-Chinese, Chinese, Tangus, Mongols, and Turks are so many branches of another single family, namely the Turanian.

Of the many articles in this series I will consider two, "The aborigines of Central India" (1848c) and "Aborigines of Southern India" (1849), which together make a case for the "general prevalence of the Tamulian type of speech" in India prior to the advent of Sanskrit, in which group, however, he did not include the Himalayan languages, some of which he had studied very closely (Hodgson 1849:350). Thus any unity of the Tamulian aborigines of the Indian landmass with the "Aboriginal Alpine Indians" would have to be put much further back in time; a belief in such unity was essentially an article of faith, since vocabulary lists could not provide proof. Leaving aside the Himalayan borderland, then, and coming to India proper in the second of these articles, Hodgson states that the "Kol" or Kolarian languages (nowadays called the Munda family) were a part of the "Tamulian" or Dravidian aboriginal language. Soliciting vocabularies conforming to his standardized word list from army officers in central and east-central India and from the Orientalist Walter Elliot in Madras, he compiled a "comparative vocabulary of the aboriginal languages of Central India," of which four are in fact Munda languages (Singhbhum Kol, Santal, Bhumij, and Mundala) and three are Dravidian languages (Uraon or Kurukh, "Rajmahali" (i.e., Maler), and Gondi). The historical scenario he proposes is in some respects like Stevenson's, but there is one striking difference: The aborigines are civilized at the outset and are oppressed into barbarism by the Aryan conquest. This seems to reflect the degenerative theory of savagery that was so prominent in mid-century England.

Hodgson sums up by saying that "all the Tamulians of India have a common fountain and origin" like all the Aryans, and the innumerable diversities of their languages have come about because of their having been dispersed and isolated from one another owing to the savage tyranny of the Aryans in early days. The Aryan population of India, he continues, had entered the country about 3,000 years before from the northwest and conquered all the open and cultivated parts of Hindustan and Bengal and adjacent parts of the Deccan but had failed to extend their power farther south—these being quasi-historical deductions "confirmed daily more and more by the results of ethnological research." In the Deccan, where the original inhabitants of the soil have been able to retain possession of it, the aboriginal (Dravidian) languages show much integrity and refinement—the doctrine of agriculture fostering civilization—while in the north where the aborigines have been "hunted into jungly and malarious recesses" their languages "are broken into innumerable rude and shapeless fragments." Nevertheless, science can bring these fragments back together by careful comparative study, "for modern ethnology has actually accomplished elsewhere yet more brilliant feats than this, throwing upon the great antihistoric movements of nations a light as splendid as useful" (1848c: 551–552).

The idea of aboriginal unity—more exactly the unity of Dravidian and Munda—was never more than a hypothesis awaiting its decisive test, but it was a hypothesis so widely and hopefully shared by British ethnologists at mid-century that it amounted to an article of faith. What bedeviled the problem of proof was the difficulty of separating *areal* effects—the traits that Indian languages share as a result of centuries of intercommunication—from *genetic* ones—those which languages of a family of languages share because of their descent from a common ancestor language. Evidence for a unitary aboriginal language often came from what are in fact areal features which, in the absence of an analytical method for separating them out, could be misinterpreted as genetic in character. In a sense, the difficulty of separating areal and genetic phenomena made the problem of proof too easy, and it prolonged the belief in aboriginal unity for some time.

The other striking feature of this ethnology is the authors' easy confidence that physiology and language tell the same story and are alternate means to the same end. Stevenson readily identifies the Aryan languages with whiteness and the aboriginal with darkness of skin. Hodgson often appends physiological descriptions of the speakers of the languages he reports. One gets no sense from these writings that the classifications that result by application of linguistic and physiological means may be at odds and might be difficult to reconcile.

## The Third Linguistic-Ethnological Entity

In the period following the writings just described, the ethnologists tended to perpetuate the favored doctrine of aboriginal unity, but the Dravidian-Munda identity on which it rested could not survive the close scrutiny of the philologists. George Campbell's overview of Indian ethnology, published by the Asiatic Society in 1867, is the most authoritative synthesis of its day and a leading advocate of the aboriginal unity thesis. Bishop Robert Caldwell's *Comparative grammar of the Dravidian or South-Indian family of languages* (1856), one of the truly outstanding accomplishments of British Orientalism, is its most effective opponent.

George Campbell (later Sir George) was educated at Haileybury and went out to India in 1842, where he served in a variety of posts, among them judge of the high court in Calcutta and lieutenant-governor of Bengal. His *Ethnology of India* (1866) was published as a special number of the *Journal of the Asiatic Society of Bengal*. It was intended as a handbook to assist the government in its attempt to collect comprehensive lists of races and classes of India through its local officers, assisting, that is, "in making classified and descriptive lists in such a uniform manner, and with such a uniform nomenclature and arrangement, that it may be afterwards possible to weld together the whole of the information thus obtained" (G. Campbell 1866:1).

Campbell's classification scheme rests principally upon five criteria: physical appearance, language, religion, laws (especially caste and marriage), and manners and mental characteristics. When we examine the actual workings of his scheme, however, we see that language is subordinate and that the overall drift of the work is to establish a relation between physical form and the remaining "civilizational" criteria, so to call them. Thus Campbell's scheme is an example of race science, in which race in the sense of physical appearance is a sign of something deeper: an outward and visible sign of an inward and invisible state of grace or, rather, of "civilization." Like Mill's multivalent scale of civilization, this ethnology follows many criteria at once in the hope, more or less untroubled, that most of them will run together and in the conviction that an informed good judgment can settle all questions. He pays lip service to the language criterion ("in 19 cases out of 20 it tells a true tale"), but it gets overruled at the strategic juncture. The Dravidian family is sacrificed to race science and divided in two.

Campbell's classification scheme has three main categories: the modern Indians, the aborigines, and the borderers. The latter are essentially Hodgson's Himalayan and sub-Himalayan peoples; suffice it to state that, unlike Hodgson, Campbell is very doubtful that they are related to the aborigines of the Indian interior, and he is skeptical of the superclasses that unite them, such as the Turanian class of Max Müller or the Mongolidae of Latham (which I will address in the next chapter). Setting this group aside reveals the basic dichotomy of his thinking, in which the modern is opposed to the aboriginal. The fundamental dividing line is that which delimits "the black aboriginal tribes of the interior hills and jungles" (1866:13) from the "modern Indians" of north and south, and although there are Dravidian-speaking peoples who are tribal and others who are "modern" under this scheme, Campbell does not hesitate to separate them from one another, joining the tribal speakers of Dravidian languages with Munda-speaking tribes, and modern Dravidians with modern northerners speaking Indo-Aryan languages. "I draw no wide ethnological line between the Northern and Southern countries of India, not recognising the separate Dravidian classification of the latter as properly ethnological" (1866:14). The civilizational divide becomes a racial one; the modern Indians of the south, although Dravidian in language, have become Aryanized in physical appearance because of the "tendency of the higher, more marked, and more prominent type to predominate": "I have no doubt that the Southern Hindoos may be generally classed as Arians, and that the Southern society is in its structure, its manners, and its laws and institutions an Arian society" (the same). The aborigines, in turn, are evidently of two classes by the test of language—the Dravidian aborigines and the "northern division" (the Mundas)—but here Campbell ventures reasons to think that there is a similarity of structure between their languages. In short, the language criterion gives way to the civilizational logic of race science.

Race science (to adopt the useful phrase of Nancy Stepan [1982]) in Victorian Britain and British India may be described as an attempt to classify human groups according to this civilizational logic, the logic whose coherence is given by the relation that joins the two terms of the Victorian notion of the dark-skinned savage in opposition to the light-skinned civilized European, and whose terms objectify a sense of otherness that had been constituted by history. The second term (civilized/savage) is so closely identified with the first (light-skinned/dark-skinned) that it tends to be engulfed by the latter in Campbell's prose, and "physical appearance" becomes a category in which words like "fine" and "high-featured" applied to the Aryan physical type contrast with words used to describe the aborigines: "crude," "coarse," "ugly," "of the African type," and the like: Civilization thus is imported into race. Upon these two pegs a limitless cumulation of particular traits can be hung, and race science is their catalog. The conception is new,

but in its result the race science solution for the problem of Indian ethnology turns the clock back, undoing the work of the Madras school,
obliterating the distinction between Dravidian and Indo-Aryan languages, and coming to rest in the civilizational ecology of the eighteenth century according to which the cultivation of the soil makes
people modern and the "interior hills and jungles" are the resort of
aborigines.

Robert Caldwell, in his *Comparative grammar* (1856, 1875), refutes the unity-of-the-aborigines doctrine, disposing of Hodgson and
Stevenson in turn. It is quite natural, Caldwell says, to suppose, with
Hodgson, that the "Kolarian" (or Munda) languages of Central India
and Bengal (whom Hodgson put in his "Tamulian" class), are allied to
the Dravidian tribal languages Gondi, Oraon (Kurukh), or Rajmahali
(Maler), but although one may perhaps detect a few Dravidian words
in some of them, their grammatical structure shows them to be of a
totally different language family (1875:38). Caldwell notes that Hodgson
had put the Bodos, Dhimals, and other tribes of the mountains and
forests between Kumaon and Assam in his Tamulian class "on the supposition that all the aborigines of India, as distinguished from the Aryans, or Sanscrit-speaking race and its offshoots, belonged to one and
the same stock; and that of this aboriginal race, the Tamilians of Southern India were to be considered the best representatives." But, he continues, their relation to the Dravidian family "is unsupported by the
evidence either of similarity in grammatical structure or of a similar vocabulary" (1875:39). In much the same spirit Max Müller wanted to call
all the non-Aryan languages of India, including the sub-Himalayan,
the Kol, and the Tamilian families by the name Niṣādas, a tribal name
from the Purāṇas. Caldwell objects that the use of a common term is in-
appropriate inasmuch as the Dravidian languages differ so widely from
the others that they possess very few features in common, and he promotes the use of a purely negative term such as "non-Aryan" or "non-
Sanskritic."

In the course of a long review of Stevenson on the notion of a unitary aboriginal language as the source of non-Sanskritic elements in
Hindi and other northern languages, Caldwell accepts the possibility
that the northern vernaculars have a grammatical structure "which in
the main appears to be Scythian," which is more or less what Jones had
suggested. But Caldwell rejects Dravidian as a substratum language to
Hindi. "Whatever relationship, in point of blood and race, may originally have subsisted between the northern aborigines and the south-

ern—whatever *ethnological* evidences of their identity may be supposed to exist—when we view the question *philologically*, and with reference to the evidence furnished by their languages alone, the hypothesis of their identity does not appear to me to have been established" (1875:55). It was Caldwell's achievement not only to have put the unity and non-Sanskritic character of the Dravidian family on a firm footing but also to have distinguished it definitively from Munda, so putting an end to the theory of the unity of the aborigines of India.

The current view of the separate identity of Indo-Aryan, Dravidian, Munda, and Tibeto-Burman language families in India was clearly articulated in Caldwell. But it is equally clear from his text, as it is from George Campbell's when we look at its inner workings, that strains were beginning to show between the classifications of languages and the classifications of races. Those with a taste for race science were beginning to disengage their ethnologies from the authority of philology, and philologists were beginning to sense that the assumption inherited from the Babel narrative, that the differences among languages and ethnic groups run together and are reflections of one another, as the song says, "ain't necessarily so."

# CHAPTER 6

# Race Science versus Sanskrit

The debate about the internal composition of the Indian people that I reviewed in chapter 5 was an ethnological issue pursued through philological means—the comparison of parallel columns of vocabulary lists—and it unfolded and expanded itself in the first half and a bit more of the nineteenth century. It was in the same period that, back in the metropole, anthropology as a discipline was taking shape. I return to Britain in this chapter, showing how the methods and preoccupations of British Indian ethnologies were central to the formation of anthropology, but how, in the end, what Nancy Stepan (1982) has named "race science" in Britain defined itself by disengaging from the tutelage of Sanskrit and Indo-Europeanist philology and putting itself in opposition to them.

## British Anthropology in the Nineteenth Century

Of the many contributions of George W. Stocking, Jr., to the history of anthropology in Britain (culminating in his great synthesis, *Victorian anthropology*, 1987), one of the most important for our subject is his discovery of the central role of James Cowles Prichard in the first half of the nineteenth century. Two excellent studies by Stocking are of particular help in examining the relation of the Prichardian paradigm to the work of the British Sanskritists. "What's in a name?" (1971) traces the institutional origins of the Royal Anthropological Institute, whose founding in 1871 was effectively the beginning of British anthropology as we know it, and the introduction to his edition of the leading work of J. C. Prichard (1973) presents a masterly analysis of Prichardian anthropology.

In the first of these writings Stocking shows a developmental sequence involving four organizations: the Aborigines Protection Society, the Ethnological Society of London, the Anthropological Society of London, and the Royal Anthropological Institute. The Aborigines Protection Society was founded in 1837, a philanthropic organization with Quaker and Evangelical roots, the more scientifically oriented members of which formed the Ethnological Society of London in 1843; a breakaway group of the latter formed a rival, the Anthropological Society of London in 1863. After years of tension between the two, they united in 1871 under a new, Darwinist leadership in the Royal Anthropological Institute.

The Ethnological Society of London (ESL) tended to support monogenism, consistent with the motto of the Aborigines Protection Society whence it came: *ab uno sanguine,* "of one blood." The goal of its vision of ethnology was to demonstrate the original unity of the human race, "to fill the gap between the dispersion of the tribes of man over the earth and the first historical records of each present nation, and in doing so to tie all men together into a single ethnological family tree." The model of explanation was diffusionary and historical, the method of choice was "the comparison of languages to establish affinities between physically dissimilar groups" (Stocking 1971:372–373)— the Mosaic ethnology, in fact. This style of ethnology was that of James Cowles Prichard (1786–1848), who was the leading British ethnologist of his age, his career spanning nearly the first half of the nineteenth century, and the one who introduced the name ethnology into Britain.

The breakaway group, the Anthropological Society of London (ASL), had to some degree an overlapping membership and range of interests with its parent, the Ethnological Society of London, but its overall style was set by the preoccupations of its leader, James Hunt. Hunt was a polygenist, who strongly emphasized the differences between the races and asserted their permanence. His racial views imbibed from the notorious Robert Knox, author of a toxic book called *The races of men: A philosophical enquiry into the influence of race over the destinies of nations* (1862), and his conception of anthropology was taken from the French physical anthropologist Paul Broca, who emphasized the connection of the physical and the psychological. It was with Prichard and the Prichardian ethnology of the ESL that Hunt picked his quarrel. In the event, the monogenetic thesis of the ESL and the polygenist antithesis of the ASL found their synthesis in the Royal Anthropological Institute, founded in 1871, which brought about a peace under the leadership, Darwinist and evolutionary, of John Lubbock.

Such was the success of the new evolutionary and Darwinist synthesis that Prichard and his works fell at length into a deep obscurity, and so complete was that darkness that Stocking rightly speaks of a blind spot. Anthropology's field of vision in respect to its own past has all but blocked out the ethnology of the first half of the nineteenth century, finding its intellectual ancestors among the "stage" theorists of the eighteenth century and among the social evolutionists of the later nineteenth century, but with little memory for anything that fell chronologically in between, Prichard's work above all. This is an important insight, improving upon J. W. Burrow's notion of a lost generation of evolutionism between the eighteenth and late nineteenth centuries (Burrow 1966).

Consider, on the one hand, the publishing record of Prichard's now unknown works as a sign of their reception in his own day. The central item, the *Researches,* was first published in 1813 and was based upon his Latin doctoral dissertation of 1808 with its Blumenbachian title, *De generis humani varietate.* Prichard continued to revise and expand this work: A second edition in two volumes came out in 1826, a third edition in five volumes in 1836–47; a German translation was published in 1840–48; and a fourth edition, "actually a reprinting" (Stocking 1973:cxv), was issued in 1851, after Prichard's death. A single-volume summary for a wider audience, *The natural history of man,* did very well indeed: The first edition and a French translation appeared in 1843, the second edition in 1845, the third in 1848, and, after his death, the fourth, a two-volume edition, in 1855. His many other books and articles on ethnological and medical subjects (for which I direct the interested to Stocking's bibliography of Prichard [1973:cxi ff.]) include an important contribution to Celtic studies, *The eastern origin of the Celtic nations proved by a comparison of their dialects with the Sanskrit, Greek, Latin and Teutonic languages,* a full-blown piece of Indo-European comparative philology, written as a supplement to the *Researches* and published in 1831. The publishing history, however, comes to an end in the 1850s, and that is a sign of the eclipse of Prichard's reputation and also the eclipse of an ethnology led by the issues and methods of language study.

Consider, on the other hand, the structure of anthropology's own sense of its history in the twentieth century, taking the posthumously published lectures of E. E. Evans-Pritchard (not to be confused with James Cowles Prichard) as a particularly clear example (Evans-Pritchard 1981). Each lecture takes up a different scholar; the work surveys the social theorists of eighteenth-century France (Montesquieu, Condorcet) and Scotland (Lord Kames, Adam Ferguson, John Millar), and the later nineteenth-century luminaries John McLennan, Robertson Smith, Sir Henry Maine, E. B. Tylor, and others, but the early nineteenth century is nearly a blank, with only August Comte included as chronological connective tissue between the two sets of proto-anthropologists. J. C. Prichard is not so much as mentioned. The early nineteenth century is a black hole into which Prichard disappeared with a completeness that is astonishing in view of the preeminence of his authority and the wide readership of his works in his own lifetime. It is not just a question of the lost reputation of an individual; because the two series of ethnological thinkers mentioned above, the eighteenth-century series and the late-nineteenth-century one, are both committed to some form of a theory of social stages, the story appears to be one of very substantial continuity and progress over a long period, interrupted at best by a "lost generation" between them. But that simple story gets greatly complicated when we examine Prichard closely, for the Prichardian paradigm is rather different from both, and the story of anthropology's formative years seems, rather, to be one of Kuhnian rupture and discontinuity.

## The Prichardian Paradigm and the British Sanskritists

With the Stocking thesis as our starting point we now come to the work of this chapter, which is to probe the two contradictory relations of Prichardian ethnology to the ethnological methods of the India hands and to India as an object of ethnological study. In Prichard himself we see that the Calcutta Sanskritists play a large role in the formation of his ethnological framework, and India is central to his ethnology, but by mid-century Prichardian ethnology, represented by the younger Prichardians R. G. Latham and John Crawfurd, was at loggerheads with Sanskrit, as symbolized in the person of Friedrich Max Müller. In the work of these writers (much as in George Campbell's), although language remains the leading principle of classification at the surface level, in fact the claims of physical features are advanced to defeat the authority of the Indo-European doctrine and of Sanskritists for ethnological classifications.

We begin with Prichard himself. Stocking's excellent guide to Prichard's references (1973) makes it easy to trace the influence of the Calcutta Sanskritists and to determine that their writings were of major import in the formation of Prichardian ethnology. *Asiatic researches* is cited repeatedly, and Stocking lists ten different authors, among whom Jones, Colebrooke, and Wilford are notable. Hamilton's anonymous review of Wilkins's Sanskrit grammar is also cited. Prichard's rather extensive reading of Indological works included other British and British Indian writers as well as Anquetil and some of the missionary writers of the older Orientalism. He also cites Jacob Bryant, the writer of *Analysis of antient mythology* which had such a pronounced effect on the formation of Jones's ethnological system, prominently and more than once. Indeed, examination of Prichard's text and references leads me to conclude that at the very heart of Prichard's interest in the Orientalist literature lay the Jones-Bryant theory of the original unity of the ancient civilized peoples—the Indians, Egyptians, Greeks, Romans, and others—as descendants of Ham. Two of the nine chapters of the *Researches* are specifically devoted to proving the unity of Indians and Egyptians. To explain the centrality of India and the new Orientalism in this curious book, it may be helpful to begin with another contemporary reaction to the Jonesean ethnology, that of an anonymous reviewer in the *Monthly review*.[1]

The reviewer lists several serious obstacles to Jones's system. The first is that Jones says nothing of where the Negroes fit into the scheme of things, "and if, by implication, we suppose them descended from the same stock as the Indians, Romans, and Goths, the difficulty is enhanced by the Indian emigrants of the same country retaining their original configuration, while the negroes have lost it" (*Monthly review* 1797:413–414). Another concerned the Curse of Ham: "The malediction of the Patriarch seems to have operated in a manner diametrically opposite to his wishes," since the sons of the reprobate Ham have taken possession of the fairest fields and richest countries of the habitable globe, the civilized parts of Europe and Asia, "while the descendants of the dutiful sons are condemned to the burning sands of Arabia [i.e., Shem], or to the inhospitable regions of frozen Tartary [i.e.,

1. See note 7 for chapter 1 on the identity of the author of this review.

Japhet]" (*Monthly review* 1797:414). In short, skin color stood in the way of combining the Europeans, Indians, and Egyptians with one another and, as sons of Ham, with black Africans. And while for Jones color of skin was a fairly fast-acting effect of climate, for others who assumed it to be less mutable, it was a stumbling block to the acceptance of the Hamian theory of Bryant and Jones.

Prichard, however, was drawn to the Bryant-Jones theory because he believed he saw a different way to synthesize the Biblical teaching of the unity of the human kind with the fast-growing stock of new information about human societies around the world. The three parts of his make-up were his personal religion (Quaker turned Anglican), his profession as medical doctor, and his interest in languages and in the progress of philology. These three combine in the composition of Prichardian ethnology, in which the Biblical narrative is scientifically grounded by a sustained inquiry into the relation of language and physical features. The fundamental idea of the *Researches* is that civilization and skin color covary, that the human race is descended from a single pair (Adam and Eve) who were black of skin, and that change of skin color was brought about not by climate (the more usual view) but by civilization, the effect of which, it is claimed, is to lighten the skin.

This surprising conclusion was in a sense a new reading of the Hamian theory of Bryant and Jones. Prichard's chapters on Indian-Egyptian unity go to show that both peoples, who are taken to be the very first to become civilized, were in ancient times black of skin and gradually became lighter, as have other civilized descendants of Ham. For the Egyptian side he cites ancient authors such as Herodotus on the black skin and woolly hair of the Egyptians and Ethiopians, whom he regards as of one race. For the Indian side he cites Wilford:

In several parts of India the mountaineers resemble Negroes in their countenance, and in some degree in their hair, which is curled and has a tendency to wool. . . . It is reasonable to suppose that the barbarous tribes preserve most of the original character of the nation, for the first colonists were in all probability rude people. The better orders in India, as in other countries, have gradually improved by civilization, and have acquired a different aspect. . . . It cannot reasonably be doubted, that a race of Negroes formerly had pre-eminence in India. (Wilford 1792; quoted in Prichard 1813:391)

Physical features combine with mythology, architecture, and other evidence set forth to prove the original unity of India and Egypt. Prichard argues that in the times of the patriarch Abraham the empire of Elam was Indo-Persian or Hindu in character and bordered the kingdom of Egypt, so that it is no longer difficult to imagine Indians and Egyptians connected in race and origin (Prichard 1813:471).

Thus in Prichard's early ethnological synthesis the central argument is that race is a sign of civilization because civilization is the *cause* of race, and the India-Egypt connection is the hinge upon which the argument turns because it mediates between the dark-skinned savage and the fair-skinned civilized European. As Stocking remarks, however, Prichard's theory of the original negritude of the human race was not popular, and in many ways the subsequent editions of the *Researches* are marked not only by the additions of vast amounts of new ethnological data but also by a series of small retreats from the central thesis of the first edition; the cumulative effect is to reverse its direction. The most striking of these retreats is that Prichard gradually falls in with the traditional theory of climate as the cause of complexion, which he had originally set aside. In *The natural history of man,* for example, he says that the most compelling proof that the complexion of the Hindus is connected with the climate they inhabit is found among the Indians settled in the high Himalayas, some of whom are very fair, with blue eyes and auburn or red hair (Prichard 1843:169). On the other hand, Prichard now juxtaposes a fair Aryan race to the aboriginal races, all of them of different languages and distinct from the Hindus, who belong to the Indo-European or Aryan stock (1843:240). He identifies these aborigines as the Sinhalese (wrongly, since their language is Indo-European), the "Tamulian race," the mountain tribes of the Deccan, and a number of "petty barbarous tribes between the Indian and the Indo-Chinese Peninsulas" (1843:241). He inclines toward the prevailing doctrine of the unity of the Indian aborigines. It is possible, he thinks, that the "wild races in the Dekhan are allied to the Tamulian tribes" and descended "from people of that stock who refused to receive the apostles of the Hindoo theology, and of civilisation and slavery," but they are now very different from each other in moral and physical characters, "some being vigorous and finely formed, others diminutive and puny. The difference may be explained in many instances by reference to the climates and local influences under which the several tribes exist" (1843:248).

The early Prichard had assumed the unity of the Indians *inter se* and with the Egyptians and their original negritude; the late Prichard abandons the unity of the Indians and tentatively adopts the unity of the Indian aborigines, or a part of them, in opposition to a light-skinned

Hindu or Aryan race. The early Prichard adopted civilization itself, and not climate, as the cause of racial differences; the late Prichard turns automatically to climate when there is a difference of physical features to be explained. And the early Prichard had said in a note at the conclusion of the *Researches,* "This part of our scheme, and indeed the whole of it, perfectly coincides with the system of Mr. Bryant, though built entirely on different principles" (Prichard 1813:558). The later Prichard abandons Bryant and the Hamian theory that had been the source of his early attraction to Bryant—and to Jones.

## Friedrich Max Müller on Aryan Brotherhood

Friedrich Max Müller was the creator of the notion of the Aryan race, and he was the most ardent and consistent advocate of the idea of the brotherhood of the Aryan peoples, more especially of the kinship between Indians and Europeans.[2] He was very well known in India even though he never traveled there, and his friendships with Indians were important to him in his self-representations. He took up the Aryan love story and told it with verve and passion. He had a gift for public performance and for colorful expression. The highly visible position he occupied in English public life—he was *the* celebrity scholar for Sanskrit and comparative philology during the greater part of the Victorian period—makes him a central actor in the story of the attacks upon Sanskrit by race science. He became the embodiment of that which race science sought to overthrow, its Public Enemy Number One. In the latter half of his life the development of race science, both in England and on the Continent, made Max Müller regret that he had spoken of race, and he proposed a divorce, amicable if possible, between philology and ethnology.

It is difficult to capture the exact character of Max Müller's place in English public life. Perhaps I could say that he was one of the great Outsider-Insiders. Born in the tiny German duchy of Anhalt-Dessau, he studied Sanskrit with Hermann Brockhaus in Leipzig, Bopp in Berlin, and Bernouf in Paris, coming finally in 1846 to London and Oxford

---

2. Friedrich Max Müller wished people to take "Max Müller" as his last name, and this has caused endless confusion. I treat him as Max Müller, Friedrich, but his name is often listed alphabetically as Müller, Friedrich Max. There is no good solution to this problem.

to carry out the great project of his youth, the editing of the text of the *Ṛg Veda*. He married an English woman and he remained in Oxford to the end of his life in 1900, first as professor of modern languages and, from 1868, in a professorship of comparative philology created especially for him. The latter was a kind of consolation prize for the fact that when H. H. Wilson died and the Boden Professorship of Sanskrit became vacant, in 1860, it went after a hotly contested election to Monier Monier-Williams, who had been the Sanskrit professor at Haileybury when it was closed two years before (the same who composed the Sanskrit inscription we examined in chapter 1). The Boden Professorship had been privately endowed for the purpose of promoting the spread of Christianity by the translation of the Bible into Sanskrit. It was awarded to Monier-Williams by vote of convocation following a period of heavy lobbying, in which Max Müller's broad religious views and foreign birth worked against him even though he was much the better Sanskritist. It was a bitter defeat for him and had the effect of turning him toward comparative philology, a field in which he never became a major contributor but for which he became a most prominent and effective publicist, purveying to the English public the fruits of Continental scholarship. His lectures at the Royal Institution in 1861 and 1863 were immensely successful and were published as *Lectures on the science of language* (1861), which became a standard authority in English for the results of comparative philology. His later work on comparative mythology also has this popularizing character. Max Müller had a career of great public visibility and many, many honors, but it was built upon Oxford's exclusion of this talented and prodigiously productive Sanskritist from teaching in his own field. Max Müller was by inclination and force of circumstance a great internationalist, but he could always be seen, instead, simply, as a foreigner.

A youthful Friedrich Max Müller—not yet twenty-three—gave his maiden speech in English, after much prodding by his patron, Baron Christian Bunsen, Prussian ambassador and writer on universal history, at a session of the 1847 meeting of the British Association for the Advancement of Science held in Oxford. The session brought together in one room most of the figures of this chapter, for it was presided over by Prichard, then at the end of his life, and attended by "some not very friendly ethnologists" (1901:210), as Max Müller recalls in a memoir, particularly R. G. Latham and John Crawfurd, who was known by the name of "the Objector General." Prince Albert was present, drawing a large audience, which made Max Müller "fearfully nervous." In the event, Prichard protected Max Müller "most chivalrously against the somewhat frivolous objections of certain members, who were not overly friendly towards Prince Albert, Chevalier Bunsen, and all that was called German in scholarship" (Max Müller 1901:211).

Max Müller's paper "On the relation of the Bengali to the Arian and aboriginal languages of India" (1847) takes up the central issue of British Indian ethnology. He sets out with a spirited counterattack upon the party of the English Christian missionaries in their opposition to Orientalist scholarship, and I cannot help but think that the description fits the Rev. John Stevenson (though a Sanskritist as well as a missionary) rather well:

The hostile spirit of a party, which has been working for the last years, particularly in this country, to attack all the theories of the Sanscrit antiquarians, has chosen the modern languages of India as a weak point, in order to prove that, as they have no connexion by their grammatical system with the pretended old language of India, the Sanscrit, this sacred language itself has never exercised any real influence upon the people, just as they have tried to prove that the literature, the religion, morals and philosophy of the Brahmins have never historically existed but in the hands of some foreign intriguing priests. (1847:325)

The intent of these partisans was no doubt philanthropic, he thought, and perhaps it had the negative benefit of opposing the extreme of Indomania, which "found Brahmins as the real founders of civilization over the whole world, connected not only with the religious systems of Egypt and Greece, but even at the bottom of the Christian doctrine" (the same); here Wilford would be the leading example. Max Müller positions himself against both extremes, identifying himself, and Orientalism, with the Orientalist party and its leader, the Oxford professor of Sanskrit H. H. Wilson; that is, he reasserts the Sanskritists' position that the vernaculars of northern India, Bengali in this instance, are derived in the main from Sanskrit and are hence a part of the Indo-European family, but he invests this fact with great moral and policy significance, and adopts the Orientalist position against the Anglicists on educational policy.

The paper develops what we might call the two-race theory of Indian civilization, the two races being Cushite or Hamite or Negro, and Japhetite or Caucasian. Indians are "one great branch of the Caucasian race [not Hamians as Jones and Bryant had it], differing from other branches of the same race merely by its darker complexion" caused by the climate (1847:347). Max Müller describes a different race in the mountainous districts of the north, however, which resembles the Negro in physical and intellectual type; the same dark race is present in the south, although the "noble stamp of the Caucasian race" is seen in the brahmins and in the great mass of the inhabitants of the Deccan. How is it that the southerners do not speak an Indo-European language (Max Müller says Indo-Germanic; he has not yet become champion of the name Aryan), but rather the Dravidian languages which, according to recent research, resemble most "the dialects spoken by the savage tribes, like the Bhillas and Gondas," thought to be of Cushite origin?

In answer to this question Max Müller unfolds the racial history of India in terms of the relations between the lighter civilized race and the darker savages. The story aims to accomplish two things at once. It aims to show that India is civilized and that its civilized Aryan invaders have not (as in the view of the hostile missionary party) become uncivilized by mingling with the dark race. Moreover, it draws from the history of relations of light and dark races within India a moral for the relations of light Britons to darker Indians in the present. The tale proceeds from North India to South India, showing differing race histories, the south being the most fruitful outcome and representing the moral of the story for Britain.

In North India, says Max Müller, when the Aryan tribes immigrated they came as a warrior people, vanquishing, destroying, and subjecting the savage and despised inhabitants of the country. "We generally find that it is the fate of the negro race, when brought into hostile contact with the Japhetic race, to be either destroyed and annihilated, or to fall into a state of slavery and degradation, from which, if at all, it recovers by the slow process of assimilation" (1847:348). Max Müller asserts that this assimilation has been accomplished in the north: The greater part vanished before the approach of the Aryans, and others were enslaved and adopted the manners, religion and language of the Aryans. "The lower classes of the Hindus consist of those aboriginal inhabitants, some continuing in a state of the utmost degradation as outcastes; but others have intellectually and physically undergone a complete regeneration, so that after three thousand years it would be difficult to trace the Sudra origin of many highly distinguished families of India" (the same). The notion that civilization brings about physical regeneration, that is, lightening of the complexion, is distinctly Prichardian.

But the Aryan conquerors of India did not settle the whole of Hindustan, Max Müller continues, leaving large tracts under the rule of aboriginal tribes, the dark race of the mountainous and afforested regions of the north. The dark aboriginal race includes the peoples of the Gondwana region of Central India, whose pillage and human sacrifices had been recently suppressed by the English armies, "and it is curious to see how the [English] descendants of the same [Aryan] race, to which the first conquerors and masters of India belonged, return, after having followed the northern development of the Japhetic race to their primordial soil, to accomplish the glorious work of civilization, which had been left unfinished by their Arian brethren" (1847:349). The phrase "Aryan brethren" is Max Müller's contribution to the Orientalist love story of British India, although it was often taken in vain by its opponents.

It was in the south, however—to continue Max Müller's argument—that the civilizing process proceeded farthest, not by conquering armies but through peaceful colonization by the brahmins. In the south, the Aryans—that is, the brahmins—"followed the wiser policy of adopting themselves the language of the aboriginal people, and of conveying through its medium their knowledge and instruction to the minds of uncivilized tribes," and in so doing they refined the language and raised it to a perfection that rivals even the Sanskrit. Because of this concession to the local language there was a much more favorable assimilation between the Aryan and the aboriginal races, and the south became a bastion of brahminical science "when it was banished from the north by the intolerant Mohammedans." The story had a moral for the current rulers of India: "The beneficial influence of a higher civilization may be effectually exercised without forcing the people to give up their own language and to adopt that of their foreign conquerors, a result by which, if successful, every vital principle of an independent and natural development is necessarily destroyed" (the same). In short, the ancient history of India demonstrated the greater wisdom of the Orientalist educational policy over the Anglicist one.

The two-race theory of Indian civilization, in Max Müller's version, was meant to promote the solidarity of the two partners of empire as Aryan brethren to each other, based on the identity Japhetic = Caucasian = Aryan. Complexion thus is a malleable property, caused by climate. Darkness of complexion, it is true, is associated with savagery in this argument. But race is not destiny; a civilizing "regeneration," moral and physical, is possible through long, preferably peaceful, association.

For the race-is-destiny view I shall turn to the ethnologists Latham and Crawfurd and their attack upon the philologists, especially Max

Müller himself. These were the "not very friendly ethnologists" Max Müller remembered at his first public performance in English. Their hostility grew as Max Müller's career developed and came to fasten upon a couple of the more vivid metaphors of his later writings, which I will now enter into the record.

Having become a professor at Oxford, Max Müller was asked to give advice to British officers engaged in the Crimean War as to how best to go about acquiring the languages of the region. The result was a short book, *Suggestions for the assistance of officers in learning the languages of the seat of war in the East* (1854b). In it he takes the opportunity to stress again the inclusive side of the Indo-European concept, and he does so in the following remarkable statement from the second edition.

No authority could have been strong enough to persuade the Grecian army [of Alexander] that their gods and their hero-ancestors were the same as those of [the Indian] King Porus, or to convince the English soldier that the same blood was running in his veins, as in the veins of the dark Bengalese. And yet there is not an English jury now-a-days, which, after examining the hoary documents of language, would reject the claim of a common descent and a legitimate relationship between Hindu, Greek, and Teuton. Many words still live in India and in England that witnessed the first separation of the northern and southern Arians, and these are witnesses not to be shaken by any cross-examination. The terms for God, for house, for father, mother, son, daughter, for dog and cow, for heart and tears, for axe and tree, identical in all the Indo-European idioms, are like the watchwords of an army. We challenge the seeming stranger, and whether he answer with the lips of a Greek, a German, or an Indian, we recognize him as one of ourselves. Though the historian may shake his head, though the physiologist may doubt, and the poet scorn the idea, all must yield before the facts furnished by language. There was a time when the ancestors of the Celts, the Germans, the Slaves [*sic*], the Greeks and Italians, the Persians and Hindus, were living together beneath the same roof, separate from the ancestors of the Semitic and Turanian races. (Max Müller 1855:29)

This arresting image of an English jury deciding in favor of Aryan brotherhood was much talked about, for and against. Almost as memorable were his words to the same effect in his *Lectures on the science of language:*

As sure as the six Romance dialects point to an original home of Italian shepherds on the seven hills at Rome, the Aryan languages together point to an earlier period of language, when the first ancestors of the Indians, the Persians, the Greeks, the Romans, the Slaves, the Celts, and the Germans were living together within the same enclosures, nay, under the same roof. . . . Before the ancestors of the Indians and Persians started for the south, and the leaders of the Greek, Roman, Celtic, Teutonic, and Slavonic colonies marched towards the shores of Europe, there was a small clan of Aryans, settled probably on the highest elevation of Central Asia, speaking a language, not yet Sanskrit or Greek or German, but containing the dialectic germs of all; a clan that had advanced to a state of agricultural civilisation; that had recognised the bonds of blood, and sanctioned the bonds of marriage; and that invoked the Giver of Light and Life in heaven by the same name which you may still hear in the temples of Benares, in the basilicas of Rome, and in our own churches and cathedrals. (1861:219–220)

It is worth adding that Max Müller continued to sound this note throughout his life, speaking out repeatedly against both anti-Semitism and the denigration of Indians by Britons. In his presidential address to the Ninth International Congress of Orientalists, toward the end of his life, he accounted it one of the great advances of Orientalism that not only had the inhabitants of India "ceased to be mere idolaters or niggers, they have been recognised as our brothers in language and thought" (1892:34). The thesis of the Aryan brotherhood of Britons and Indians was far more than a proposition of science for Max Müller; it was also an ethic.

## Robert Latham and John Crawfurd Attack the Sanskritists

The attack upon Max Müller and upon the Sanskritists generally by Robert Latham and John Crawfurd is remarkable for its acrimony, and for the fact that it came from an ethnology of the Prichardian kind that was otherwise so very congenial to comparative philology. Indeed, both Latham and Crawfurd, in their very different career paths, came via philological work of their own to a language-based ethnology, but then turned *against* the Sanskritists. Crawfurd (1783–1868) spent five years in North India as an army medical officer, but he passed the greater part of his career in Southeast Asia, at Penang, Java, and Singapore and as envoy to Siam, Cochin China, and Ava, before retiring to England in 1827. He is especially known for his *Grammar and dictionary of the Malay language* (1852) and his diplomatic memoirs, quite apart from his many ethnological articles published in the journal of the Ethnological Society of London. The stay-at-home Latham wrote on the English language and on the *Elements of comparative philology* (1862) as well as his more properly ethnological works of which the major ones are *The natural history of the varieties of man* (1850) and *Descriptive ethnology* (1859a). Both were active in the Ethnological Society of London—Crawfurd was a president—and both are leading examples of Prichardian ethnology. Between them they illustrate how the claims of race overruled the claims of language in the representative theories of the ESL, and not only in the rival Anthropological Society of London with its anti-Prichardian leadership. By mid-century the relations between philology and ethnology were in crisis.

Latham classes the populations of contemporary India as Mongoloid (Mongolidae) and not among the Japhetites (Iapetidae), which is his equivalent for the Indo-Europeans (1850). The ancient speakers of Sanskrit, then, are of a race quite different from that of the Indians proper, and his argument obliges him to minimize all connection between Sanskrit and the modern languages of India, as he does in his chapter on Sanskrit in *Elements of comparative philology* (1862:chap. 64.) To this end he argues that the homeland of Sanskrit is on the eastern or southeastern border of Lithuania in the Baltic region, far from India; that none of the modern languages of India are true daughters of Sanskrit, and Sanskritic words in them may as easily be indigenous Indian loanwords; that the Devanagari script in which Sanskrit is written has no specimen older than the Muslim conquest (!); that Sanskrit has a series of true aspirates wanting in its European congeners (!) and cerebrals; that it is not proved that the brahmins, the expositors of the Sanskrit language, are the descendants of those who first spoke it as their mother tongue; and that the character of Sanskrit literature is such that it cannot have been the product of a vernacular, and thus it can have no true vernaculars as its descendants. It hardly needs saying that these "facts" are highly contentious interpretations.

Latham comes, then, to the nub of the thing, which is a portrayal of the opposing view as un-English. As against "the extreme Sanskrit scholars"—and there can be no doubt that he considered Max Müller as the type case—Latham presents himself not as an expert but as an intelligent English juryman reading the evidence by the light of common sense, "who, knowing that he is no judge, putting a wholesome distrust in the barrister, and ignoring anything which he may or may not know *aliunde*, simply looks to the evidence" and finds it "insufficient for the present." Beyond this purely negative conclusion "he is not afraid of committing himself to the doctrine that, when philologers make the Vedas 3,000 and odd years old, and deduce the Latin and its congeners from Asia, they are wrong to, at least, a thousand miles in space, and as many years in time" (1862:619). Thus does plain English common sense triumph over the learned folly of the Sanskritist, and the fundament of that common sense, it would appear, is mere contempt for dark-skinned peoples. It is surprising to find such an argument coming from the pen of a philologist, and a Prichardian at that. It is a sign that the Prichardian paradigm is being abandoned for a "race science" view.

In Crawfurd's transformation, Prichardian ethnology finds the testimony of language and of race at odds with each other, and he jettisons the claims of language. In an 1861 article provoked by Max Müller's immensely popular lectures on the science of language, Crawfurd characterizes the "Aryan or Indo-Germanic theory" as a theory "that had its origin in Germany"—so much for Jones—"and which has since had a wide acceptance among the learned in other parts of Europe" (1861:268). According to this theory, all the nations and tribes from Bengal to Europe are of one race, the only material exception being the Arabs, Jews, and others speaking cognate (Semitic) languages. The fault of this theory, Crawfurd argues, is that it is founded on a supposed essential conformity of language and nationality "without regard to physical form or intellectual capacity" (the same). The burden of the article is to show, to the contrary, that consideration of physical form and intellectual capacity overturns the evidence of language. As in Latham, the conclusion mockingly recalls Max Müller's metaphor of the English jury:

From the facts I have adduced in the course of this paper I must come to the conclusion that the theory which makes all the languages of Europe and Asia, from Bengal to the British Islands, however different in appearance, to have sprung from the same stock, and hence, all the people speaking them, black, swarthy, and fair, to be of one and the same race of man, is utterly groundless, and the mere dream of learned men, and perhaps even more imaginative than learned. I can by no means, then, agree with a very learned professor of Oxford, that the same blood ran in the veins of the soldiers of Alexander and Clive as in those of the Hindus whom, at the interval of two-and-twenty ages, they both scattered with the same facility. I am not prepared, like him, to believe that an English jury, unless it were a packed one of learned Orientalists, with the ingenious professor himself for its foreman, would, "After examining the hoary documents of language," admit "the claim of a common descent between Hindu, Greek, and Teuton," for that would amount to allowing that there was no difference in the faculties of the people that produced Homer and Shakespear, and those that have produced nothing better than the authors of the Mahabharat and Ramayana; no difference between the home-keeping Hindus, who never made a foreign conquest of any kind, and the nations who discovered, conquered, and peopled a new world. (1861:285)

The vehemence and sarcasm of this rejection of Max Müller's "Aryan brethren" thesis is as notable as the contempt for Indians and Indian civilization that accompanies it. Elsewhere Crawfurd writes of the dangers of intermarriage between races widely apart on the scale of civilization (Crawfurd 1865). Evidently he believed that philology is bad for racial hygiene. The irony of this sad story is that the destruction of the authority of language comparison in ethnological classifications, and the substitutions of the claims of race science, was in great part the work of the two leading philologically pedigreed ethnologists from the Prichardian stable.

## Race Science

In Crawfurd we meet the race doctrine in its strong form, that is, as the doctrine of the necessary and permanent association of different levels of intelligence with different races defined by physical form. Let us call it the doctrine of racial essentialism. In this belief, race is an inescapable doom or destiny, as the case may be.

Neither Evangelicals intent on turning Hindus into Christians, nor Utilitarians seeking to liberate Hindus from their own civilization by education in the arts and sciences of Europe, could hold to racial essentialism, for that would be to assert that the Indians were doomed to remain forever inferior; both groups were committed to a belief in the possibility of ameliorating the Indian condition. Thus the Indophobia of the Evangelicals and Utilitarians is not racial-essentialist but has to do with unflattering comparisons of Hinduism with Protestant Christianity and of Indian civilization with European. What we generally encounter in such circles, therefore, is some form of the climate doctrine as an explanation of physical features. Thus when Macaulay delivered a dissertation on the Bengali character—in terms that amount to character assassination at the level of the nation—he explains in climactic, not racial-essentialist, terms: "The Bengali lives in a vapour bath" (1835) which makes his character what it is. The doctrine of racial essentialism of the emerging race science had to make its way against these religious and progressivist positions, but the evident weakness of climate as a cause of complexion told in its favor.

On one thing Max Müller and Crawfurd were agreed, namely that the evidence of language and the evidence of physiology were at odds with each other. Where they differed was over the respective claims of philology and physiology to govern ethnological inquiry. Underlying the difference was a difference in beliefs about the fixity or malleability of complexion and intelligence, and the relation, necessary or variable, between the two.

India was at the center of the growing quarrel between ethnology and philology or, to put it more exactly, between race science and the Sanskritists. We can picture the development of race science in nineteenth-century Britain somewhat schematically (and more in conceptual terms than in chronology) as a movement from the extremes toward the center. At opposite extremes lay the light-skinned civilized European and the dark-skinned savage. The results of anatomical investigation of Europeans and Negroes were read not as parallel departures from simian forms (as under the tree paradigm), but as establishing the top and bottom of a progressive series of human races (as in the figure of a scale or staircase of human races), with comparable mental endowments and civilizational achievements. Thus, part one of the program of race science, so to say, was to define the extremes, and its activities lay completely outside India—in Europe on the one hand, and, on the other, in Africa, Australia, Tasmania, or wherever the elusive missing link between humans and animals might be sought. Part two of the program was to divide up the interval between the extremes into a fixed number of discrete races. The growing mass of measurements that race science made in the latter half of the nineteenth century, which was to have secured that result, made it, in fact, ever more elusive, showing continuous variation where discontinuities were looked for, and the existence of races became a faith in ideal types underlying the messiness of the actual measurements.[3]

---

3. That is the impression one gets from examining Paul Topinard's (1885) thousand pages on the scientific measurement of racial characteristics (discussed in the next chapter). Multiplication of the means of exact measurement does not result in certainty but in the need to choose a few measurements that confirm prior notions of the scale of races and eliminate others that produce results that do not conform. Race science seemed like a new key to history for its advocates, but in hindsight it appears simply to confirm prejudices rather than to uncover new and unexpected truths.

India was the critical battleground for the claims of ethnology and philology exactly because of its intermediate location, both in the scale of civilization as defined by Mill and for its variety of complexions lying between the extremes of the scale of physical types defined by race science. The Indo-European concept established a kinship between Indians and Europeans that was increasingly at odds with the search for discrete races.

The terms of the argument were radically altered in the 1860s by Darwinism and the collapse of the short six-thousand-year Biblical chronology for human history, which was due to the discovery of human remains adjacent to long-extinct animals. Now it became clear that the racial differences among humans had come about over a timescale vastly longer, measurable in the tens and hundreds of thousands of years at least, than the period in which the Indo-European languages differentiated themselves from one another and from their common ancestral language. It became clear as well that the formation of the Indo-European languages was an event that lay not near the beginning of human life, but was, in light of the newly discovered antiquity of man, comparatively recent. The effect of the suddenly expanding human timeframe was to disengage the study of race in the biological sense from the study of language. Thomas Huxley's view (1865) was that biology was now in charge of ethnological questions, philology supplying only supplementary findings over only the most recent period of human history; in any case it was apparent that language and race had no necessary connection, since people speaking the same language might be of different races and vice-versa. Max Müller accepted this conclusion fully, and he repented of not having distinguished between racial and linguistic groups.

But if in the new intellectual climate brought about by Darwinism and the time revolution the relation between race and language was seen to be arbitrary and contingent, what then became of the claim that the same blood flowed in the veins of Clive's soldiers and the dark Bengalese? Herbert Hope Risley, who applied calipers to Bengali heads and noses, believed it possible to reconcile the Indo-European concept of a relation between Britons and Indians with the findings of physical anthropology based on its improved means of measurement (Risley 1892, 1908). He found a direct relation between the proportion of Aryan blood and the nasal index, along a gradient from the highest castes to the lowest. This assimilation of caste to race proved, as we shall see in the next chapter, very influential.

## Isaac Taylor on the Aryan Race

In the meantime, let us see how the notion of the Aryan race in Britain changed as it was wrested from the hands of the Sanskritists by the anthropologists. The exposition of this issue by Isaac Taylor (not to be confused with the anthropologist E. B. Tylor), called *The origin of the Aryans; an account of the prehistoric ethnology and civilisation of Europe* (c.1889) is exceptionally clear and telling.

Taylor thought that Max Müller, "owing to the charm of his style, to his unrivalled power of popular exposition, and to his high authority as a Sanskrit scholar," had done more than any other writer to popularize the erroneous notion that the primitive unity of Aryan speech implied a primitive unity of race. On the passage in which Max Müller says that there was a time "when the first ancestors of the Indians, the Persians, the Greeks, the Romans, the Slaves, the Celts, and the Germans were living together within the same enclosures, nay, under the same roof" (1861:219), Taylor commented, "Than this picturesque paragraph more mischievous words have seldom been uttered by a great scholar" (c.1889:3). The error was the old assumption of the philologists that relationship of languages implies relationship of race. This assumption is false on the face of it; so much so that twelve English tradesmen in a jury box (to trot out Max Müller's metaphor once again) would readily see through linguistic evidence purporting to show, like the linguistic evidence for the notion that the same blood flowed in the veins of Clive's soldiers and those of the dark Bengalese, the common descent of the Alabama Negro and the New Englander of Massachussetts (1861:6).

Where English common sense rejected the authority of the Sanskritist in matters of race, science, in the form of what we now call archaeology and physical or biological anthropology, brought new findings to its aid. The burden of Isaac Taylor's book is to popularize the new findings for an English audience, concentrating upon the prehistoric archaeology of Europe and the latest writings on race science by the French anthropologists Paul Broca and Paul Topinard and the Germans Theodor Pösche and Karl Penka.

Taylor's argument is as follows. The discoveries of prehistoric archaeology, in the vastly expanded timespan for human history that it revealed, completely undermine the older scenario of the philologist, according to which Aryan peoples migrated from Central Asia to Europe near about the beginning of human history. Archaeology now reveals abundant evidence of a long human occupation of Europe and shows that the races of Europe were long established in the places they now occupy. Thus the question becomes, which of the four races of prehistoric Europe is the original Aryan race, whose language it imposed upon the others—for craniology has revealed that those who speak the Aryan languages are not of one race, but many. Of the four races of Europe, the Iberians were Hamitic, and the Ligurians were Euskarian (Basque); this leaves the Scandinavians and North Germans (represented by the northern dolichocephalic Row Grave race), or the Celts (the northern brachycephalic Round Barrow people). The German scholars had identified the Aryans with the Germanic long-heads, the French with the Celtic broad-heads. Taylor notes and deplores the chauvinistic element in this debate and sides with the French.

One would like to dwell on this text, rich document as it is of the new English common sense that had been building for several decades, that race is the hitherto hidden key to all of history, an idea that united people as different as Thomas Carlyle, Benjamin Disraeli, and the virulent anti-Irish race scientist Robert Knox. Before taking leave of it let us at least note how it makes of European history a double of the racial history of India:

The Aryan invaders, few in number, who were settled on the banks of the Upper Indus, are found gradually advancing to the south and the east in continual conflict with the Dasyu or dark-skinned aborigines, who spoke a strange language, worshipped strange gods, and followed strange customs, till finally the barbarians are subdued and admitted into the Aryan state as a fourth caste, called the "blacks," or Sudras. The higher civilisation and the superior physique of the northern invaders ultimately prevailed, and they imposed their language and their creed on the subject tribes; but the purity of the race was soiled by marriage with native women, the language was infected with peculiar Dravidian sounds, and the creed with foul Dravidian worships of Siva and Kali, and the adoration of the lingam and the snake.
The Aryanisation of Europe doubtless resembled that of India. The Aryan speech and the Aryan civilisation prevailed, but the Aryan race either disappeared or its purity was lost. (c.1889:212)

In Taylor's nimble fingers the race doctrine becomes the explanation of everything, including class (the landed gentry, for example, are Teutons, phelgmatic in temperament, dull of intellect, brave, warlike, and given to field sports and athletic exercises). The confessional geography of Europe takes on entirely new significance, according to which dolichocephalic Protestants reject the Roman Catholicism with which they had been civilized by the brachycephalics. Some fancy stitching is needed here to show that the Presbyterian lowland Scots are actually Teutons, not Celts, and the Celtic but Protestant Welsh and Cornish have become so by political accident and "have transformed Protestant-ism into an emotional religion, which has inner affinities with the emotional faith of Ireland and Italy." England, on the other hand, is a rare true mixture of two races; being orthocephalic, it of course "neither Catholic nor Protestant, but Anglican" (c. 1889:248).

Taylor's closing word is flung against the Sanskritists. The discoveries of the last decade have overthrown the work of the previous half-century, he says, demolishing ingenious but baseless (philological) theories of race and clearing the ground for the raising of more solid structures. "The whilom tyranny of the Sanskritists is happily overpast, and it is seen that hasty philological deductions require to be systematically checked by the conclusions of prehistoric archaeology, craniology, anthropology, geology, and common sense" (c.1889:332).

In the end, examination of Taylor's version of the meanings of the Aryan idea in late Victorian England yields an unearned increment of understanding of the formation of racist ideologies in Europe generally that was not looked for. It is not my ambition to clarify the story of the Aryan idea on the Continent, but one cannot help seeing that Taylor's reading of the current European, and especially German, scholarship captures the Aryan idea in process of becoming a politically usable and racially exclusive conception in the late nineteenth century. That is, the Aryan idea is now not merely linked to whiteness—that had been so to a degree already in the early Max Müller—but whiteness itself is now narrowed down to some conception of a small, pure, original "white" Aryan race that spread the Indo-European languages to different races in very early times. Thus the Indians came to be excluded from the Aryan concept to which they had supplied the name. That the Indians were excluded from the newly conceptualized originary Aryan race and were now no longer concerned with it was a by-product, of more importance to Britons than to other Europeans, of an argument about the underlying racial strands in the European population. This narrowing of the bounds of whiteness within Europe itself was accomplished by the archaeologists and craniologists, masters of the new race science, developing their own authority claims in *opposition* to the comparative philologists and Sanskritists.

It is only by grasping this crucial development, I believe, that we can unpack the paradox that Aryanness came to be deployed by the Nazi regime to murderous effect not only against the Jews but also against the Gypsies—whose Indian origin and Indo-European linguistic credentials had been conclusively established by philologists and Sanskritists so long previous, and that it expressed no bond of sympathy between Germans and Slavs. The racialization of the Aryan idea made the Aryan race an exclusive group very much smaller than the Indo-European speaking population as a whole.

In the liberal United States Max Müller's theme of Aryan brotherhood fared no better. The Supreme Court decision in *U.S. v. Bhagat Singh Thind* (1923) held that a Punjabi immigrant, although an Aryan, was not a "free white person" within the meaning of the 1917 act governing naturalization, no matter what the Sanskritists and the language-led ethnologies of the experts might argue; it is common usage that determines the intent of Congress in making naturalization available to "free white persons," not the lucubrations of philologists and ethnologists.[4] In this decision the construction of "whiteness" excluded Indians in another way, by disengaging whiteness from (linguistic) Aryanness.

## Against the "Tyranny of the Sanskritists"

Taken together, the British hostility to Sanskrit had two conceptually distinct sources: British Indophobia, which was essentially a developmentalist, progressivist, liberal, and non-racial-essentialist cri-

---

4. *United States v. Bhagat Singh Thind*, 202 U.S. 209–210 (1923). Mr. Justice Sutherland's opinion says, "The words of the statute are to be interpreted in accordance with the understanding of the common man from whose vocabulary they were taken. . . . It may be true that the blond Scandinavian and the brown Hindu have a common ancestor in the dim reaches of antiquity, but the average man knows perfectly well that there are unmistakable and profound differences between them today" (p. 209). The applicant claimed eligibility based on the fact that he is a high-caste Hindu born in the Panjab and is classified by certain scientific authorities as of Caucasian or Aryan race. But the term *Aryan* has to do with linguistic, not physical characteristics, and under scientific manipulation *Caucasian* has come to include far more than the common man supposes. The opinion also invokes the race-mixture theory of Indian civilization: "In the Punjab and Rajputana, while the invaders seem to have met with more success in the effort to preserve their racial purity, intermarriages did occur, producing an intermingling of the two and destroying to a greater or less degree the purity of the 'Aryan' blood" (p. 210). Thus the effect of the racialization of the Aryan theory is to deny the kinship of Indians and Europeans upon a new basis.

tique of Hindu civilization in aid of a program for the improvement of India along European lines; and race science, which theorized the English common-sense view that the Indians, whatever the Sanskritists might say, were a separate, inferior, and *unimprovable* race—in this they were often likened to the Irish by the purveyors of this way of thinking. But although conceptually distinct and logically incompatible, the two sources often combined in an unstable and volatile mixture, forming the attitude that said to the people of India, "Admire us; emulate us; become like us," then added, "but you can never be one of us."

An index of that hostility is the marginal position that Orientalism held in Britain throughout the nineteenth century. The teaching of Sanskrit and modern Indian languages had been institutionalized at an early date, first at the College of Fort William and then at the East India College. But it planted no roots in the universities for quite some time. The Oxford chair was established not through the initiative of the university but by a private benefaction, from James Boden in 1827, to promote the translation of the Bible into Sanskrit, and it was not filled (by H. H. Wilson) until 1832. A professorship of Sanskrit at University College, London, was held as early as 1852 by Theodor Goldstücker. Edinburgh (in 1862) and Cambridge (in 1867) created chairs of Sanskrit only after Haileybury was closed in 1858, leaving civil service training to the universities, and Edinburgh's was created by the private endowment of the noted British-Indian Sanskritist John Muir. Friedrich Max Müller pursued efforts to create a school of Oriental studies throughout his life to no effect,[5] and London University's School of Oriental and African Studies opened its doors only in 1917, when the British Indian empire had passed its zenith and had little more three decades of life remaining.

I would not wish to diminish the very real accomplishments of the

---

5. In an autobiography Max Müller recalls a youthful visit to Macaulay, who said that he wanted to know all Max Müller had to say on the real advantages to be derived by young Civil Service members from study of Sanskrit. Without waiting for his answer Macaulay

began to relate his own experiences in India, dilating on the difference between a scholar and a man of business, giving a full account of his controversy while in India with men like Professor Wilson and others, who maintained that English would never become the language of India, expressing his own strong conviction to the contrary, and relating a number of anecdotes, showing that the natives learnt English far more easily than the English could ever learn Hindustani or Sanskrit. Then he branched off into some disparaging remarks about Sanskrit literature, particularly about their legal literature, entering minutely into the question of what authority could be assigned to the Laws of Manu, and of what possible use they could be in determining lawsuits between natives, ending

British Sanskritists, which were considerable. Succeeding to the brilliant opening generations of Jones, Wilkins, Colebrooke, Wilson, Prinsep, Hamilton, and Ellis were many fine scholars in British India such as A. C. Burnell, the South India hand, a man of vast learning; Robert Childers, the Pali scholar; John Muir, whose compendia of Sanskrit sources on early Indian history and social institutions served to consolidate the new theory of India's history; and the epigraphists John Faithful Fleet, Benjamin Rice, and Walter Elliot. We find others in the metropole whose scholarship deserves our admiration, such as E. B. Cowell, Thomas and Caroline Rhys Davids, Arthur Anthony Macdonell, and Arthur Barriedale Keith, to name a few of the several dozen British Sanskritists. Nevertheless it is striking that foreign Sanskritists played prominent and distinguished roles both in the institutions of British India (e.g., Georg Bühler, Martin Haug, Eugen Hultzsch, Franz Keilhorn, and Heinrich Lüders) and in British universities (Theodor Aufrecht and Julius Eggeling at Edinburgh, Theodor Goldstücker at U.C. London, and, of course, Friedrich Max Müller at Oxford). German overproduction of Sanskritists was one part of the picture; British underproduction the other. In a way, Max Müller's situation was emblematic: He was allowed to represent Sanskrit, in his person, as a foreign kind of learning, but not to reproduce it on British soil by teaching it to Britons.

While the teaching of Oriental languages flourished in Europe, especially in the Germanies and in France, it limped along in Britain. So far from there being a thick institutionalized connection between Orientalism and empire, as readers of Said might be led to imagine, one could say, roughly, that the study of Sanskrit varied *inversely* with imperialism, certainly when Britain and Germany are compared. It is as if the British had been persuaded by James Mill's preposterous argument that ignorance of Indian languages was a positive aid to the formation of unclouded views on imperial policy.

---

up with the usual diatribes about the untruthfulness of the natives of India, and their untrustworthiness as witnesses in a court of law. (Max Müller 1898:162)

This monologue went on for about an hour, and at the conclusion of "this so-called conversation" Macaulay thanked Max Müller for the useful information he had given him. Max Müller reflects on the perverse disinclination of the English to support their Oriental empire with a school for teaching Oriental languages (unlike the French, Italians, Prussians, Austrians and Russians), having closed down Haileybury. He characterizes the governing attitude thus: "We can always find interpreters if we pay them well, and if we only speak loud enough the natives never fail to understand what we mean" (the same).

CHAPTER 7

# The Racial Theory
# of Indian Civilization

Around 1850 one begins to hear voices, soon swelling to a chorus, expressing the belief that language and race do not necessarily correlate. "Language no test of race," the title of a paper delivered before the British Association in 1858 (cited in Muir 1874–84, 2:277), epitomizes the rising theme, the new Big Idea of the day. It is an idea that has become so normalized for later generations that it takes an effort of the historical imagination for us to recapture the power it had for its first audience, the sense of a long hidden error suddenly exposed to public scrutiny. The abrupt decoupling of race and language was a reaction against the Aryan idea itself, especially against the assertion that Indians were kin to Europeans, and it attacked the authority of the comparative philologists and Sanskritists. Their proofs of the racial unity of the Indians and Europeans had henceforth to be qualified and drawn back to meet the new skepticism. We see the effects of this new skepticism in John Muir's influential collection, *Original Sanskrit texts on the origin and history of the people of India*. In the first edition (1858ff.) he had argued from the evidence of language that the Indians were kin to the Europeans on grounds that "affinity in language implies affinity in race" and went on to demonstrate that "there is no objection arising from physiological considerations, *i.e.* from colour or bodily structure, to classing the Hindus among the Indo-European races." But in the second edition (1868–73), in response to criticism, he scaled that back to the view that "affinity in language affords *some presumption* of affinity in race" (emphasis added) and treated it as a question of whether physiological considerations prevented classing the Indians among the Indo-

European races (Muir 1874–84, 2:277–286). The retreat of the Sanskritists had begun.

That a truth which to us is obvious and commonplace had to be articulated with such force tells us two things. It tells us that the belief in the correlation of language and race had been for a very long time an unexamined assumption, governing in fact the previous half-century of ethnological writing, whose signature was the subordination of physical traits to linguistic ones and to the method of compiling word lists in the enterprise of forming ethnological classifications. And it tells us that the accumulating strain in the relation between linguistic and physical-anthropological methods was now driving the two apart. Increasingly, the authority claims of race science were being advanced against the authority of philology in general and the Sanskritists in particular.

We have seen in the last chapter how the revolt of race science against "the whilom tyranny of the Sanskritists" ended the subordination of human physiology to language within the conversation that constituted British ethnology. I do not wish to leave the impression that the race science crowd were the bad guys and the Sanskritists the good guys. The disarticulation of race and language was not a solution but a problem, and the problematizing of that relation at mid-century meant that Sanskritists as well as race science types had to reconsider what the relation was in fact, more especially the relation of race to the Indo-European concept. In this reconsideration racial essentialism found a place at the heart of the work of the British Sanskritists in the formation of what I call the racial theory of Indian civilization.

One of the many signs of the times is the way in which the terms of the discussion had changed. *Nation* and *race* had so changed their meanings that it is scarcely paradoxical to say that they are nineteenth-century inventions. *Nation, race,* and *stock* in the writings of Sir William Jones are words which are approximately equivalent, and *nation* is preferred as the name of the unit of ethnological discourse. In Jones's anniversary discourses the subject of world history is the nation, but the word means something quite different from what it means to us. Our present-day sense that popular sovereignty is the only legitimate basis for political authority, to which governments of all kinds appeal (even ones that are very unpopular in fact), has been immensely influential and by now has become nearly universal. The success of the concept of the people's will as the source of sovereignty—the only legitimate source—has imbued the idea of nation with the sense that it is the necessary precondition of the state, and makes the state the political destiny of the nation. In Jones's time, however, the nation-state was just being invented, and the surcharge of political significance that comes with it had not yet invaded the idea of nation. For Jones, *nation* had on the one hand a genealogical aspect, an aspect of codescent and membership by birth, whence he speaks interchangeably of the Indian nation, stock, or race. On the other hand, he also speaks interchangeably of the Indian or Hindu nation, giving a religious tincture to the idea of nation. It reminds us that the nation is the unit of the story in the English Bible upon which his style of ethnology is based. *Nations* in the English Bible answer to *ethnoi,* the Greek translation of the Old Testament, and the Hebrew word *goyim,* that is, the gentiles or heathens. The sense that the largest ethnological units are the great religions remains strong as late as the works of James Mill, as we have seen. A final difference between current and older senses of the word *nation* is the segmentary character of the nation idea at the beginning of the British-Indian period, by which Colebrooke, as we have seen, finds it natural to speak of the ten polished nations of India, which itself is a nation. By comparison, we would have to say that the modern idea of nation does not have this relativistic, contextualist character; it is, we may say, substantialist. All these differences taken together account for the curious fact that at the beginning of their Indian empire the British regularly referred to the Indians as a nation, and at the end of it, as Indian nationalists were laying claim to independence, they were denying that Indians constituted what could properly be called a nation. Much the same is true of British writings on Egypt over the same period. Thus, to catch the Jonesean sense of *nation* we must empty it of the political content it acquired through nationalism.[1]

*Race* changes meaning too, and equally drastically. As *nation* comes to have a heightened political significance, *race* becomes less interchangeable with it and takes on a more specialized meaning, coming to signify the visible, physical characteristics of the human body—or rather, to stand for that invisible entity of which the physical characters are the signs and upon which the taxonomist depends in the making of classifications. The most telling changes to the conception of race came about through the double revolution that overtook British intellectual life be-

---

1. Similarly, American Indian groups were regularly called nations in eighteenth-century writings in English, but they were increasingly referred to as tribes in the nineteenth century. Nationalist leaders of today are reviving the word *nation,* imbuing it with a political content (nation-state as the teleology of the nation) that it did not have in the earlier usage.

ginning in the late 1850s: the revolution in ethnological time, and the Darwinian revolution.

Up to about 1860 most learned opinion in Britain, and in Europe generally (some notable skeptics apart), adhered to a short chronology for human history that was based on the Bible. By the chronology of Archbishop Ussher, which prevailed in Britain, the world and the life within it had been created in 4004 B.C. Although early in the nineteenth century geologists had begun developing a timeline for earth history and for the history of fossilized plants and animals that was not constrained within this narrow limit, the ethnological time in which the human species diversified and covered the earth remained within the short Biblical chronology until the discovery of human remains in association with long-extinct animal forms forced the issue. The Brixham Cave excavation of 1859 was the breakthrough event. More or less simultaneously, Darwin's *On the origin of species* (1859) appeared and precipitated vast changes in the story of living forms.

The new Orientalism had come into existence under the short chronology, and it explored an India whose culture of time could not have been more different, positing vast cycles of time through which the world had passed. As a Muslim scholar of the eleventh century had noted, Hindus did not even believe in creation as such, since the world was made anew of the "same clay" from the ruin of the old, after its dissolution (al-Bīrūnī 1964:321–322). After a period of experimentation during which several British-Indian writers took up the idea of a longer chronology suggested by Indian ideas of world time, Jones more or less established the terms upon which the Oriental renaissance was based, rejecting Indian time in favor of Biblical time, but in every other respect drawing upon Indian antiquities as independent evidence of the truth of the Biblical narrative. The effect of rejecting the vast timeframe proper to ancient Sanskrit literature, and of situating that literature within the short chronology of the Bible, was to make of that literature, most especially the Veda as its oldest work, one of the earliest testimonies of human life, of "man's primitive state" and of "primitive monotheism" in the original meaning of the word *primitive*. It was specifically within a short Biblical timeframe that India and the Veda acquired their heightened significance for Europeans as a window upon the original condition of mankind and of ancient wisdom.

The breaking open of the short chronology for human history and the new Darwinian reading of the history of biological forms had a variety of effects in the minds of Europeans, of which the leading one as it concerns our subject was that India's ancient literature was no longer a testament of the primitive state and was now seen to be quite recent in human history; the period of Indo-European origin of which it was the oldest evidence was no longer at the beginning of the human story. As a long period of prehistory opened out behind the oldest written records—the Veda, the Greek and Latin classics, and the Bible—the Ancients suddenly became very young, Indians among them. At the same time it became increasingly clear that the formation of races followed a much slower tempo than the formation of language families, putting strains on an ethnology that attempted to correlate race and language. In a curious way, even as Darwinism made it clear that race was not fixed and permanent, the deepening time of race formation acted to solidify the idea of race as an entity independent of language, an entity that was far more durable and had a far deeper history.[2]

The paradox of these developments is that in spite of the growing distrust between Sanskritists and race science, the two sides of an often noisy dispute nevertheless collaborated, without really meaning to, in the creation of an enduring synthesis, what I call the racial theory of Indian civilization. By this I mean the theory, which by century's end had become a settled fact, that the constitutive event for Indian civilization, the Big Bang through which it came into being, was the clash between invading, fair-skinned, civilized Sanskrit-speaking Aryans and dark-skinned, barbarous aborigines. It was a local application of the double binary that guided all nineteenth-century European ethnologies, the double binary of the fair and the dark, the civilized and the savage. We can best explore this formation through the leading representatives of the sides of this fraught relation: Friedrich Max Müller and H. H. Risley.

## Friedrich Max Müller on Language and Race

Max Müller's dictum that the same blood ran in the veins of the soldiers of Clive as in the veins of the dark Bengalese, as a finding

2. On the time revolution, see Trautmann 1992b; on the deepening of race history and persistence of polygenist thought after Darwin, see Stocking 1968:chap. 3.

of philology, was much attacked for the very good reason that identifying race ("blood") with language and pitting them against complexion was a direct provocation to a nascent race science in which complexion was at the forefront. Max Müller had surely gone too far in
asserting the claims of language, and the very year in which that provocation was issued (1854) he began his retreat, proposing something like
a nonaggression pact between the two sciences according to which each
would go about its business without interfering with the other. This
theme, which appears in his writings with increasing frequency, develops into direct opposition to a racial conception of the Aryan, a rejection of the idea of "dolichocephalic languages" and the like.

But for purposes of elucidating Max Müller's unintended collaboration with Risley in the working out of an ethnological master narrative
for India, I must begin at the beginning. The foundational text is Max
Müller's long contribution to Christian Bunsen's *Outlines of the philosophy of universal history, applied to language and religion* (1854a), which
is concerned with the "last results of the researches respecting the non-
Iranian and non-Semitic languages of Asia and Europe, or the Turanian
family of languages" (1854:263). In the course of his exposition he considers the evidence advanced by Hodgson and Stevenson concerning an
"aboriginal" element in the Indian population and its languages, the
element that Hodgson called "Tamulian," which Max Müller regarded
as a section of the larger "Turanian" group.

In a section titled "Ethnology v. phonology," Max Müller asserts
that the proper relation between the two sciences in question should
be one of providing each other with advice and suggestion, nothing
more, and that much confusion of terms and indistinctness of principles
have come from mixing these "heterogeneous sciences" together: "Ethnological race and phonological race are not commensurate, except in
ante-historical times, or perhaps at the very dawn of history. With the
migrations of tribes, their wars, their colonies, their conquests and al-
liances . . . it is impossible to imagine that race and language should
continue to run parallel." The physiologist should study skulls, hair
color, and complexion but be deaf to language, and the phonologist
should collect his evidence and arrange it into classes "as if no Blumenbach had ever looked at skulls, as if no Camper had measured facial angles, as if no Owen had examined the basis of a cranium" (Max Müller
1854a:349). The phonologist will not scruple to classify the English language with the Low German as Teutonic even though the physiologist
informs him that the skull is of Celtic type or the family arms are Nor-

man. He adds that although ethnological suggestions of an early substratum of Celtic inhabitants in Britain and historical information as
to a Norman conquest will be useful, the phonologist can detect the
resulting admixture of languages in English without this outside help.
"With the phonologist, English is Teutonic, and nothing but Teutonic,
and that because what we may call its soul—the grammar—is Teutonic"
(1854:350).

Applying this reasoning to India, Max Müller goes on to argue, the
phonologist needs no physiological or historical evidence to determine
that the languages of India were not derived from one uniform language. The ethnological division of the inhabitants of India into Aryan
and non-Aryans was at first chiefly based on linguistic evidence without
recourse to physical features. Thereupon, tribes speaking languages deriving from Sanskrit were set down as Aryans; others speaking non-
Sanskritic languages were classified as of the Turanian race. This has
led to confusion and futile controversy, he says. On the one hand it is
undeniable that millions of people in North India speak modern languages descended from Sanskrit, although they are decidedly "Tamulian" in physical type; on the other hand it is equally certain that
many brahmins of the Deccan, now speaking Dravidian languages,
were of Aryan extraction. This has led to the error of trying to prove
that the Bengali and Hindustani languages have a "Tamulian" grammar, or, in an opposite direction, that the tribes speaking Assamese, a
Sanskritic dialect, "had Caucasian blood in their veins, and were Cau-
casians modified and deteriorated by the influence of climate and diet"
(the same).

But although the majority of people who speak Bengali may be of Tamulian
extraction, does it follow that the grammar of their language is Tamulian?
Or does it follow that the original inhabitants of Asam were Arians, because
the language at present spoken in that country is Sanskritic in its grammar?
(1854:351)

The answer is in both cases plainly "no," and in reaching this conclusion
Max Müller as plainly cancels his provocative statement about the racial
brotherhood of the soldiers of Clive and the dark Bengalese.

In another section of this text, however, Max Müller just as plainly
violates his own edict of separation and investigates what historical
traces of the aboriginal races of India (for whom he proposes the label
Niṣāda instead of Hodgson's Tamulian) in the *Ṛg Veda*. He was at that
time engaged in preparing the first published edition of the *Ṛg Veda*,

and his discussion of this topic therefore carried a great deal of authority and served to set the direction of discussion for a very long time.

The ethnological facts Max Müller gathers from the *Ṛg Veda* are few
and modestly put forward. The four castes, Brāhmaṇa, Kṣatriya, Vaiśya,
and Śūdra preexisted the collection of the *Ṛg Veda* (RV), and (according to later, Brāhmaṇa texts) only the first three are Aryan, the Śūdra
being an-ārya. In addition to the four castes are frequent allusions to
the Dasyus, a name which means simply "enemy" as, for example, when
Indra is praised because he destroyed the Dasyus and protected the Aryan "color" (*varṇa*). The Dasyus of the *Ṛg Veda* mean non-Aryan races
in many hymns, but it is not always clear that this is meant. Other epithets that are applied to barbarous nations or wild tribes are "devil" in
the sense of "giant" and "barbarian" (*rakṣas*); "they who do not keep
the fire" (*anagnitra*); and flesh-eaters, that is, "eaters of raw meat"
(*kravyād*). "All these epithets seem to apply to hostile, and most likely
aboriginal races, but they are too general to allow us the inference of
any ethnological conclusions." The composers of the Vedic hymns certainly distinguish between Aryan and non-Aryan enemies, but "there is
no allusion to any distinct physical features such as we find in later writings" (1854:344–345). He then tentatively offers a possible reference to
a difference of noses (I normalize the transliteration of Sanskrit words):

The only expression that might be interpreted in this way is that of "suśipra," as applied to Arian gods. It means "with a beautiful nose." As people
are fain to transfer the qualities which they are most proud of in themselves,
to their gods, and as they do not become aware of their own good qualities
except by way of contrast, we might conclude that the beautiful nose of
Indra was suggested by the flat-noses of the aboriginal races. Tribes with
flat or with even no noses at all, are mentioned by Alexander's companions
in India, and in the hymns of the Rigveda Manu is said to have conquered
Viśiśipra (Pada-text, viśi śipra), which may be translated by "nose-less." The
Dāsa or barbarian is also called vṛṣaśipra in the Veda, which seems to mean
goat or bull-nosed, and the "Anāsas" enemies whom Indra killed with his
weapon (Rv. V,29,10), are probably meant for noseless (a-nāsas), not, as the
commentator supposes, for faceless (an-āsas) people. (1854:346)

This first effort to find direct evidence of the physical features of the
Indian aborigines in the Sanskrit text dating from the time of the Big
Bang that brought Indian civilization into existence, therefore, boiled
down to a matter of noses. Max Müller himself later abandoned his
own interpretation of the word *śipra*, so that the evidence as to noses
was reduced to a single word (*anāsa*) in a single passage (RV 5.29.10),

to which we shall return. But Risley, for quite different reasons, put noses right at the center of his ethnology of India.

## H. H. Risley on Noses

Herbert Hope Risley (1851–1911) was but a toddler when this passage by Max Müller was published, and his rise to eminence as the leading ethnologist of India came much later, in the 1890s, with the publication of his pattern-making *Tribes and castes of Bengal* (1892). Thereafter, as census commissioner he injected ethnological content into the 1901 census, became director of ethnography for India in 1901, published, among many books, *The people of India* in 1908, and became president of the Royal Anthropological Institute in 1910.

Risley was very much the India hand, a member of the Indian Civil Service who served in India from 1873 to 1910. He had a preference for rural India, and his ethnological interests first developed themselves in the surveying of land tenures and the writing of gazetteers. His advocacy of fieldwork is modest but more prophetic than he knew. Writers on ethnology when writing on Indian subjects, he once wrote, rely too much "on mere literary accounts which give an ideal and misleading picture of caste and its social surroundings" (Risley 1891:237). Risley himself would not be so unreasonable as to ask that all ethnographical evidence be gathered at first hand through fieldwork, but he often senses in the writings of European ethnologists that "the writers were a long way removed from the subjects they were dealing with, and had never quite got into touch with their facts." It was not for him "to lay down a course of preliminary training for distinguished ethnologists, and to demand that Mr. Herbert Spencer should get himself enrolled, like Mr. Frank Cushing, in the sacred societies of the Zunis, or that Sir John Lubbock should follow the example of Mr. Lewis Morgan in joining himself to the Iroquois," the prospect of which would perhaps turn people away from the new science. But in ethnology a little firsthand knowledge is a very good thing, "and some slight personal acquaintance with even a single tribe of savage men could hardly fail to be of infinite service to the philosopher who undertakes to trace the process by which civilization has been gradually evolved out of barbarism" (1891:238). Both in his career and in his taste for fieldwork, Risley was as different as can be from Max Müller, which makes their unwilling collaboration all the more intriguing.

Risley's grand syntheses of Indian ethnology are contained in the 1901 census report and in *The people of India*, but a programmatic article on "The study of ethnology in India," published in the *Journal of the Anthropological Institute* (1891), gives an exceptionally clear view of his project at the state of what we might call its early maturity. In this article, Risley opens by deploring "the comparatively scanty use that has been made of the great storehouse of ethnographical data which British rule in India has thrown open to European inquirers" (1891:235). After reviewing the shortcomings of Indian ethnographic literature and its methods he asserts the advantages of India for ethnology, which are mainly two. In the first place, it gives access for scientific study to "the wilder tribes" who, however, have not been exposed to European colonists "which has proved so destructive to the aborigines of Australia and America." Moreover, the so-called non-Aryan races of India show no tendency to disappear and in some parts of India their numbers appear to be on the increase (1891:239).

In the second place, however, not only do "the administrative conditions of the country"—colonialism—lend themselves readily to the collection of evidence, but the caste system of India is so constituted as to render that evidence peculiarly telling (the same). In Europe and elsewhere *métissage* or crossing of races complicates investigation and obscures and confuses the results. In India, however, the institution of caste breaks up the population into mutually exclusive aggregates of homogeneous composition and forbids marriage outside the group. The bond of caste is in fact *race,* and when new occupational specialties arise within a caste the difference of profession leads to a new matrimonial aggregate, "being held by a sort of unconscious fiction to be equivalent to the difference of race, which is the true basis of the system" (1891:240).

The conviction that caste is race, and that the differences among Indian castes and tribes are racial in character, makes Indians uniquely appropriate objects for the newly developing anthropological subscience of anthropometry. The appeal of the new methods is that they might "enable us to detach considerable masses of non-Aryans from the general body of Hindus" and to refer them at the least to the general category of non-Aryans and perhaps to more specific stocks as the Kolarian, Dravidian, Lohitic, Tibetan, and so forth (1891:247).

For the needed injection of improved methods into the ethnological study of India, Risley turns to metropolitan science in the person of Paul Topinard, pupil of Broca and secretary of the Société d'Anthropologie of Paris, and, particularly, to the thousand densely printed pages of Topinard's *Éléments d'anthropologie générale* (1885) with its dozens of anthropometric techniques. From these Risley selects twelve, plus two others (the bimalar and nasomalar dimensions of Oldfield Thomas) under advice from Professor William Flowers. Chief among the measurements that Risley got from Topinard was the nasal index, a ratio of the breadth of the nose to its height, which serves to assign individual noses into leptorrhine (narrow), platyrhine (broad), or mesorhine (medium) classes.

We come again, then, to the matter of noses. Reading through Topinard's treatment one gets the impression that the nature of the exercise is to assess anthropometric methods not according to what new knowledge they yield but by the degree to which they confirm what is already known. By this test the nose is by far the preferred site, as it had been for Geoffroy Saint-Hilaire (Topinard 1885:264), much to be preferred to the uncertain skin color and the confusing results of the study of hair, which puts the Australians with the Europeans. By combining the nasal index of living subjects with the nasal profile and nasal index of the skull, according to Topinard, we can achieve Linnean classifications which we know to be correct:[3]

Lepto (living). White races.
    very lepto (living)            Kymris
    less lepto
        non-aquiline           Celts
        aquiline              Semites

Meso (living). Yellow races.
    nose flattened
        lepto (skull)          Eskimo
        meso (skull)          Yellow races of Asia
    nose prominent          American Indians

Platy (living). Black races.
    nose relatively fine        Negroes of Africa
    nose large, nostrils enormous   Melanesians and Australians

---

3. The nose has a further bonus as ethnographic indicator, according to Topinard: "Encore un avantage que possède le nez: il est le seul caractère qui permette de classer le Sémite" (Topinard 1885:306).

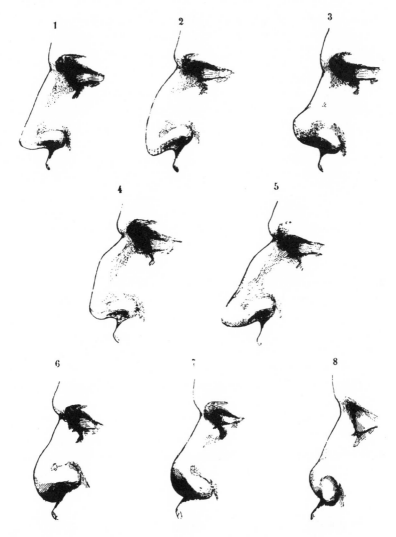

Figure 10. Topinard's types of noses. (From Topinard 1885:298.)

Topinard's scheme is useful both in its exactness of application and in the reassuring way in which it conforms itself to what is already known to be true rather than presenting us with information that requires us to part with existing beliefs. Risley has other reasons to go for the nose, derived from his reading of the received wisdom about the ethnological information contained in the Veda and the unconscious convergence of Max Müller and Topinard:

No one can have glanced at the literature of the subject and in particular at the Vedic accounts of the Aryan advance, without being stuck by the *frequent* references to the noses of the people whom the Aryans found in possession of the plains of India. So impressed were the Aryans with the shortcomings of their enemies' noses that they *often* spoke of them as "the noseless ones," and their keen perception of the importance of this feature seems almost to anticipate the opinion of Dr. Collignon that the nasal index ranks higher as a distinctive character than the stature or even than the cephalic index itself. In taking their nose then as the starting point of our present analysis, we may claim to be following at once the most ancient and the most modern authorities on the subject of racial physiognomy. (1891:249–250, emphasis added)

In doing so he has of course greatly overstated the Vedic evidence; Risley's *frequent* references to the aboriginal nose which he says the Aryans *often* spoke of comes down, as we have already mentioned, to a single passage. Both Risley and Max Müller show a tendency to exaggerate the significance of noses in the ancient Indian evidence.

In Risley, as in Topinard, the purpose is to show the reliability of anthropometric tests by showing that their results conform to existing knowledge. For Risley the conventional wisdom concerns the formation of the Indian population, and his reading of it is a fully racialized one. The standard theory of the making of the Indian people holds that the Aryans, "a tall, fair-complexioned dolicho-cephalic [long-headed] and presumably lepto-rhine race," entered India from the northwest and moved down the great river valleys of north India. At an early stage of this advance they collided with "a black snub-nosed race" who were partly absorbed by the conquerors and partly driven away into Central and South India, where their descendants may still be found (1891:249).

In addition to confirming the standard theory, the new anthropometric methods have a positive contribution of their own, namely to controvert the view of E. T. Dalton and J. F. Hewitt, who "discover among the remnants of the black race two distinct types or groups of tribes, known as the Dravidian and the Kolarian," supposed to have entered India from the northwest and the northeast, respectively (the same). The burden of Risley's paper is to set out statistics of the nasal index going to show that the supposed Dravidian and Kolarian tribal peoples of Santal Parganas and Chota Nagpur are racially identical and differ as a group from narrower-nosed leptorrhines and mesorhines. The evidence of the nasal index establishes the existence in India of two distinct racial types, the one broad-nosed to a degree closely approach-

ing that of the Negro, the other narrow-nosed in much the same measure as people of southern Europe. Between the extremes are intermediate types whose physical characteristics show that they must have
arisen from intermixture of the extreme types and their descendants.
The troublesome and contrary evidence that derives from measuring
crania instead of noses, which puts the Kol with the Aryan, has to be
set aside, and Risley is at pains to argue that "the Kol gets his long head
from the non-Aryan races while the Brahman's dolichocephaly comes
to him from the Caucasian stock" (1891:252). The difference between
Dravidians and Kolarians is merely linguistic, corresponding to no ap-
preciable differences of physical type. Thus anthropometry saves the
unity of the aborigines against the linguists, and sustains a two-race
theory of the making of the Indian people.

The value of the nasal index, then, is that it bifurcates the Indian
population into its two original constituents. But there is more. In identifying the populations that fall between the extremes it tracks the gra-
dations of the caste system, as Risley says in what has become an epi-
gram: "The social position of a caste varies inversely as its nasal index"
(1891:253). Finally, the structure is completed with consideration of Risley's other special preoccupation: totemism, especially exogamous clans
with totemic names, in contrast to exogamous clans named after ancestors typical of caste Hindus. This, too, correlates with the breadth of
the nose. In Bengal proper, castes with a platyrhine index have totemistic exogamous divisions, castes with a leptorrhine index have eponymous clans, and those with nasal indices intermediate between the extremes show a mixture of totemistic, eponymous, and local clans. Thus
the measurement of noses infallibly locates the distinction between
tribes and Hindu castes.

Risley's conclusion is that "community of race, and not, as has frequently been argued, community of function, is the real determining
principle, the true causa causans, of the caste system" (1891:260). The
caste system of India is a highly developed expression of the primitive
principle of tabu when the Aryans first came into peaceful contact with
the so-called Dravidians, a platyrhine race. The tabu derived its initial
force from the difference of race as indicated by difference of skin color.
Its great subsequent elaboration is due to a series of fictions by which
heterogeneous sources of difference (occupation, religion, habitat, tri-
fling departures from the established standard of custom) have been
taken as denoting difference of blood and endogamous groups. Race,
then, is the true origin of caste and the fictional idiom of its continuing

differentiation of units. For Risley, caste is race, in origin and by meta-phorical extension.

## Race and Language in the
## Camp of the Sanskritists

Risley must suffice as example of race science in India, for I now return to the British Sanskritists and their allies to see how race came to figure in their ethnological thinking.

Max Müller had proposed an amicable divorce between the study of language and the study of race, but the divorcing parties had been mar-ried for a long time, and as is so often the case, divorce served not to end the relationship but simultaneously to prolong it and make it very thorny. British Sanskritists could not ignore race and were obliged to come to their own determination about the actual relation of language and race in Indian history. The racial theory of Indian civilization was their construction, a compromise formation that recognized the claims both of language and of race so effectively that it endures to this day. We must now see how it was built.

A good place to start is not with the Sanskritists themselves but with Sir Henry Maine. At the beginning of this book I referred to his 1875 essay, *The effects of observation of India on modern European thought*, in which he expressed the conviction that the evidence of language, more especially the Indo-Europeanist theory emanating from the European encounter with Sanskrit, had revolutionized European ideas about race. Maine never learned Sanskrit, but he was an avid and intelligent con-sumer of the work of the Sanskritists. In his many books on compara-tive law he adopted an essentially Indo-Europeanist frame of reference in which Indian Dharmaśāstra played a large role. What makes his proj-ect useful as an index of the changes that were overtaking the Euro-pean study of India is that all three of the interpretive issues—race, language, and time—are implicated with special clarity.

"From status to contract" was the famous maxim in which Maine epitomized his essentially social-evolutionist project. "Status" referred largely to the statuses conferred through kinship, and accordingly Maine's first book shows how in ancient Rome the statuses deriving from membership in the patriarchal, slave-owning family was the source of most legal relations and how contractual relations that are status-

blind, so to say, arise later and against the claims of the family. This is
his sense of the evolutionary progression of laws.

That first book was called, tellingly, *Ancient law,* and it was published
in 1861. Mostly it speaks of early Roman law, with considerable reference to Greece and slight reference to India; nevertheless, as the unqualified title implies, the movement from status to contract that Maine
finds at Rome has a universal significance and is the evolutionary path
to modernity for human societies generally. I have shown elsewhere that
Maine's own sense of his project at this point was based on the short
chronology and the belief that early Rome was close to the beginning
of human history, such that from it we could learn of the "primitive
condition of man," as the phrase was. The project quickly fell victim
to the newly lengthened chronology for human history that was breaking about the same time (Trautmann 1987:180–186). The result was that
as a long period of human prehistory opened out, the ancient Roman
family law was increasingly seen to be not primitive at all but very recent
in human history. Accordingly Maine redefined his findings as having
to do principally with the Indo-European–speaking peoples, not ancient law in general, and the representative, evolutionary character of
those findings was rendered less certain. His project, then, was now one
of the comparison of the laws of ancient Indo-European legal systems,
conceived as historically related to one another by codescent, modeled
on the way philologists analyzed the Indo-European languages. Having
been posted to India as the Law Member of the colonial government,
his subsequent books became much more comparative, with increasing
amounts of Dharmaśāstra material in them.

As Maine adjusted to the newly enlarged frame of human time, the
place of India within his project of Indo-European comparative law
became larger and more intellectually productive. But it was largely as
a museum of the past of Europe that India exercised its revolutionary
effects upon European thought and contributed to its new theory of
race. That had been true for the first of the British Sanskritists, for Sir
William Jones and his contemporaries at Calcutta. In some ways nothing had changed; in another, everything. By that time the idea of ancient wisdom had been purged from Orientalism and a progressive and
coolly scientific style prevailed; Indomania had long since been margi-
nalized and confined to vegetarian societies, Theosophists, and others
outside the academy.

In Maine, then, the kinship of the early Indo-European–speaking
societies is the working assumption behind a comparison of their laws,

especially as the law affects the family and the "village community" that increasingly fascinates him; within that undoubted kinship, difference is accounted for by a new principle, that some branches of the Indo-European family are progressive, to wit Greece and Rome, and others, especially India, are stagnant and stuck in archaic legal forms. Thus in a curious way the social-evolutionary principle becomes a principle of racial essentialization at the interior of Maine's project.

## The Veda and the Racial Theory of Indian Civilization

The racial theory of Indian civilization was constructed by narrativizing the encounter of the polar opposites of Victorian racial thought, the fair-skinned civilized Aryan and the dark-skinned savage, and by finding evidence for their encounter in the Vedic texts. It was the work of Sanskritists, and British Sanskritists were at the forefront in its construction. The leading texts were those of Max Müller, which I have discussed, and John Muir's *Original Sanskrit texts on the origin and history of the people of India* (1874–84) to which I have alluded. The latter is a very important product of British Sanskrit study, which lays out the new, Orientalist reading of the Indian past with extensive citation of proof texts from Sanskrit literature, meant both as a contribution to European discussion and to propagate the new knowledge among Indians. I will concentrate my attention on a somewhat later text that can be taken as the end point and culmination of the formation of the racial theory of Indian civilization founded upon the study of the Veda, a work that is still much in use. This is the *Vedic index of names and subjects* (1912) of Arthur Anthony Macdonell and Arthur Berriedale Keith.

In all these texts the conception of an aboriginal population of India is given a Vedic foundation by identifying the aborigines with the Dāsas and Dasyus of the Vedic texts, who are the enemies of the Aryans. In the *Vedic index* the difference between the new interpretive frame of the Orientalists and those that preceded is illustrated by references to the interpretations of Sāyaṇa, a commentator on the *Ṛg Veda* of medieval times. When Sāyaṇa wishes to explain a reference to "the black skin" (*kṛṣṇa tvac*) he does so not by reference to racial difference between aborigines and invading Aryans but by assimilating it to the view of the past that is familiar to him, the world of Puranic mythology.

Thus he alludes to a story of a demon (*asura*) named The Black (*kṛṣṇa*) from whom Indra strips "the black skin." For the Orientalists, by contrast, the first interpretive move is not to assimilate the words of a difficult archaic text to a familiar mythological world but rather to *remove* what can be construed as fact from the realm of mythology, to rescue history from myth; indeed the "facts" are constructed by that act, as at the same time the mythological residue is drained of factuality. The Vedic text does not always cooperate, because Dāsas and Dasyus are often described in superhuman form; whence discussion of the question must at the outset address the question of which passages if any may be taken to refer to human beings and to constitute ethnological facts.

We must keep in mind as we approach passages from the *Vedic index* that the language of the Veda is archaic and its meanings are often hard to make out because of its poetic character and religious purpose. Extracting ethnographic facts from sources so recalcitrant and obscure is evidently a difficult enterprise calling for great expert knowledge and a nice judgment. The interpretation of such facts is always subject to a shading up or down, a magnification or a minimizing of their drift. We see this in Risley's reading of the Vedic evidence as to noses, and it shows itself not so much in the substantives as in the adjectives and adverbs: A *single* reference elicited by Max Müller becomes in Risley "the *frequent* references to the noses of the people whom the Aryans found in possession of the plains of India," whom they "*often*" spoke of . . . as 'the noseless ones' " (1891:249–250). I shall, accordingly, talk both of "adjectival" as well as "substantive" aspects of interpretation.

The Orientalists brought many new tools to the interpretation of the Vedic texts that are valuable and that we would not wish to discard, and could not discard if we wished, including the comparative study of Indo-European languages which illuminates the language and, in part, the mythology and ritual of the Veda, and its chronological positioning in relation to other literatures, of which the most salient for Vedic interpretation is the *Avesta* of Iran. Reasons we should read the proof texts of the racial theory of Indian civilization skeptically lie not in faults of method proper to Orientalist production but in the ideas of race on which they draw, ideas that were generally held in Europe, especially in Britain, and in the United States. The racial theory of Indian civilization alludes to racial attitudes of whites toward blacks, found in the segregated southern United States after the Civil War and in South Africa, as a kind of constant of history, or rather as a transcendent fact immune to historical change, that is as operative in the Vedic period as now. We need to keep it in mind that the racial theory of Indian civilization is a formation of the late nineteenth century when, in the wake of slave emancipation, white-black relations in the Anglo-Saxon world were being restructured with ideological support from a rush of racial essentialism.

The argument I should like to make, then, is not that the racial theory of Indian civilization is a fabrication, a tissue of lies, or that the Veda has nothing useful to say (or nothing that we can reasonably draw from it) about the ethnological situation of its time. What I want to show is that the Vedic evidence that has been brought forward has been subjected to a consistent overreading in favor of a racializing interpretation, and that the image of the "dark-skinned savage" is only imposed on the Vedic evidence with a considerable amount of text-torturing, both "substantive" and "adjectival" in character.

We come, then, to its expression in articles of the *Vedic index*. This book is an encyclopedia of historical and sociological knowledge extracted by study of the Vedic texts. It is based on a thorough review of Orientalist research, including especially the work of German Orientalists, but it is at the same time very much a British reading of the Vedic texts and the Orientalist interpretation of them.

We begin with entries for the non-Aryan enemies of the Aryans, the Dasyus or Dāsas. As we review these entries it will be seen that Macdonell and Keith wish to impose the "dark-skinned savage" on what the *Ṛg Veda* says about the Dasyus/Dāsas, but that the text does not entirely cooperate with the two parts of this image: First, darkness of skin was not a salient marker of Dasyu/Dāsa identity to the hymn writers, for whom the most important attributes of these enemies had rather to do with language and religion; the matter of flat noses is limited to a single disputed passage. Second, the Dasyus/Dāsas are depicted as wealthy and powerful opponents, but Macdonell and Keith minimize this evidence and represent them instead as marginal, barbarous hill tribes, consistent with their image of the dark-skinned savage. Here, in summary, are the two relevant articles.

*Dasyu:* The word, though clearly applied to superhuman enemies in many passages of the *Ṛg Veda,* is, in several others, applied to human foes, probably the aborigines, especially in those in which the Dasyu is opposed to the Aryan, who defeats him with the aid of the gods. The great difference between the two is their religion; the Dasyu are styled "not sacrificing," "devoid of rites," "addicted to strange vows," "god-hating," and so forth. That the Dasyu were real people is shown by the epithet *anās* applied to them in one passage of the *Ṛg Veda*. The sense is not absolutely certain; Pada text and Sāyaṇa take it as "without face" (*an+ās*), but "noseless" (*a+nās*) is possible and would accord well with the flat-nosed aborigines of the Dravidian type, whose language still persists among the Brahuis of the northwest. (1912, 1:347–349)

*Dāsa:* Like Dasyu, the word sometimes denotes demonic enemies in the *Ṛg Veda*, but in many passages it refers to human foes of the Aryas. They are described as having forts (*puraḥ*) and clans (*viśaḥ*); the forts, called "autumnal" (*śāradīḥ*) may allude to their being resorted to in the autumn season. The Dāsa color (*varṇa*) is probably an allusion to the black skin of the aborigines, which is also directly mentioned (*kṛṣṇa tvac*, two passages). The aborigines, as Dasyus, are called *anās* "noseless" (?) and *mṛdhravāc*, "of hostile speech," and are probably meant by the phallus-worshipper (*śiśna-devāḥ*, "whose deity is a phallus") of the *Ṛg Veda*. It is significant that constant reference is made to the differences in religion between Aryan and Dāsa or Dasyu. "The wealth of the Dāsas was no doubt considerable, but in civilization there is no reason to suppose that they were ever equal to the invaders." (1912, 1:356–358)

To these we must add the article concerning Śambara, evidently a Dasyu/Dāsa chief.

*Śambara:* An enemy of Indra in the *Ṛg Veda*, called a Dāsa in one passage, said to have deemed himself a godling (*devaka*). "His forts, ninety, ninety-nine, or a hundred in number, are alluded to, the word itself in the neuter plural once meaning 'the forts of Śambara.' His great foe was Divodāsa Atithigva, who won victories over him by Indra's aid. . . . It is impossible to say with certainty whether Śambara was a real person or not. . . . Śambara was quite possibly an aboriginal enemy in India, living in the mountains." (1912, 2:321).

What is remarkable about these articles is the way in which they extract the dark-skinned savage from a very recalcitrant Vedic text. The first half of the image is drawn from a grand total of two passages referring to dark skin and a single one interpreted to mean "flat-nosed" against ancient authorities. But, as the articles themselves make abundantly clear, the significant social markers separating Aryas from Dāsas or Dasyus for the writers of the texts are religion, above all, and language, while complexion is barely mentioned. The second half of the image, savagery, is completely contrary to the evidence of wealth and many forts possessed by these enemies, which the authors dismiss without evidence. The image of them as mountaineers is perhaps constructed on the interpretation of "autumnal" (a word that has never been satis-factorily explained) in relation to forts; it in any case draws upon the prevailing notions that the mountaineers or hill tribes of contemporary India are the non-Aryan aborigines.

There is yet the word *varṇa*, which is critical to the theory that caste is race. The ordinary meaning of the word is "color," but it is also the word for the four main castes or estates of the Indian social system: *Brāhmaṇa* ("priest"), *Kṣatriya* ("warrior"), *Vaiśya* ("yeoman farmer" or "merchant"), and *Śūdra* ("dependent laborer"). These four are evi-dently not racially different among themselves, so it is by no means ob-vious how *varṇa* can signify complexion. But Max Müller in the 1854 piece discussed previously had constructed a racial reading of the sec-ond use of *varṇa* by combining two facts: The first is that the first three *varṇas* are called the "twice-born" because their males take the Vedic initiation and have the religious competence to offer sacrifice, in con-trast to the "once-born" Śūdra. In some later texts the "twice-born" are contrasted with the Śūdra as Aryan to non-Aryan. The second fact is that the *Ṛg Veda* contains mention of the *Ārya-varṇa* in contrast with the *Dāsa-varṇa*. Putting these two points together he concludes that *varṇa* in reference to human social categories indicates a difference of complexion between Aryas and Dāsas.

This interpretation is elaborated upon by Macdonell and Keith in the corresponding article, which I give at some length (in paraphrase) in view of its importance:

*Varṇa*: The word (lit. "color") in the *Ṛg Veda* is applied to denote classes of men, the Dāsa and the Ārya Varṇa being contrasted, as (two) other pas-sages show, on account of color. A footnote adds that there is no trace in Vedic literature of any real distinction of color save this main one, Arya v. Dāsa. There is a later, heraldic sense in which colors are assigned to the social groups called *varṇas*, the authors citing passages giving the brahmin's color as white (*Gopatha Brāhmaṇa*), the *vaiśya* as white and the *rājanya* as swarthy (*Kathaka Saṃhitā*); "and the later view makes the four castes black, yellow, red and white respectively."

The ultimate cause of the extreme rigidity of the caste system probably comes from the sharp distinction drawn from the beginning between the Aryan and the Śūdra. The Vedic Indians felt a sharp contrast to exist be-tween themselves and the conquered population, and which probably origi-nated from the difference of color between the upper and the lower classes, and it tended to accentuate "the natural distinctions of birth, occupation and locality which normally existed among the Aryan Indians, but which among other Aryan peoples never developed into a caste system like that of India." The doctrine of hypergamy marks the practical working of the caste system, and seems clearly to point to the feeling that Aryan males could marry Śūdra females but not the reverse. This distinction probably lies at the back of all other divisions, its force being illustrated by "the peculiar state of feeling as to mixed marriages" in the South of the United States and in South Africa, or even in India itself, "between the new invaders from Europe and the mingled population which now peoples the country." "Marriages between persons of the white and the dark race are disapproved in principle, but varying degrees of condemnation attach to (1) the marriage of a man of the white race with a woman of the dark race; (2) an informal connexion between these two; (3) a marriage between a woman of the white race and a man of the dark race; and (4) an informal connexion between these two. Each category, on the whole, is subject to more severe reprobation than the preceding one. This race element, it would seem, is what has converted social divisions into castes." There appears to be a large element of truth in the theory of Risley and others that explains caste as mainly a matter of blood, and holds that the higher the caste, the greater the proportion of Aryan blood. (1912, 2:247–271)

In this fantastic back-projection of systems of racial segregation in the American South and in South Africa onto early Indian history, the relations of the British "new invader from Europe" with the peoples of India is prefigured thousands of years before by the invading Aryans. But what the British encountered was not their Aryan brethren, as Max Müller wanted to have it, but a "mingled population" toward whom a supposed perduring prejudice of whites against interracial sexual relations (or rather a perduring mixture of repulsion and desire) structured those relations in a certain, hypergamous way. We witness here the closing steps in the development of a conception of racial whiteness.

## Back to the Veda

Let us briefly examine the evidence of the *Ṛg Veda*, and make the experiment of subjecting it to an evaluation that is minimizing and skeptical in respect of the racializing interpretations that have prevailed and prevail still. I can be brief, for, as we have seen, the evidence of the *Ṛg Veda* amounts to three passages. I begin with the matter of noses.

Returning to Max Müller's passage cited previously, we find that he himself later abandoned the meaning "nose" for *śipra,* upon which he had constructed evidence of a physical contrast between the Aryan and the Dasyu/Dāsa (*suśipra,* "with a beautiful nose," of the gods; *Viśiśipra,* "noseless," proper name of someone conquered by Manu; *vṛṣaśipra,* "bull-nosed," applied to Dāsas) (RV 1891:301–302); *śipra* is now "jaws" and *suśipra* "posessed of strong jawbones." By the time of the *Vedic index,* the initial interpretation is completely exploded: *Śipra* is "a word of somewhat uncertain sense: it seems to mean 'cheeks' in several passages; in others it appears to designate the 'cheek-pieces' of a helmet, or of the 'bit' of a horse," and taking the authorities, ancient and modern, together give its meaning variously as cheek, lip, jaw, and nose (Macdonell and Keith 1912, 2:s.v. *śipra*).

And so the supposed noselessness of the Dasyu/Dāsa comes to rest upon Max Müller's interpretation of a single passage, *Ṛg Veda* 5.29.10. In this verse Indra with his weapon kills the Dasyus who are described as *anāsaḥ* and *mṛdhravācaḥ.* Sāyaṇa, whose commentary Max Müller published with his edition of the *Ṛg Veda* text, analyzes the first as *an+ās-,* that is, a-privative followed by *ās,* "face, mouth," which by metonymy stands for *śabda,* "speech." Thus the Dasyus are "without speech," coordinate with *mṛdhravāc,* which Sāyaṇa glosses as *hiṃsitavāgiṃdriyān,* "having defective organs of speech." Now Sāyaṇa's commentary is by no means infallible, but at the very minimum it goes to show that a learned Indian commentator of the Middle Ages did not understand the Dasyus to be described as "noseless, i.e. flat-nosed," which itself tends against the significance of noses for ancient Indian ethnological notions. What is more, Sāyaṇa's explanation of the half-verse in question is rather good and convincing, as it coordinates the two characterizations of the Dasyu. As H. H. Wilson said in rejecting Max Müller's interpretation, the word possibly alludes "to the uncultivated dialects of the barbarous tribes, barbarism and uncultivated speech being identical, in the opinion of the Hindus, as in the familiar term for a barbarian, *mlechchha,* which is derived from the root *mlechchh,* to speak rudely" (*Ṛg Veda* 1854–57, 3:276 n.). Thus there is good reason to assimilate the expression in question into the well-known obsession with proper Sanskrit speech as an ethnic marker, abundantly evident in the *Ṛg Veda* itself.

That leaves the two passages that speak of hostile persons of black skin (*kṛṣṇa tvac*), *Ṛg Veda* 1.130.8 and 6.40.1. Here as elsewhere in the *Ṛg Veda* it is unmistakable that the verses in question are describing enemies of the Aryans and of their gods in the most unflattering terms.

But it is not always clear whether the persons being described are human or supernatural. Sāyaṇa takes the first of the passages to refer to a legend according to which a demon (*asura*) named Kṛṣṇa ("The Black"), having advanced with ten thousand followers to the banks of the Aṃśumati River where he caused great devastation, was defeated and stripped of his skin by Indra, who had been sent with his Maruts by Bṛhaspati. Thus even accepting that the Dasyus/Dāsas are human enemies of the Aryans—which does not seem to be doubtful—some uncertainty attaches to the substance of the racial interpretation. Beyond that, even if the racial interpretation is right on this point substantively, it is wrong adjectivally, since the two passages on skin color are very few on which to base a theory of a systematic color prejudice and, in salience, are far outweighed by references to the shortcomings of the Dasyus/Dāsas in respect of religion and language.

At most, then, the racial interpretation of the relation between Aryans and Dasyus/Dāsas in the *Ṛg Veda* appears to have two verses in its support. But there is also the question of *varṇa* which, as I have said, is the ordinary Sanskrit word for "color." The proponents of the racial interpretation have been unable to bring forward a single passage in the entire body of Sanskrit literature that comes after the *Ṛg Veda* that shows that the system of four *varṇas* is based upon color of skin, or that *varṇa* in this context is given any other color-related significance than a heraldic one. Since usage rather than etymology must be our guide to meaning, it is evident that *varṇa* in this sense means, as Monier-Williams's dictionary has it, "class of men, tribe, order, caste." It is quite clear, then, that skin color would not have come into Orientalist discussion of the four *varṇas* but for the fact that in the *Ṛg Veda* we find mention of the Ārya-varṇa in contrast with the Dāsa-varṇa. But here again usage does not show that skin color is in question, and *varṇa* could as well mean no more than "class of men," "tribe," and so forth, in the absence of corroborating reference to skin color in such passages. We find once more that there is a doubt as to whether the racial interpretation is correct substantively, and it is in any case clear that it is wrong adjectivally.

In sum, without adopting an excessive degree of skepticism, this brief experiment of subjecting the evidence for the racial interpretation of Indian civilization to a minimizing reading shows just how soft that evidence is and gives some gauge as to the amount of overreading upon which it rests.

But, readers may ask, is not the minimizing interpretation guilty of the opposite fault, of underreading the evidence for color prejudice? That Indians of all historical periods took an interest in variations of complexion can be amply documented. Madhav Deshpande, for example, cites a passage from Pantañjali's *Mahābhāṣya* to the effect that a brahmin is *gaura*, "fair," and that no dark person can normally be identified as a brahmin (Deshpande 1993:chap. 6). He gives a fascinating view of the complexion geography of India in Rājaśekhara's *Kāvyamī-māṃsa*, according to which the people of northern India are *gaura*, "fair," those of eastern India are *śyāma*, "dusky," those of the south are *kṛṣṇa*, "dark," and those of the west are *pāṇḍu*, "pale, yellowish-white," whereas the people of the Middle Country are a mixture of *gaura*, *śyāma* and *kṛṣṇa*. Indian preference for a bride of fair complexion is attested in texts as ancient as *Vāsiṣṭha Dharma Sūtra* (18.18) and as recent as the matrimonial advertisements in last Sunday's newspaper. In the face of this and similar evidence it would seem foolish to argue against the entrenched racial interpretation.

It is important not to be misled by this evidence. That Indians have a lively interest in complexion is not in doubt, nor that Indians generally prize a fair complexion over a dark one. Complexion is not race in and of itself, but it may be *construed* as a *sign* of race; what is in question is whether complexion was in fact taken by the authors of the Veda to characterize large and opposed groups that we may call races. The racial interpretation of Indian civilization says that it was, and in examining its case we become aware not only that its makers overread the evidence but also that they did so out of a sense of the objective character of race, especially of white and black races, and of the permanent, transhistorical nature of certain attitudes of whites toward blacks. It is this belief that justified taking the Jim Crow system of the American South and the segregation of South Africa as evidence of the reactions, deemed natural, of Aryans to Dasyus thousands of years earlier.

My minimizing interpretation of the same evidence has its deeper roots in a view that race is socially constructed, that it is not objective but conventional, and that, therefore, it has a contingent, historical character that is not perduring but governed by forces in play at a given time. That is not to deny that variation of complexion has an existence independent of the observer, but so far as history is concerned, what is important is how those features are read and socially construed by humans. They are or are not construed racially for a host of contingent reasons which it is the business of scholarship to try to identify. It is with this changing sense of what race is that the racial interpretation of Indian civilization is increasingly out of step. The view I propose does not, it is true, entirely rule out that a difference of complexion between Aryan and Dasyu may have existed, but it insists at the least that in the *Ṛg Veda* text the social construction of the difference stresses language and religion, and that complexion, if it is in fact referred to, has little salience.

The evidentiary base of the racial theory of Indian civilization was never very firm, and subsequent developments have only served to weaken it further. Its great appeal for Europeans had been that it attributed the civilizing of India to peoples related to themselves. But, by the 1920s, it became plain that mounds of old brick being excavated in the Indus valley were the remains of an urban civilization that was older than the chronological horizon of the Veda. The discovery of the Indus Civilization should have put paid to the racial theory of Indian civilization. Coordinating the evidence of archaeology and textual study is never easy and what successors to the Indus Civilization may have been meant by the Vedic expressions "Dāsa" and "Dasyu" is uncertain, but it is clear enough from the texts themselves that these peoples were in some ways more economically advanced. What is more, race science has completely changed its nature since the 1950s; the evidence that races shade imperceptibly into one another is no longer resisted by appeal to ideal-type races, such that the races (as technical constructs of biology, and not the social entities we have been discussing) themselves have only a fleeting and statistical shape, and the correlation between race and civilization is given up as a bad job. That the racial theory of Indian civilization still lingers is a miracle of faith.

Is it not time we did away with it? I should like to suggest that the concept of race does nothing to illuminate our understanding of the ancient sources of Indian history and, on the contrary, has only served to corrupt our reading of them. What we know of the human resources out of which Indian civilization was built includes the following: We know that Sanskrit was brought to India from without and was spoken by people calling themselves Arya. We know that in India Sanskrit speakers encountered the speakers of distinct language families, including the Dravidian and the Austro-Asiatic. We know that there is a variety of complexions and physical features in the population of the Subcontinent today, and we grant that it is a perfectly legitimate scientific activity to study such variation. But, as has been argued since the 1850s, there is no necessary connection between race and language, or between race and civilization, so of what value is "race" as a biological concept for history? What we need to know is whether ancient Indians socially constructed "races" in the way Macdonell and Keith assumed they did, that is, like "whites" in the American South or in South Africa. I suggest that they did not. It was Macdonell and Keith who engaged in a project of social construction, and the construct is that of a changeless racial "whiteness" accompanied by changeless attitudes toward nonwhites.

For Britons and Americans it is different. "Race" and "race relations" are meaningful terms with which they talk about the socially constructed "races" in their populations. But when they go to India, Britons and Americans cannot help being struck that these expressions disappear and that their functional equivalents in Indian discourse are "communities" and "communalism." The markers of such communities are language, religion, and caste, but not complexion. Why then project an alien discourse onto the distant Indian past? It is more than three passages of the *Ṛg Veda,* one of them of disputed significance, can reasonably be said to prove.

# CHAPTER 8

# Epilogue

Before bringing this essay to a close there are three remaining issues that I should like to touch on even though I cannot hope to do them justice in this brief coda. The first is the relation of the people of India to all of this. The second has to do with the social construction of race. The third is the question of what of value remains of the accomplishments of the British Sanskritists.

## Indians and the New Orientalism

We have been examining British ideas about the place of India. These ideas were dialogically constructed by Britons and Indians, subject to British guiding purposes, but Indian purposes governed the way Indians read the Orientalist scholarship in which they collaborated, of which they were consumers, or which they produced themselves. It is time to consider what is in some ways the more important question of the meaning of Orientalism to Indians and how the interaction of British Sanskritists and Indian scholars produced both shared and opposed meanings.

At the opening of the book I referred to the contradictory images of Orientalism one finds in Proust and in Said. Is the Orientalist an academic dry old stick, pursuing an obscure subject that no one cares about? Or is the Orientalist the intellectual spearhead of Western imperialism?

It is hard to believe that the two portraits depict the same object, but perhaps, in the end, they do. Perhaps the reason for the discrepancy is to be found in the fact that while the work of the new Orientalism enjoyed a huge vogue in Europe, the excitement about the prospect of an Oriental renaissance faded and Orientalism's heroic age was over before the nineteenth century had ended; at the same time, the importance of Orientalism has become and remains of great interest and importance in the countries that have been its object. Certainly that is true for India, where the British Sanskritists are better known than they are in Britain, and where, at this writing, one may purchase reprints of works of the Asiatic Society, of Jones, Max Müller, Caldwell, Muir, and Macdonell and Keith, among others. Max Müller was a celebrity scholar in Victorian England, but he is far better known today in India than in England, both by those who praise him and those who vilify him.[1]

As we have seen, Indians were not inert objects of study for the new Orientalism but the teachers of Sanskrit to the first British Sanskritists. They participated in the "dialogic construction" (Irschick 1994) of the new Orientalism, although by no means as equals in that process and without at first any control over the finalities that governed the project. The Asiatic Society, for example, was in its first fifty years a talking club for Europeans. Jones, in his opening address, proposes that "all curious and learned men be invited to send their tracts to our secretary" for publication, which publication might also include "such unpublished essays or treatises as may be transmitted to us by native authors." In this way several Indian authors appear in early issues of *Asiatic researches,* notably Govardhan Kaul and Ali Ibrahim Khan, and Jones is careful to mention the names of his Indian teachers and collaborators in his own writings. In the same address Jones adds, "but whether you will enrol as members any number of learned natives, you will hereafter decide" (1807:9). For whatever the reason (no discussion of the matter is given in the proceedings of the Society), it was not until 1829 that, on the nomination of H. H. Wilson, Indians were first elected to membership. They were Prasanna Thakur, Dwarakanath Thakur, Sib Chandra Das, Rasamaya Dutta, and Ram Comal Sen; later the same year came

---

1. For the latter I offer in evidence the accusing title of a recent book by Brahm Datt Bharti (1992): *Max Muller: A lifelong masquerade (the inside story of a secular Christian missionary who masqueraded all his lifetime from behind the mask of literature and philology and mortgaged his pen, intellect and scholarship to wreck Hinduism).*

the election of Maharaj Baiyanath Ray, Kashikanta Mullick, Maharaja Bunwari Govinda Rai, Santosh De, Radhamadhab Banerji, Rajchandra Das, Harachandra Lahiri, and Shyamal Thakur (Asiatic Society 1980:31). The Indianization of the Asiatic Society proceeded apace. Well before the end of the nineteenth century Indians such as R. C. Dutt and Rajendralal Mitra had mastered the new learning and its idiom and were publishing their versions of the historical ethnology of India in English in the pages of the *Calcutta review* and in books.

The effects of the new Orientalism on India were large and complex, far larger than their effects, significant though they had been in the age of the Oriental renaissance, upon Europe. The Indians who participated in the making and dissemination of the new Orientalism comprised a small elite, narrowly circumscribed by class, gender, and education, yet it would fairly take a book by itself to do justice to the Indian discussion of the new ethnological ideas. Fortunately, the book has already been written, at least the Bengali aspect of it: Tapan Raychaudhuri's *Europe reconsidered: Perceptions of the West in nineteenth-century Bengal* (1988).

I draw several observations from Raychaudhuri as to the Bengali reaction to the new Orientalism and the Aryan idea. In the first place the outstanding representatives of European Orientalism for Bengalis of the nineteenth century were, above all, Max Müller, and, somewhat surprisingly, Colonel Alcott and Annie Besant of the Theosophical Society. Secondly, the Aryan idea had in part the same significance for Bengalis as for Britons, as a sign of their kinship, although it functioned differently:

Max Müller's scholarly theories concerning the common origin of all Indo-Aryan [i.e., Indo-European] races based on his linguistic studies were received with incredible enthusiasm. The belief that the white masters were not very distant cousins of their brown Aryan subjects provided a much needed salve to the wounded ego of the dependent elite. A spate of "Aryanism" was unleashed. The word "Aryan" began to feature in likely as well as unlikely places—from titles of periodicals to the names of street corner shops. (Raychaudhuri 1988:8)

Thirdly, the "Aryan brother" theme seemed to have provoked a variety of reactions, from enthusiasm to revulsion, in Bengal as it did in England; not all Bengalis wished to be cousin to beef-eating, whiskey-drinking Englishmen.[2] Fourthly, while both Indians and Britons found

2. So says a Bengali publication of the period, according to Tapan Raychaudhuri (personal communication).

in the Aryan idea a new conception of the relation of India to Europe and to the world, in nineteenth-century Bengal the idea seemed to be subject to a kind of slippage, such that Aryan meant India plus Europe in some contexts but India versus Europe in others:

Aryanism and the Hindu reaction found some powerful protagonists though their influence proved to be short-lived. The most effective among them were Sasadhar Tarkachudamani and Krishnabihari Sen. Chandranath Bose was a milder exponent of the same tendency. Its literary lions included Indranath Bandyopadhyay and Jogindranath Basu. The central message of the movement was clear and simple: Hindu superiority and the unacceptability of western civilization. Indian Hindus were the most superior Aryans, no, even the only true Aryans. Everything in popular Hindu practice was based on higher reasoning and could be explained in a scientific way. All the discoveries of western science and technology had been anticipated by the ancient Aryans. (1988:34)

Finally, and most important to the Bengali intellectuals of whom Raychaudhuri speaks, the new Orientalism was of intense interest because it was the most intimate and the most sensitive point of contact between the civilizations. Bankimchandra Chattopadhyay especially (also Swami Vivekananda) wrote at length, with both deep admiration of Orientalism and sharp criticism of the distorting force of prejudice in even the most able of its practitioners. "There is no study which does not yield its secrets to the European scholar when he takes it up," said Bankim (quoted in Raychaudhuri 1988:178). Raychaudhuri comments:

In his later years Bankim was convinced that with rare exceptions the European scholars were deeply prejudiced against India and that racial arrogance was a mainspring of their academic judgements. They took great pains to prove that only the Buddhist texts, hostile to Hinduism, contained some truth. The rest of India's literary heritage was either false or borrowed from other cultures. The Ramayana to such men was but an imitation of the *Iliad,* the Gita an adaptation of the Bible, Hindu astronomy borrowed from the Chinese and the Greeks and their script was learnt from the Semitic race. Such conclusions derived from a method based on a clear principle: anything favourable to Indians found in Indian texts were either false or interpolated. The heroism of the Pandava brothers was but a poet's imagination, but the legend of Draupadi's five husbands was true for it proved that Indians were polyandrous and hence barbarous. (1988:180)

A new Bengali word—*jāti-vairitā*—had been coined (from Sanskrit) in the nineteenth century to name the new feeling of racial hatred that kept intruding between ruler and ruled, and it became for Bankim and others the explanatory principle that accounted for the tension between European and Indian views of India's history and India's place in the history of the world. The feeling that India's true place could only be found through the new Orientalism coexisted for Bankim and like-minded Indians with the belief that feelings of racial superiority had led European Orientalists to deprive India of its true place.

From this brief review of Raychaudhuri I conclude that the Aryan idea had the same inclusive sense for Indians—or at least for Bengali writers of the nineteenth century—that it had for the British, that is, it stood as a sign of kinship between Indians and Europeans. I must immediately qualify this, taking note of the tendency for the word *Aryan* to slip back to its Indian orbit and become a synonym for *Hindu,* in which case the kinship with Europe is lost. This slippage itself suggests that we may need a line of interpretation that pays greater attention to differences.

I have argued that the Indo-European or Aryan idea, while it has a (segmentary) structure of its own, was viewed differently in Britain than on the Continent, being a sign of inclusion (of Indians) for Britons and a sign of exclusion (of Jews, Asians, Africans, and so forth) more notably elsewhere. I have argued, furthermore, that this was because of differing angles of vision, Britons being preoccupied with the question of the relation between themselves and Indians, Germans with, perhaps, the frontiers of Europeanness.

Elaborating this line of reasoning, one might say that among Indians the same issues are again seen differently. Insofar as Indian writers concern themselves with the relation of India to Europe, the Aryan idea seems to be susceptible to different readings, a source of kinship (Aryans = Indians + Europeans) for some writers and of difference, superiority, and greater antiquity (Aryans = Hindus) for others. This appears clearly in Raychaudhuri's discussion.

By far the greater part of the fascination of the Aryan idea for Indians has to do not with India's relation to Europe and the world—the project that launched the new Orientalism—but with the question of the composition of the Indian people. In the latter half of the nineteenth century the idea of popular sovereignty and the prospect of electoral politics came to exert a powerful effect upon ethnological ideas, politicizing all ethnological classifications in a new way as it posed the all-important question: If government shall be the voice of the people, who, exactly, are the people? In South India, the newly revealed Aryan/Dravidian difference, fruit of the collaboration of Ellis, Campbell, Woodiagherry Vencatanarrain Ayah, Patabhirama Sastri, and others of the College of Fort St. George at the beginning of the nineteenth century, came in the nationalist struggles of the twentieth century to stand as a sign of the brahmin/non-brahmin difference and was taken up as a banner by the non-brahmin movement.[3] In Sri Lanka today the Aryan/Dravidian difference has been assimilated to the Sinhala/Tamil and Buddhist/Hindu differences, themselves deeply politicized, with tragic consequences playing themselves out before us with no end in sight. In these instances the Aryan idea becomes exclusionary in a different way. But in other Indian readings the Aryan idea becomes a sign of intra-Indian unity or of Indian expansion, as when S. R. Rao (1982) gives an Aryan interpretation of the Indus Civilization materials, or Shrikant Talageri (1993), reversing the directional arrows of the philologists, makes India the original Aryan homeland from which the Indo-European languages spread. None of these outcomes—it needs saying again—is predetermined by the structure of the Indo-European idea, and all are creatures of emergent circumstance and purposes.

## The Social Construction of Race

In this book I have assumed that race, insofar as it is a matter of human belief and action, is socially constructed, not given by nature. I need to elaborate a bit.

Under this assumption it is not just the conception of particular races that is socially constructed but race itself as a category of thought. Indianists will be familiar with Louis Dumont's argument (drawing on Gunnar Myrdal's *An American Dilemma*, 1944) that racial essentialism is a recent and Western phenomenon, a pathology or dark side of the Enlightenment and the egalitarian values that had been put at the center of the idea of political modernism by the French Revolution (Dumont 1966:app.). According to this view, when the belief in universal human equality replaces the hierarchical values of the old regime, ideas of inequality are banished to the (newly constituted) realm of the biological and reappear as racism.

This view is well known and I need not recite it at length. It is pow-

3. Nicholas Dirks (n.d.) thinks that Caldwell's anti-brahminism played a role in this formation, as shown in Caldwell's 1819 sketch of the Tinnevelly Shanars.

erfully attractive, and it holds out the prospect of putting an end to the large literature on race and caste that has grown up over the last century by locating the very idea of race in the recent history of the West and denying that it existed elsewhere, specifically denying that it existed in India before British rule. It rests on the view that the French Revolution marks the beginning of what in Thomas Kuhn's phrase is a paradigm shift, instituting a new configuration of thought that gives every inherited idea changed meanings (Kuhn 1962). I have already noted how the very words *race* and *nation* gradually but distinctly change their sense from the eighteenth century to the nineteenth in the writings examined. Indeed, we can see race in its modern sense being constructed before our eyes through the writings covered in this book.

And yet, attractive and useful as the idea of race as a modern and Western invention is in many ways, there is another way of looking at the question. Dumont's most interesting contribution to the problem of race and caste emerges from a certain framework that has two principal features: Europe and India are juxtaposed as polar opposites (the analytic of the self:other binarism), standing, moreover, for modernity and tradition in good Orientalist or, for that matter, modernist fashion; and, modernism is treated as a sudden leap from tradition (the analytic of the paradigm shift or the discontinuity view). The texts that I have read and the thoughts that I have had in the course of making this book suggest to me the value of trying a different framework, one in which binarism is replaced by a more segmentary sense of the subject and the subject-object relation, and one that stresses continuities with the deeper past in the formation of modernity and downplays discontinuities.

I should like it to be clear that I do so not to reject the Dumontean view of race—I have already indicated that I believe it is largely true and that it illuminates certain things such as the changing meaning of *race*—but to find what next step may take us beyond the point to which Dumont's immense contributions have taken us. I believe that the next step will have to be at an angle to the previous compass heading. I do so as a committed eclectic (dare I admit something so scandalous?), who believes that we need a variety of tools for differing ends and who holds that a pluralism of perspectives is the only corrective we have for the perverse nature of our generalizations to distort the world while making it intelligible.

I have said that the project of British ethnology in its formative phase was to sort the growing abundance of ethnographic information that empire had created into categories constructed from the double opposition of the dark-skinned savage and the fair-skinned civilized European, and that India was the central problem for that ethnology, which presented the conundrum of a dark-skinned people with an ancient civilization, throwing in doubt the consistency of the central oppositions. I was prepared to believe that the whole problematic was created by the British conquest of Bengal when I came across an eleventh-century book of Ṣāᶜid ibn Aḥmad Andalusī, an Arab writer of Spain, which the translators call *Science in the medieval world* (1068).

What Andalusī says about science in India is this: India is the first nation to have cultivated science. It is a powerful, wealthy, and populous nation known for the wisdom of its people and their abilities in all branches of knowledge.

The Indians, as known to all nations for many centuries, are the metal [essence] of wisdom, the source of fairness and objectivity. They are peoples of sublime pensiveness, universal apologues, and useful and rare inventions. In spite of the fact that their color is in the first stage of blackness, which puts them in the same category as the blacks, Allah, in His glory, did not give them the low characters, the poor manners, or the inferior principles associated with this group and ranked them above a large number of white and brown peoples. (1068:11)

Andalusī goes on to say that some astrologers have tried to account for this anomaly by stating that the destiny of the Indians is under the control of both Saturn and Mercury, the former turning their color black and the latter imbuing them with intellectual power and spirit (1068:11–12). Both the darkness and Hamian descent of the Indians, and their wisdom and special contributions to science, are widely held ideas among Islamic writers of the Middle Ages, and in this passage, which prefigures the project of British ethnology by the better part of a millennium, the anomalous character of the union of these two orders of fact is directly addressed. These and other reasons lead me to think that early British writers on India had an ethnological framework some aspects of which they shared with the Persian writers on India that they read and the Muslim savants with whom they conversed.

Why should this have been so? Why should this problematic, and the sense of color prejudice on which it is based, have so deep a history and so wide a geography, if it is, as we want to believe, socially constructed? It seems to me that an important article by William McKee Evans, "From the Land of Canaan to the land of Guinea: The strange odyssey of the 'Sons of Ham' " (1980), shows how it is that racial essentialism can be both socially constructed and nevertheless very, very old. Evans shifts the discussion from complexion to the color-independent concept of a "slavish nature" that comes to be attributed to enslaved groups to explain and justify their enslavement. Thus the Israelites who had conquered and enslaved the Canaanites (who were probably not different in complexion) attributed to them a slavish nature that is rationalized by the story of Noah's curse. The ancient slave trade of the Mediterranean and Near Eastern peoples drew upon fair-skinned Slavs and Celts among others, such that "Rufus" (redhead) became a stereotypical slave name for the Romans and red hair a sign of a slavish nature. It was only with the closing off of the sources of light-skinned slaves and the concentration of the international slave trade upon black Africans that the idea of a slavish nature got firmly attached to blackness in Muslim and Christian countries, a process that began in the early Middle Ages, long before the creation of the Atlantic slave trade in which the English and the Americans participated so largely. To the old question of whether slavery created color prejudice or color prejudice created slavery, Evans gives a clear and persuasive answer: The fact of enslavement is the seed-bed of the notion of a slavish nature. What aspects of the human body, language, religion, and so forth such a concept will fasten upon for its signs depends upon the contingent circumstances of slave taking.

Like the Slavs, whose enslavement by other Europeans in the long past turned their name into the English word *slave*, the Dāsas of the *Ṛg Veda* show every sign of being an ethnic group whose enslavement gave Sanskrit its word for *slave*. There is abundant evidence that these Dāsas among whom we presume the Aryans took slaves were strongly marked as different by language and religion. There is slight evidence to think that they were of dark complexion, so that there may be some beginnings of a linkage between darkness and a slavish nature in Vedic times. But nothing like the African slave trade of the Muslim Middle East and Christian Europe develops in India to thicken the linkage of slavery with dark complexion and project it across the centuries.

## An Evaluation

Finally and in conclusion I ask: What of value remains of the accomplishments of the British Sanskritists?

The question is not which accomplishments of the British Sanskritists survive today, but which survive the critique of the racial theory of Indian civilization just given and appear likely to endure in the foreseeable future. The answer has the nature both of a judgment and of a prediction, with all the uncertainties that must attend each. Given the provisional nature of all our knowledge, that is the best we can hope for.

The accomplishments of the British Sanskritists fall under the heading of what for Jones was a unitary inquiry he called "civil history" or the history of civilization (often called universal history), and which has since been divided up into specialized disciplines of history, ethnology, and linguistics. The Indians, of course (as the British discovered), had a vivid interest in the past, and in that sense can be said to have had a well-developed history, contained in the great epics and in the many mytho-historical compendia called Purāṇas ("Antiquities"). What the British Sanskritists did was to create a new way of looking at the Indian past by pushing a distinction between the "strange time" of mythology and the historical time of events and by developing a set of criteria for distinguishing the two.[4] The space of history, then, was given an ontology of its own, one that was different from that of myth, and it was created by identifying and clearing away the mythological elements from the historical ones. In addition, the British Sanskritists brought this space of history for India into connection with the history of the world by finding synchronisms with the Old World chronology that had been built up by many hands since the time of Eusebius and his chronological table.

Even a brief summary such as this, however, needs to note some of the complexities. First complexity: The distinction between myth and history is already notable in Muslim writers on India's history such as Firishtah, which is only to remind us that there is a deeper past to this constituting of history, one in which belief in the Biblical God and nonbelief in the gods of others play roles in constituting a realm of paganism and mythology opposed to the realm of eventful, factual history. Second complexity: The realm of history thus constituted by distinguishing and banishing mythology from it nevertheless included, for a time, the Mosaic narrative of creation, flood, confusion of tongues, and dispersal of the nations as its point of origin, regarded as ontologically homogeneous with recent history and only later, with much pain

---

4. "Strange time": This phrase and the idea it embodies comes from Peter Hughes, "Ruins of time: Estranging history and ethnology in the Enlightenment and after" (1995).

and controversy, reclassified as mythology. Here again there is a deeper history to this move, and again Firishtah serves as an instance, dismissing the Indians' own account for their origins and fitting them into the Biblical narrative. But the substitution of one mythology for another in the new history of India did not survive the nineteenth century.

The other side of the accomplishment was ethnological and linguistic. The identification of the three major language families of South Asia, namely Indo-Aryan, Dravidian, and Munda or Austro-Asiatic, together with the Iranian and Tibeto-Burman families which define the frontiers of Indian civilization, is very well grounded and remains the most meaningful set of building blocks for scholars trying to account for the development of Indian civilization and how it acquired its distinctive configuration of traits. The study of human physical features can offer only indirect help to these questions at best, as signs of non-physical cultural entities, and the results so far are of little use, for the reasons given in the previous chapter. A history of Indian civilization in which group differences of physical features play no part is readily imaginable, but it is hard to see how one could write intelligently about the formation of Indian civilization today without giving a large role to the major language families as clues to the originating constituents of that civilization.

Finally, of course, linking India's history with the world's in another way, there is the discovery of the Indo-European language family, in which the British Sanskritists played an initiatory role, although the leadership in Indo-European philology quickly passed to the Continent. The unexpected connection of Sanskrit and its descendants with Persian and the languages of Europe produced, as Maine remarks in the passage I quote at the beginning of this book, a revolutionary new view of "race" (read "ethnology") quite unlike any of the older ideas about the relations among the nations. It has profoundly affected the way in which we now read the oldest writings of Rome, Greece, Iran, and India, and make it a principle of method that the illumination of any one must include, in part, comparison with the others. It is unlikely that we will soon cease to find this result both true and useful.

It seems to me that these things need saying just now. We have become intensely interested in the politics of knowledge these days, and we are persuaded that the notion of disinterested knowledge is a dream from which we have awakened. We think a lot about power, and tend to take it as a naturally occurring ubiquitous thing that may readily form a preideological baseline from which to measure the ideological element in other forms of knowledge (a presumption that we had better not examine too closely). Foucault's eloquent suggestion has proved very—to use that word—powerful, an iron "perhaps":

Perhaps, too, we should abandon a whole tradition that allows us to imagine that knowledge can exist only where the power relations are suspended and that knowledge can develop only outside its injunctions, its demands and its interests. Perhaps we should abandon the belief that power makes mad and that, by the same token, the renunciation of power is one of the conditions of knowledge. We should admit rather that power produces knowledge (and not simply by encouraging it because it serves power or by applying it because it is useful); that power and knowledge directly imply one another; that there is no power relation without the correlative constitution of a field of knowledge, nor any knowledge that does not presuppose and constitute at the same time power relations. (Foucault 1979:27)

It is beyond question that our interest in the politics of knowledge has illuminated many dark corners of science, not least in the highly suggestive ideas Foucault develops in his own historical writings, where the power/knowledge idea is brilliantly deployed. But any source of illumination throws its own shadows and leaves in obscurity the other side of the objects its light falls upon. Because the politics of knowledge fixes its gaze upon power it tends to leave in darkness whatever falls outside the power relation—the world, in short. It tends to view knowledge as if it confronts a world that is infinitely plastic and of which anything may be said and to treat knowledge as if it were shaped by power alone. When Said puts all question of the content of Orientalism and its value—its relation to the world it claims to represent—outside the bounds he draws for his analysis of Orientalism, it seems to me that such an outcome is guaranteed.

Everything said in this book goes to show that the political consequences of the Aryan or Indo-European idea do not reside within the idea itself as a kind of hidden virus or all-determining genetic code but vary with circumstance and are the creatures of historical conjuncture and human purpose. I suggest that we would do well to keep this faith. If we lose it we may suppose that political problems can be resolved by supressing ideas we deem to be bad; or we may lose heart, and think that evil conjunctures are permanent and beyond remedy.

# References

Aarsleff, Hans
  1967        *The study of language in England, 1780–1860.* Princeton: Princeton University Press.
  1982        *From Locke to Saussure: Essays on the study of language and intellectual history.* Minneapolis: University of Minnesota Press.

Abu'l Fazl
  1783–86     *Ayeen Akbery, or, The institutes of the Emperor Akber.* 3 vols. Trans. Francis Gladwin. Calcutta: n.p.
  1908        *The Akbar Nāma of Abu-l-Fazl.* 2 vols. Trans. H. Beveridge. Reprint, Delhi: Ess Ess Publications, 1977.

Andalusī, Ṣāʿid ibn Aḥmad
  1068        *Science in the medieval world: "Book of the categories of nations"* (Tabaqāt al-ʾumam). Trans. Semaʿan I. Salem and Alok Kumar. Austin: University of Texas Press, 1991.

Anquetil-Duperron, Abraham Hyacinthe
  1771        *Zend-Avesta, ouvrage de Zoroastre, contenant les idées théologiques, physiques & morales de ce législateur, les cérémonies du culte religieux qu'il a établi, & plusieurs traits inportants relatives à l'ancienne histoire des Perses.* 3 vols. Paris: N. M. Tilliard.
  1808        Le Premier fleuve de l'Inde, le Gange, selon les anciens, expliqué par le Gange, selon les modernes. *Mémoires de littérature, tirés des registers de l'Académie Royale des Inscriptions et Belles-Lettres,* 1784–93, vol. 49, 512–646; Supplément au mémoire qui précède, 647–712. The Supplément publishes correspondence of Père Coeurdoux with the Académie des Inscriptions of about 1768.

Arberry, A. J.
1942        *British contributions to Persian studies*. London, New York, Toronto: Longmans Green & Co. for the British Council.
1943        *British Orientalists*. London: William Collins.

Asiatic Society
1980        *Proceedings of the Asiatic Society*. Ed. Sibadas Chaudhuri. Vol. I. Calcutta: The Asiatic Society.

Augustine
1950        *The city of God*. Trans. Marcus Dods. New York: Modern Library.

Bailly, Jean-Sylvain
1775–82     *Histoire de l'astronomie ancienne, depuis son origine jusqu'a l'établissment de l'école d'Alexandrie*. 4 vols. Paris: Les freres Debure.
1787        *Traité de l'astronomie indienne et orientale*. Paris: Debure l'ainé.

Ballantyne, James R.
1856        *A synopsis of science, in Sanskrit and English, reconciled with the truths to be found in the Nyáya philosophy. By James R. Ballantyne LL.D., Principal of the Government College, Benares*. Mirzapore: Government N.W.P.

Ballhatchet, Kenneth
1980        *Race, sex and class under the Raj: Imperial attitudes and policies and their critics, 1793–1905*. New York: St. Martin's Press.

Basham, A. L.
1954        *The wonder that was India* 3d. rev. ed. London: Sidgwick & Jackson.
1961        Modern historians of ancient India. In *Historians of India, Pakistan and Ceylon*, ed. C. H. Philips, 260–293. London: Oxford University Press.

Bayer, Gottlieb Siegfried
1738        *Historia regni Graecorum Bactriani in qua simul Graecarum in India coloniarum vetus memoria explicatur*. St. Petersburg: Academy of Sciences.

Bayly, Chris
n.d.        Colonial Star Wars: The politics of the heavens in India, c. 1780–1880. Forthcoming in *Festschrift for Tapan Raychaudhuri*, ed. J. M. Brown, Delhi: Oxford University Press.

Bernal, Martin
1987        *Black Athena: The Afroasiatic roots of classical civilization*. Vol. I: *The fabrication of ancient Greece 1785–1985*. New Brunswick: Rutgers University Press.

Bernier, François
1656–68        *Travels in the Mogul empire*, A.D. 1656–1668. Trans. Archibald
               Constable. Delhi: S. Chand, 1968.

*Bhagavad Gītā*
1785           *The Bhagvat-geeta, or dialogues of Kreeshna and Arjoon*. Trans.
               Charles Wilkins. Reprint, Gainesville, Florida: Scholars' Fac-
               similies & Reprints, 1959.

Bharti, Brahm Datt
1992           *Max Muller: A lifelong masquerade (the inside story of a secular
               Christian missionary who masqueraded all his lifetime from be-
               hind the mask of literature and philology and mortgaged his pen,
               intellect and scholarship to wreck Hinduism)*. New Delhi: Era-
               books.

Bīrūnī, Abū Raihān Muhammad ibn Ahmad
1964           *Alberuni's India*. 2 vols. Trans. Edward C. Sachau. Delhi: S.
               Chand & Co.

Blumenbach, Johann Friedrich
1776           *De generis humani varietate nativa liber*. Göttingen: A Van-
               denhoeck.

Bopp, Franz
1816           *Über das Conjugationssystem der Sanskrit sprache in Verglei-
               chung mit jenem der griechischen, persischen und germani-
               schen Sprache*. Frankfurt: Andreäischen Buchhandlung.
1833           *Vergleichende Grammatik des Sanskrit, Zend, Griechischen,
               Lateinischen, Littausischen, Gothischen und Deutschen*. Berlin:
               F. Dummler.
1845–53        *A comparative grammar of the Sanskrit, Zend, Greek, Latin,
               Lithuanian, Gothic, German and Slavonic Languages*. 3 vols.
               Trans. Lieut. Eastwick, ed. H. H. Wilson. London: Madden
               and Malcolm.

Borst, Arno
1957–63        *Der Turmbau von Babel: Geschichte der Meinungen über Ur-
               sprung und Vielfalt der Sprachen und Völker*. 4 vols. Stuttgart:
               Anton Hiersemann.

Breckenridge, Carol A., and Peter van der Veer, eds.
1993           *Orientalism and the postcolonian predicament: Perspectives on
               South Asia*. Philadelphia: University of Pennsylvania Press.

Bryant, Jacob
1807           *A new system; or, an analysis of antient mythology*. 6 vols. Lon-
               don: J. Walker. First published 1744–76, 3 vols.

Brydone, Patrick
1774           *A tour through Sicily and Malta*. 2d ed. London: W. Strahan
               and T. Cadell.

Bunsen, Christian Charles Josias
1854        *Outlines of the philosophy of universal history, applied to lan-
            guage and religion.* 2 vols. London: Longmans, Brown,
            Green, and Longmans.

Burnett, James (Lord Monboddo)
1773–92     *Of the origin and progress of language.* 6 vols. Edinburgh: A.
            Kincaid & W. Creech; London: T. Cadell.
1779–99     *Antient metaphysics; or, the science of universals.* 6 vols. Lon-
            don: T. Cadell; Edinburgh: J. Balfour.

Burrow, J. W.
1966        *Evolution and society: A study in Victorian social theory.* Cam-
            bridge: Cambridge University Press.

Burton, Isabel
1893        *The life of Sir Richard Burton.* 2 vols. New York: D. Appleton
            & Co.

Caldwell, Robert
1819        *The Tinnevelly Shanars: a sketch of their religion, and their
            moral condition and characteristics, as a caste; with special
            reference to the facilities and hindrances to the progress of
            Christianity amongst them.* Madras: Christian Knowledge So-
            ciety.
1856        *A comparative grammar of the Dravidian or South-Indian
            family of languages.* London: Harrison.
1875        *A comparative grammar of the Dravidian or South-Indian
            family of languages.* 3d ed. London: Trübner.

Campbell, Alexander D.
1816        *A grammar of the Teloogoo language, commonly termed the
            Gentoo, peculiar to the Hindoos inhabiting the North Eastern
            provinces of the Indian Peninsula.* Madras: College Press of
            Fort St. George.

Campbell, [George]
1866        Ethnology of India. *Journal of the Asiatic Society of Bengal* 35,
            pt. 2, special number on Indian ethnology, 1–152.

Cannon, Garland
1979        *Sir William Jones: A bibliography of primary and secondary
            sources.* Amsterdam Studies in the Theory and History of
            Linguistic Science, 5; Library and Information Sources in
            Linguistics, vol. 7. Amsterdam: John Benjamins B.V.
1990        *The life and mind of Oriental Jones: Sir William Jones, the fa-
            ther of modern linguistics.* Cambridge: Cambridge University
            Press.

Carey, William
1804        *A grammar of the Sungscrit language, composed from the works
            of the most esteemed Hindoo Grammarians. To which are added,*

*examples for the exercise of the student, and a complete list of the Dhatoois, or Roots. By W. Carey, teacher of the Bengalee and Sungskrit languages, in the College of Fort William.* Serampore: Mission Press.

1814　　　*A grammar of the Telingana language.* Serampore: Mission Press.

Clifford, James
1988　　　*The predicament of culture: Twentieth-century ethnography, literature, and art.* Cambridge, Mass., and London: Harvard University Press.

Clive, John
1973　　　*Macaulay: The shaping of the historian.* New York: Alfred A. Knopf.

Cloyd, E. L.
1969　　　Lord Monboddo, Sir William Jones, and Sanskrit. *American anthropologist* 71:1134–1135.
1972　　　*James Burnett, Lord Monboddo.* Oxford: Clarendon Press.

Coeurdoux, Gaston-Laurent
c.1768　　　"Réponse au mémoire de M. l'Abbé Barthélemy." Published in Anquetil-Duperron 1808:647–667.

Cohn, Bernard S.
1968　　　Notes on the history of the study of Indian society and culture. Reprinted in Cohen 1990:136–171.
1985　　　The command of language and the language of command. In *Subaltern studies IV: Writings on South Asian history and society,* ed. Ranajit Guha, 276–329. Delhi: Oxford University Press.
1990　　　*An anthropologist among the historians and other essays.* Delhi: Oxford University Press.

Colebrooke, Henry Thomas
1801　　　On the Sanscrit and Pracrit languages. *Asiatic researches* 7:199–231.
1805　　　*A grammar of the Sanscrit language.* Vol. 1. Calcutta: The Honorable Company's Press.

Court de Gebelin, Antoine
1773–82　　　*Le monde primitif, analysé et comparé avec le monde moderne.* 9 vols. Paris: The author.

[Craufurd, Quentin]
1790　　　*Sketches chiefly relating to the history, religion, learning, and manners, of the Hindoos. With a consise account of the present state of the native powers of Hindostan.* London: T. Cadell.

Crawford, John
1852　　　*A grammar and dictionary of the Malay language.* 2 vols. London: Smith, Elder and Co.

1861          On the Aryan or Indo-Germanic theory. *Transactions of the Ethnological Society of London*, n.s., 1:268–286.

1865          On the commixture of the races of man as affecting the progress of civilization. *Transactions of the Ethnological Society of London*, n.s., 3:98–122.

Darwin, Charles

1859          *On the origin of species*. Facsimile reprint. Cambridge, Mass., and London: Harvard University Press, 1964.

Derrett, J. Duncan M.

1968          The British as patrons of the Sastra. In *Religion, law and the state in India*, 225–269. London: Faber and Faber.

Deshpande, Madhav M.

1993          *Sanskrit and Prakrit: Sociolinguistic issues*. Delhi: Motilal Banarsidass.

Dirks, Nicholas B., ed.

n.d.          The conversion of caste: Location, translation, and appropriation. Unpublished.

1992          *Colonialism and culture*. Ann Arbor: The University of Michigan Press.

Dresch, Paul

1988          Segmentation: Its roots in Arabia and its flowering elsewhere. *Cultural anthropology* 3:50–67.

1989          *Tribes, government, and history in Yemen*. Oxford: Clarendon Press; New York: Oxford University Press.

Dubois, Abbé J. A.

1906          *Hindu manners, customs and ceremonies*. 3d. ed. Trans. Henry K. Beauchamp, with a prefatory note by F. Max Müller. Oxford: Clarendon Press.

Dumont, Louis

1966          *Homo hierarchius: The caste system and its implications*. Trans. Mark Sainsbury. London: Weidenfeld and Nicholson.

Durkheim, Emile

1893          *De la division du travail social*. Paris: Alcan.

East India Company

1804          *Report of the committee appointed to enquire into the plan for forming an establishment at home for the education of young men intended for the Company's Civil Service in India, 26 October 1804*. Published in Farrington 1976: 14–21.

Eco, Umberto

1995          *The search for the perfect language*. Trans. James Fentress. Oxford and Cambridge, Mass.: Blackwell.

Elliot, Walter

1875          Mr. F. W. Ellis. In *The Indian antiquary* 4:219–221. Reprinted from *The Athenaeum*, 10 April 1875.

Ellis, Francis Whyte

n.d.            *The Ellis papers.* MS in the Bodleian Library, Oxford.

1816            Note to the introduction. In A. D. Campbell 1816, 1–20.

1818            Replies to seventeen questions proposed by the Goverment of Fort St. George relative to Mirasi right with two appendices elucidatory of the subject. Madras: Government Gazette Office. Reprinted in *Three treatises on Mirasi right . . . with remarks made by the Hon'ble the Court of Directors,* ed. C. P. Brown. Madras: D.P.L.C. Connor, 1852.

Embree, Ainslie Thomas

1962            *Charles Grant and British rule in India.* London: George Allen & Unwin.

Evans, William McKee

1980            From the land of Canaan to the land of Guinea: The strange odyssey of the "Sons of Ham." *American historical review* 85:15–43.

Evans-Pritchard, E. E.

1940            *The Nuer: A description of the modes of livelihood and political institutions of a Nilotic people.* Oxford: Clarendon Press.

1981            *A history of anthropological thought.* Ed. André Singer. New York: Basic Books.

*Ezour Vedam*

1984            *Ezourvedam, a French Veda of the eighteenth century.* University of Pennsylvania Studies on South Asia, vol. 1. Ed. Ludo Rocher. Amsterdam and Philadelphia: John Benjamins Publishing Company.

Farrington, Anthony

1976            *The records of the East India College, Haileybury, and other institutions.* India Office Records: Guides to Archive Groups. London: Her Majesty's Stationery Office.

Firishtah, Muhammad Qasim Hindu Shah Astarabadi

1768            *The history of Hindostan; from the earliest account of time, to the death of Akbar.* 2 vols. Trans. Alexander Dow. London: T. Becket and P. A. De Hondt.

Fontana, Nicolas

1799            On the Nicobar Isles and the fruit of the mellori. *Asiatic researches* 3:149–164 (London edition).

Forster, H. P.

1810            *An essay on the principles of Sanskrit grammar. Part I. By H. P. Forster, Senior Merchant on the Bengal establishment.* Calcutta: Ferris and Co.

Foucault, Michel

1979            *Discipline and punish: The birth of the prison.* Trans. Alan Sheridan. New York: Vintage Books.

Funkenstein, Amos
    1993        History, counterhistory, and narrative. In *Perceptions of Jewish history*, 22–48. Berkeley and Los Angeles: University of California Press.

Gibbon, Edward
    1776–88     *The history of the decline and fall of the Roman empire*. 7 vols. Ed. J. B. Bury. 4th ed. London: Methuen, 1906–20.

Grant, Charles
    1796        Observations on the state of society among the Asiatic subjects of Great Britain, particularly with respect to morals; and on the means of improving it, written chiefly in the year 1792. Printed as Appendix I in *Report from the Select Committee on the Affairs of the East India Company 1831–32*, 3–92. Facsimile reprint, *Irish University Press Series of British Parliamentary Papers*. Vol. 5: *Colonies: East India*. Shannon: Irish University Press, 1970.

Greenberg, Joseph
    1955        *Studies in African linguistic classification*. Bradford, Conn.: Compass Pub. Co.
    1987        *Language in the Americas*. Stanford: Stanford University Press.

Grellmann, Heinrich Moritz Gottlieb
    1787        *Dissertation on the Gipseys*. Trans. Matthew Raper from the German. London: Printed for the editor by G. Brigg.

Halbfass, Wilhelm
    1988        *India and Europe: An essay in understanding* (Indien und Europa: Perspectiven ihrer geistigen Begegnung). Albany: State University of New York Press.

Halhed, Nathaniel Brassey
    1776        The translator's preface. In *A code of Gentoo laws, or, ordinations of the pundits, from a Persian translation, made from the original, written in the Shanscrit language*. London: [East India Company].
    1778        *A grammar of the Bengal language*. Facsimile reprint, Menston, England: The Scolar Press, 1969.

Hamilton, Alexander
    1802        Review of *Asiatic researches*, vol 6. *Edinburgh review* 1, art. 4 (Oct.):26–43.
    1806        Review of *Asiatic researches*, vol. 7. *Edinburgh review* 9 (Oct.):92–101
    1807        Review of *Asiatic researches*, vol. 7 (continued). *Edinburgh review* 9 (Jan.):278–304.
    1808        Review of Francis Buchanan, *A journey from Madras, through the countries of Mysore, Canara and Malabar*. *Edinburgh review* 13 (Oct.):82–100.

1809          Review of Wilkins's *Sanskrit grammar*. *Edinburgh review* 13
              (Oct.):366–381.
1820          Sanscrit and Greek—Sanscrit Poetry. Review of Bopp. *Edin-
              burgh review* 33 (May):431–442.

Hegel, Georg Wilhelm Friedrich
1807          *The phenomenology of mind*. Trans. J. B. Baillie. New York and
              Evanston: Harper Torch Books, 1967.
1830–31       *The philosophy of history*. Trans. J. Sibree. New York: Dover
              Publications, 1956.

Hodgson, Brian Houghton
1833          Origin and classification of the military tribes of Nepal. *Jour-
              nal of the Asiatic Society of Bengal* 2:217–224.
1847          On the aborigines of the sub-Himalayas. *Journal of the Asi-
              atic Society of Bengal* 16:1235–1244.
1848a         Addenda et corrigenda of the paper on the aborigines of the
              sub-Himalayas, in the December no. of the Journal. *Journal
              of the Asiatic Society of Bengal* 17:73–79.
1848b         Ethnography and geography of the sub-Himalayas. *Journal
              of the Asiatic Society of Bengal* 17:544–549.
1848c         The aborigines of Central India. *Journal of the Asiatic Society
              of Bengal* 17:550–558.
1848d         Tibetan type of mankind. *Journal of the Asiatic Society of Ben-
              gal* 17:580–583.
1848e         On the Che'pa'ng and Ku'su'nda tribes of Ne'pa'l. *Journal
              of the Asiatic Society of Bengal* 17, pt. 2: 650–658.
1849          Aborigines of Southern India. *Journal of the Asiatic Society of
              Bengal* 18:350–359.

Hoisington, H. R.
1848          *Cotisaattiram. The Oriental astronomer: being a complete sys-
              tem of Hindu astronomy, accompanied with a translation and
              numerous explanatory notes. With an appendix.* Jaffna: Ameri-
              can Mission Press.

Holwell, John Zephaniah
1765–71       *Interesting historical events, relative to the provinces of Bengal,
              and the Empire of Indostan.* 3 vols. London: T. Becket and P. J.
              De Hondt. Vol. 1, 1765; vol. 2, 1767; vol. 3, 1771.

Hughes, Peter
1995          Ruins of time: Estranging history and ethnology in the En-
              lightenment and after. In *Time: Histories and ethnologies,* ed.
              Diane Owen Hughes and Thomas R. Trautmann, 269–290.
              Ann Arbor: The University of Michigan Press.

Huxley, Thomas
1865          On the methods and results of ethnology. In *Man's place in
              nature and other anthropological essays,* 209–252. London:
              J. M. Dent & Sons, Ltd. 1910.

Inden, Ronald
    1990          *Imagining India.* Oxford: Basil Blackwell.

Indian Institute
    1887          *Record of the establishment of the Indian Institute in the University of Oxford.* Oxford: Horace Hart.

Irschick, Eugene F.
    1994          *Dialogue and history: Constructing South India, 1795–1895.* Berkeley, Los Angeles, London: University of California Press.

Jefferson, Thomas
    c.1782        *Notes on the state of Virginia.* N.p.: n.p.

Jones, Sir William
    1770          *Histoire de Nader Chah, connu sous le nom de Thahmas Kuli Khan, empereur de Perse.* 2 vols. Trans. Jones. London: P. Elmsley.
    1771          *Grammar of the Persian language.* London: W. & J. Richardson.
    1771          *Lettre à Monsieur A\*\*\* du P\*\*\*, dans laquelle est compris l'examen de sa traduction des livres attribués à Zoroastre.* London: P. Elmsley.
    1774          *Poeseos Asiaticae commentariorum libri sex.* London: T. Cadell.
    1780          *An inquiry into the legal mode of suppressing riots, with a constitutional plan of future defense.* London: C. Dilly. Unsigned.
    1782a         *The Moallakát, or seven Arabian poems, which were suspended on the Temple at Mecca.* Trans. Jones. London: P. Elmsley.
    1782b         *The Mohamedan law of succession to the property of intestates (Bhughyat al-bahith of Ibn al-Mulaqqin).* Trans. Jones. London: John Nichols for Charles Dilly.
    1782c         *The principles of government, in a dialogue between a scholar and a peasant.* Written by a member of the Society for Constitutional Information. N.p.: Society for Constitutional Information.
    1782d         *A speech of William Jones, Esq. to the assembled inhabitants of the Counties of Middlesex and Surry, the Cities of London and Westminster, and the Borough of Southwark.* N.p.: n.p.
    1788          On the literature of the Hindus, from the Sanscrit, communicated by Goverdhan Caul, with a short commentary. *Asiatic researches* 1, art. 18:340–355.
    1792          *Sacontalá; or, the fatal ring: an Indian drama.* London: Printed for Edwards.
    1794          *Institutes of Hindu law: or, the ordinances of Menu, according to the gloss of Cullúca.* Trans. Jones. Calcutta: printed by order of Government.
    1799          *The works of Sir William Jones.* 6 vols. Ed. Anna Maria Jones. London: G. G. and J. Robinson, and R. H. Evans.
    1807          *The works of Sir William Jones.* 13 vols. Ed. Anna Maria Jones. London: John Stockdale and John Walker.

1824        *Discourses delivered before the Asiatic Society: and miscellaneous papers, on the religion, poetry, literature, etc., of the nations of India.* 2d ed. London: C. S. Arnold.

1970        *The letters of Sir William Jones.* 2 vols. Ed. Garland Cannon. Oxford: Clarendon Press.

Keiffer, Jean-Luc

1983        *Anquetil-Duperron: L'Inde en France au XVIII<sup>e</sup> siècle.* Paris: Les Belles Lettres.

Kejariwal, O. P.

1988        *The Asiatic Society of Bengal and the discovery of India's past, 1784–1838.* Delhi: Oxford University Press.

Khalidi, Tarif

1975        *Islamic historiography: The histories of Mas'udi.* Albany: State University of New York Press.

Kissinger, Henry

1979        *The White House years.* Boston: Little, Brown.

Klaproth, Julius von

c.1865      Wilford (François). *Biographie universelle (Michaud) ancienne et modern.* 2d ed. Vol. 54:608–609. Paris: Madame C. Desplaces; Leipzig: F. A. Brockhaus.

Knox, Robert

1862        *The races of men: a philosophical enquiry into the influence of race over the destinies of nations.* London: Henry Renshaw.

Kopf, David

1969        *British Orientalism and the Bengal Renaissance: The dynamics of Indian modernization 1773–1835.* Berkeley and Los Angeles: University of California Press.

Kuhn, Thomas S.

1962        *The structure of scientific revolutions.* Chicago: University of Chicago Press.

La Loubère, Simon de

1691        *Description du royaume de Siam par M. de la Loubère envoyé extraordinaire du Roy auprès du Roy de Siam en 1687 & 1688.* 2 vols. Paris. Reprint, Amsterdam: David Mortier, 1714.

Laplace, P. S.

1809        *The system of the world.* 2 vols. Trans. J. Bond. London: Richard Phillips.

Latham, Robert Gordon

1850        *The natural history of the varieties of man.* London: John van Voorst.

1859a       *Descriptive ethnology.* 2 vols. London: John van Voorst.

1859b       *Ethnology of India.* London: John van Voorst.

1862        *Elements of comparative philology.* London: Walton and Maberly.

Leach, Edmund
1990            Aryan invasions over four millennia. In *Culture through time: Anthropological approaches,* ed. Emiko Ohnuki-Tierney, 227–245. Stanford: Stanford University Press.

Lehmann, Winfred P.
1967            *A reader in nineteenth-century historical Indo-European linguistics.* Bloomington and London: Indiana University Press.

Leopold, Joan
1970            The Aryan theory of race. *Indian economic and social history review* 7:271–297.

1974a           British applications of the Aryan theory of race to India, 1850–1970. *The English historical review* 89: 278–603.

1974b           Britische Anwendungen der arischen Rassentheorie auf Indien 1850–1870. *Saeculum* 25:386–411.

*Lettres édifiantes.*
1702–77         *Lettres édifiantes et curieuses, écrites des missions étrangères, par quelques missionnaires de la Compagnie de Jésus.* 34 vols. Paris: Nicholas le Clerc, etc.

Lingat, Robert
1973            *The classical law of India.* Trans. J. Duncan M. Derrett. Berkeley, Los Angeles, London: University of California Press.

Literary Society of Madras
1827            Notice. In *Transactions of the Literary Society of Madras,* Part 1:v–vi.

Locke, John
1689            *An essay concerning human understanding.* Ed. Peter H. Nidditch. Oxford: Clarendon Press, 1975.

Lord, Henry
1630            *A display of two forraigne sects in the East Indies viz: the sect of the Banians the ancient natives of India, and the sect of the Persees, the ancient inhabitants of Persia together with the religion and manners of each sect collected into two books by Henry Lord sometimes resident in East India and preacher to the Honble Company of Merchants trading thither.* London: Francis Constable.

Lorenzen, David
1982            Imperialism and the historiography of ancient India. In *India: History and thought: Essays in Honour of A. L. Basham,* ed. S. N. Mukherjee, 84–102. Calcutta: Subarnarekha.

Ludden, David
1993            Orientalist empiricism: transformations of colonial knowledge. In Breckenridge and van der Veer 1993: 250–278.

Macaulay, Thomas Babington
1835        *Minute on Indian education.* Reprinted in *Selected writings,*
            ed. John Clive and Thomas Pinney, 237–251. Chicago and
            London: The University of Chicago Press, 1972.

Macdonell, Arthur Anthony, and Arthur Barriedale Keith
1912        *Vedic index of names and subjects.* 2 vols. London: John Mur-
            ray.

Mackenzie, Kenneth R. H., ed.
1877        *The royal Masonic cyclopaedia.* Reprint, Wellingborogh,
            Northamptonshire: The Aquarian Press, 1987.

Maine, Henry Sumner
1861        *Ancient law, its connection with the early history of society and
            its relation to modern ideas.* Reprint, Tucson: University of
            Arizona Press, 1986.
1871        *Village-communities in the east and west.* London: J. Murray.
1875        *The effects of observation of India on modern European thought.*
            The Rede Lecture, delivered before the University of Cam-
            bridge on 22 May 1875. London: John Murray.

Majeed, Javed
1992        *Ungoverned imaginings: James Mill's* The history of British
            India *and Orientalism.* Oxford: Clarendon Press.

Mallory, J. P.
1989        *In search of the Indo-Europeans: Language, archaeology and
            myth.* London: Thames and Hudson.

Manaster Ramer, Alexis
1993        On Illic-Svitic's Nostratic theory. *Studies in language* 17:
            205–250.

Manu (see also Jones 1794)
1886        *The laws of Manu.* Trans. Georg Bühler. In *The sacred books of
            the East,* ed. F. Max Müller, vol. 25. Oxford: Clarendon Press.

Manuel, Frank
1959        *The eighteenth century confronts the gods.* Cambridge: Harvard
            University Press.

Marshall, P. J.
1970        *The British discovery of Hinduism in the eighteenth century.*
            Cambridge: Cambridge University Press.

Maurice, Thomas
1793–1800   *Indian antiquities: or, dissertations, relative to the ancient geo-
            graphical divisions, the pure system of primeval theology, the
            grand code of civil laws, the original form of government, and
            the various and profound literature of Hindostan. Compared,
            throughout, with the religion, laws, government and literature
            of Persia, Egypt, and Greece. The whole intended as introductory*

*to, and illustrative of, the History of Hindostan.* 7 vols. London: The author.

1795      *An elegaic and historical poem, sacred to the memory and virtues of the honourable Sir William Jones.* London: The author.

1795–98      *The history of Hindostan; its arts, its sciences, as connected with the history of the other great empires of Asia, during the most ancient periods of the world. With numerous illustrative engravings. By the author of Indian antiquities.* 2 vols. London: The author.

1797      *Sanscreet fragments, or interesting extracts from the sacred books of the Brahmins, on subjects important to the British Isles. In two parts. By the author of Indian antiquities.* London: The author.

1800      *A dissertation on the Oriental trinities: extracted from the fourth and fifth volumes of Indian antiquities.* London: The author.

1802–03      *The modern history of Hindostan: comprehending that of the Greek empire of Bactria, and other great Asiatic kingdoms, bordering on its western frontier. Commencing at the period of the death of Alexander, and brought down to the close of the eighteenth century.* 2 vols. London: The author.

1812      *Brahminical fraud detected; or the attempts of the sacerdotal tribe of India to invest their fabulous deities and heroes with the honour and attributes of the Christian messiah, examined, exposed, and defeated. In a series of letters to the Right Reverend the Episcopal Bench. By the author of Indian antiquities.* London: The author.

1819      *Memoirs of the author of Indian antiquities; comprehending the history of the progress of Indian literature in Britain, during a period of thirty years. To be comprised in three parts. Part I.* London: The author.

1820      *Memoirs. . . .* Part II. London: The author.

Maw, Martin

1990      *Visions of India; fulfilment theology, the Aryan race theory, and the work of British Protestant missionaries in Victorian India.* Studien zur interkulturellen Geschichte des Christentums, vol. 57. Frankfurt am Main: Verlag Peter Lang.

Max Müller, Friedrich

1847      On the relation of the Bengali to the Arian and aboriginal languages of India. In *Report of the British Association for the Advancement of Science,* 1847:319–350.

1854a      The last results of the researches respecting the non-Iranian and non-Semitic languages of Asia and Europe, or the Turanian family of languages. In Bunsen 1854, 1:263–472.

1854b      *Suggestions for the assistance of officers in learning the languages of the seat of war in the East.* London: Williams and Norgate.

1855      *The languages of the seat of war in the East, with a survey of the three families of language, Semitic, Arian, and Turanian,* 2nd ed. London: Williams and Norgate.

1861      *Lectures on the science of language, delivered at the Royal Institute of Great Britain in April, May, and June.* Reprint, Delhi: Munshi Ram Manohar Lal, 1965.

1868      On the value of comparative philology as a branch of philological study. Inaugural lecture, Oxford, 27 October 1868. In Max Müller 1881, 1:108–173.

1872      On the results of comparative philology. Inaugural lecture, Strassburg, 23 May 1872. In Max Muller 1881, 1: 174–225.

1874      Opening address. Delivered by the President of the Aryan Section at the International Congress of Orientalists, London, 21 September 1874. In Max Muller 1881, 2:1–45.

1881      *Selected essays on language, mythology and religion.* 2 vols. London: Longmans, Green, and Co.

1882      *Lectures on the science of language.* New ed. 2 vols. London: Longmans, Green, and Co.

1892      *Address delivered at the opening of the Ninth International Congress of Orientalists held in London, September 5, 1892.* Oxford: Oxford University Press.

1895      Thought thicker than blood. In *Three lectures on the science of language, delivered at the Oxford University extension meeting,* 43–72. Chicago: Open Court Publishing Company.

1898      *Auld lang syne.* 1st ser. London and Bombay: Longmans, Green.

1901      *My autobiography, a fragment.* London and Bombay: Longmans, Green.

Meiners, Christoph

1780      *Historia doctrinae de vero Deo.* Lemgo: n.p.

Mill, James

1817      *The history of British India.* 3 vols. London: Baldwin, Cradock, and Joy.

1858      *The history of British India.* 5th ed. 6 vols. With notes and continuation by Horace Hayman Wilson. Facsimile reprint, with introduction by John Kenneth Galbraith, New York: Chelsea House Publishers, 1968.

Millar, John

1806      *The origin of the distinction of ranks: or, an inquiry into the circumstances which give rise to influence and authority, in the different members of society.* 4th ed., corrected. Edinburgh: William Blackwood; London: Longman, Hurst, Rees & Orme. Facsimile reprint, with an introduction by John Valdimir Price, Bristol: Thoemmes; Tokyo: Kinoduniya, 1990.

Monier-Williams, Monier

1899      *A Sanskrit-English dictionary.* New ed. Facsimile reprint, Delhi: Motilal Banarsidass, 1970.

*Monthly review*
1797        Review of *Dissertations and miscellaneous pieces relating to the history and antiquities, the arts, sciences, and literature of Asia,* vol. 3, and other works. Unsigned. *Monthly review* 23:408–414.

Moon, Penderel
1947        *Warren Hastings and British India.* London: Hodder & Stoughton for The English Universities Press.

Moore, Norman
1899        Vallency, Charles, 1721–1812. *Dictionary of national biography,* vol. 20:82–83. London: Smith, Elder.

Muir, John
1874–84     *Original Sanskrit texts on the origin and history of the people of India, their religions and institutions.* 3d. ed. 5 vols. London: Trübner & Co.

Mukerji, Abhijit
1985        European Jones and Asiatic pandits. *Journal of the Asiatic Society* 27:43–58.

Mukherjee, S. N.
1983        *Sir William Jones: A study in eighteenth-century British attitudes to India.* 2d ed. N.p.: Orient Longman.

Murr, Sylvia
1977        Nicolas Desvaulx (1745–1823) véritable auteur de Moeurs, institutions et cérémonies des peuples de l'Inde, de l'abbé Dubois? *Puruṣārtha* 3:245–267.

1983        Les conditions d'émergence du discours sur l'Inde au Siècle des Lumières. *Puruṣārtha* 7:233–284.

1987        *L'Inde philosophique entre Bossuet et Voltaire.* 2 vols. Vol. 1: *Moeurs et coutumes des Indiens (1777);* vol. 2: *L'Indologie du Père Coeurdoux: Stratégies, apologétique et scientificité.* Publications de L'École française d'Extrême-Orient, vol. 146. Paris: École française d'Extrême-Orient.

Myrdal, Gunnar
1944        *An American dilemma: The Negro problem and modern democracy.* New York: Harper.

Nangle, Benjamin Christie
1955        *The Monthly review, second series 1790–1815: Indexes of contributors and articles.* Oxford: Clarendon Press.

Newton, Isaac
1728        *The chronology of ancient kingdoms amended.* London: J. Tonson, J. Osborn, and T. Longman.

Nott, J. C., and George R. Gliddon
1854        *Types of mankind: or, ethnological researches, based upon the ancient monuments, painting, sculptures, and crania of races, and*

*upon their natural, geographical, philological, and biblical history*. 6th ed. Philadelphia: Lippincott, Grambo & Co.

Olender, Maurice
1992 *The languages of paradise: Race, religion and philology in the nineteenth century* (Les langues du paradis: Aryens et Sémites, un couple providentiel). Trans. Arthur Goldhammer. Cambridge, Mass., and London: Harvard University Press.

Pallas, P. S.
1786–89 *Linguarum totius orbis vocabularia comparativa*. 2 vols. St. Petersburg: Carl Schnoor.

Paulinus a Sancto Bartholomaeo
1790 *Dissertation on the Sanskrit language*. Ed. and Trans. Ludo Rocher. Amsterdam Studies in the Theory and History of Linguistic Science, ed. E. F. K. Koerner, ser. 3, Studies in the History of Linguistics. Amsterdam: John Benjamins B.V., 1977.

Playfair, John
1790 Remarks on the astronomy of the Brahmins. Read by the author, 2 March 1789. *Transactions of the Royal Society of Edinburgh* 2, art. 13:135–192.

Poliakov, Léon
1974 *The Aryan myth: A history of racist and nationalist ideas in Europe*. Trans. Edward Howard. London: Chatto, Heinemann for Sussex University Press.

Prichard, James Cowles
1813 *Researches into the physical history of man*. Ed. and with an introductory essay by George W. Stocking, Jr. Chicago and London: The University of Chicago Press, 1973.
1831 *The eastern origin of the Celtic nations proved by a comparison of their dialects with the Sanskrit, Greek, Latin and Teutonic languages. Forming a supplement to Researches into the physical history of mankind*. Oxford: Oxford University Press.
1843 *The natural history of man; comprising inquiries into the modifying influence of physical and moral agencies on the different tribes of the human family*. London: H. Baillière.
1855 *The natural history of man*. 4th ed. 2 vols. Ed. and enlarged by Edwin Norris. London: H. Baillière.

Rao, S. R.
1982 *The decipherment of the Indus script*. Bombay: Asia Publishing House.

Rask, Rasmus
1818 An investigation concerning the source of the old Northern or Icelandic language. Trans. Winfred P. Lehmann. In Lehmann 1967:29–37.

Raychaudhuri, Tapan
1988            *Europe reconsidered: Perceptions of the West in nineteenth-century Bengal.* Delhi: Oxford University Press.

Rendall, Jane
1982            Scottish Orientalism: From Robertson to James Mill. *The historical journal* 25:43–69.

Renfrew, Colin
1987            *Archaeology and language: The puzzle of Indo-European origins.* London: Penguin Books.

*Ṛg Veda*
1854–57         *Rig-Veda-Sanhita: A collection of ancient Hindu hymns.* 4 vols. Trans. H. H. Wilson. London: H. Allen and Co.
1890–92 [?]     *Rig-Veda-Samhitâ, the sacred hymns of the Brâhmans together with the commentary of Sâyanâkârya.* 2d ed. 4 vols. Ed. F. Max Müller. London: Henry Frowde.
1891            *Vedic hymns.* Part I: Sacred books of the East, vol. 32. Trans. F. Max Müller. Reprint, Delhi: Motilal Banarsidass, 1964.

Risley, Herbert Hope
1891            The study of ethnology in India. *Journal of the Anthropological Institute of Great Britain and Ireland* 20:235–263.
1892            *Tribes and castes of Bengal.* 2 vols. Calcutta: Bengal Secretariat Press.
1908            *The people of India.* Calcutta: Thacker, Spink & Co.; London: W. Thacker & Co.

Robertson, William
1812            *An historical disquisition concerning the knowledge which the ancients had of India; and the progress of trade with that country prior to the discovery of the passage to it by the Cape of Good Hope.* 1st American ed., from 5th London ed. Philadelphia: John Bioren & Tho. L. Plowman.

Rocher, Ludo
1961            Paulinus a Sancto Bartholomaeo on the kinship of the languages of India and Europe. *The Adyar Library bulletin* 25:321–352.
1986            *The Puranas: A history of Sanskrit literature.* Vol. 2, fasc. 3. Ed. Jan Gonda. Wiesbaden: Otto Harrassowitz.

Rocher, Rosane
1968            *Alexander Hamilton (1762–1824): A chapter in the early history of Sanskrit philology.* American Oriental Series, vol. 51. New Haven: American Oriental Society.
1970            New data for the biography of the Orientalist Alexander Hamilton. *Journal of the American Oriental Society* 90:426–448.

1980a          Lord Monboddo, Sanskrit and comparative linguistics. *Journal of the American Oriental Society* 100:12–17.
1980b          Nathaniel Brassey Halhed, Sir William Jones, and comparative Indo-European linguistics. In *Recherches de linguistique; hommages à Maurice Leroy*, 173–180. Brussels: Éditions de l'Université de Bruxelles.
1983           *Orientalism, poetry and the millennium: The checkered life of Nathanial Brassey Halhed, 1751–1830.* Delhi: Motilal Banarsidass.
1989           The career of Rādhākānta Tarkavāgīśa, an eighteenth-century pandit in British employ. *Journal of the American Oriental Society* 109:627–633.
1993           British Orientalism in the eighteenth century: The dialectics of knowledge and government. In Breckenridge and van der Veer 1993, 215–249. Philadelphia: University of Pennsylvania Press.

Roger, Abraham
1670           *La porte ouverte, pour parvenir à la connoissance du paganisme caché. Ou, la vraye representation de la vie, des moeurs, de la religion, & du service divin des Brahmines, qui demeurent sur les costes de Chormandel, & aux pays circonvoisins. Par le Sieur Abraham Roger . . . Traduite en François par le Sieur Thomas La Grue. . . .* Amsterdam: Chez Jean Schipper.

Said, Edward W.
1978           *Orientalism.* New York: Pantheon Books.
1983           *The world, the text, and the critic.* Cambridge, Mass.: Harvard University Press.

Schlegel, Friedrich
1808           *Über die Sprache und Weisheit der Indier: ein Beitrag zur Begründung der Alterthumskunde.* Heidelberg: Mohr und Zimmer.

Schleicher, August
1861           *Compendium der vergleichenden Grammatic der indogermanischen Sprachen.* Weimar: Hermann Bohlau.

Schwab, Raymond
1934           *Vie d'Anquetil-Duperron, suivie des usages civils et religieux des Parses.* Paris: Librarie Ernest Leroux.
1984           *The Oriental renaissance: Europe's rediscovery of India and the East 1680–1880* (La rennaissance orientale). Trans. Gene Patterson-Black and Victor Reinking, foreword by Edward W. Said. New York: Columbia University Press.

Scrafton, Luke
1761           *Reflections on the government, &c. of Indostan: and a short sketch of the History of Bengal, from the year 1739 to 1756.* Edinburgh: n.p.

Sen, S. N.
  c.1985          Survey of studies in European languages. In *History of astronomy in India,* ed. S. N. Sen and K. S. Shukla, 49–121. New Delhi: Indian National Science Academy.

Shaffer, Jim G.
  1984            The Indo-Aryan invasions: Cultural myth and archaeological reality. In *The people of South Asia: The biological anthropology of India, Pakistan, and Nepal,* ed. John R. Luckacs, 77–90. New York: Plenum Press.

Shore, John (Lord Teignmouth)
  1805            *Memoirs of the life, writings, and correspondence of Sir William Jones.* Philadelphia: Wm. Poyntell.

Smith, Edwin Burrows
  1954            Jean-Sylvain Bailly: Astronomer, mystic, revolutionary, 1736–1793. *Transactions of the American Philosophical Society,* n.s., 44, pt. 4.

Smith, George
  1857            India and comparative philology. *Calcutta review* 29: 229–279.

Smith, Vincent
  1904            *Early history of India, from 600 B.C. to the Muhammadan conquest.* Oxford: Clarendon Press.

Smith, W. Robertson
  1885            *Kinship and marriage in early Arabia.* Cambridge: Cambridge University Press.

Spear, Percival
  1963            *The nabobs: A study of the social life of the English in eighteenth-century India.* London: Oxford University Press.

Steel, F. A., and G. Gardiner
  1909            *The complete Indian housekeeper and cook; giving the duties of mistress and servants, the general management of the house and practical recipies of cooking in all its branches.* 7th ed. London: William Heinemann.

Stepan, Nancy
  1982            *The idea of race in science: Great Britain 1800–1960.* London: Macmillan.

Stevenson, John
  1841–44a        An essay on the vernacular literature of the Marathas. *Journal of the Bombay Branch of the Royal Asiatic Society* 1:1–10.
  1841–44b        An essay on the language of the aboriginal Hindus. *Journal of the Bombay Branch of the Royal Asiatic Society* 1:103–126.
  1843            Observations on the Maráthí language. *Journal of the Royal Asiatic Society,* pp. 84–91.
  1849–51         Observations on the grammatical structure of the vernacular

languages of India. *Journal of the Bombay Branch of the Royal Asiatic Society* 3, pt. 1:71–76; 3, pt. 2:1–7, 196–202.

1853a    Observations on the grammatical structure of the vernacular languages of India, no. 4—the pronoun. *Journal of the Bombay Branch of the Royal Asiatic Society* 4:15–20.

1853b    A comparative vocabulary of the non-Sanscrit vocables of the vernacular languages of India. *Journal of the Bombay Branch of the Royal Asiatic Society* 4:117–131.

1853d    Comparative vocabulary of non-Sanscrit primitives in the vernacular languages of India, part II. *Journal of the Bombay Branch of the Royal Asiatic Society* 4:319–339.

Stewart, Dugald
1827    *Elements of the philosophy of the human mind.* Vol. 3. London: John Murray.

Stocking, George W., Jr.
1968    *Race, culture, and evolution: Essays in the history of anthropology.* Chicago and London: Chicago University Press.
1971    What's in a name? The origins of the Royal Anthropological Institute, 1837–1871. *Man*, n.s., 6:88–104.
1973    Introduction to Prichard 1813.
1987    *Victorian anthropology.* New York: The Free Press; London: Collier Macmillan Publishers.

Stokes, Eric
1959    *The English Utilitarians and India.* Oxford: Clarendon Press.

Stone, Lawrence
n.d.    Changing sexualities in eighteenth century England. Unpublished.

Strabo
1949    *The geography of Strabo.* London: Heinemann; Cambridge: Harvard University Press.

Talageri, Shrikant G.
1993    *The Aryan invasion theory: A reappraisal.* New Delhi: Aditya Prakashan.

Taylor, Isaac
c.1889    *The origin of the Aryans; an account of the prehistoric ethnology and civilisation of Europe.* London: Walter Scott.

Thapar, Romila
1993    *Interpreting early India.* Delhi: Oxford University Press.

Thomas, William
1985    *Mill.* Oxford: Oxford University Press.

Topinard, Paul
1885    *Éléments d'anthropologie générale.* Paris: Adrien Delahaye et Émile Lecrosier.

Trautmann, Thomas R.

1981        *Dravidian kinship.* Cambridge Studies in Social Anthropology, 36. Cambridge: Cambridge University Press.

1987        *Lewis Henry Morgan and the invention of kinship.* Berkeley, Los Angeles, London: University of California Press.

1988        In memoriam Arthur Llewellyn Basham, 1914–1986. *Journal of the International Association of Buddhist Studies* 11:131–135.

1992a       Whig ethnology from Locke to Morgan. *Journal of the Anthropological Society of Oxford* 23:201–218.

1992b       The revolution in ethnological time. *Man* n.s., 27: 379–397.

1995        Indian time, European time. In *Time: Histories and ethnologies,* ed. Diane Owen Hughes and Thomas R. Trautmann, 167–197. Ann Arbor: The University of Michigan Press.

n.d.        The lives of Sir William Jones. Unpublished manuscript. To appear in a volume of lectures commemorating the life and work of Jones.

Vallancey, Charles

1770–1804   *Collectanea de rebus hibernicis.* 6 vols. Dublin: R. Marchbank; Luke White; Graisberry and Campbell.

1772        *An essay on the antiquity of the Irish language. Being a collation of the Irish with the Punic language. With a preface proving Ireland to be the Thule of the ancients,. . . .* Dublin: S. Powell.

1773        *A grammar of the Iberno-Celtic, or Irish language.* Dublin: G. Faulkner, T. Ewing, and R. Moncrieffe.

1786        *A vindication of the ancient history of Ireland.* Dublin: Luke White.

1797        *The ancient history of Ireland, proved from the Sanscrit books of the Bramins of India.* Dublin: Graisberry & Campbell.

1802        *Prospectus of a dictionary of the language of the Aire Coti, or, ancient Irish, compared with the language of the Cuti, or ancient Persians, with the Hindoostanee, the Arabic, and the Chaldean languages. By Lieut. General Charles Vallancey, Author of the Vindication of the ancient history of Ireland. With a preface, containing an epitome of the ancient history of Ireland, corroborated by late discoveries in the Puranas of the Brahmins, by our learned countrymen in the east. And An account of the Ogham tree-alphabet of the Irish, lately found in an ancient Arabic manuscript in Egypt.* Dublin: Graisberry and Campbell.

1807        *An essay on the primitive inhabitants of Great Britain and Ireland. Proving from history, language, and mythology, that they were Persians or Indo Scythae, composed of Scythians, Chaldaeans, and Indians.* Dublin: Graisberry and Campbell.

Vermeulen, Han F.

1992        The emergence of "ethnography" ca. 1770 in Göttingen. *History of anthropology newsletter* 19, no. 2:6–9.

Viswanathan, Gauri
1989          *Masks of conquest: Literary study and British rule in India.*
              New York: Columbia University Press.

Wilberforce, William
1813          *Substance of the speeches of William Wilberforce, Esq. on the*
              *clause in the East-India bill for promoting the religious instruc-*
              *tion and moral improvement of the natives of the British domin-*
              *ions in India, on the 22nd of June, and the 1st and 12th of July,*
              *1813.* N.p.:n.p.

Wilford, Francis
1792          On Egypt and other countries adjacent to the Cálí River, or
              Nile of Ethiopia, from the ancient books of the Hindus. *Asi-*
              *atic researches* 3:295–462.
1805          An essay on the sacred isles of the west, with other essays
              connected with that work. *Asiatic researches* 8:245–367 (con-
              tinued in subsequent vols.).
c.1846        *Essai sur l'origine et la décadence de la religion chrétienne dans*
              *l'Inde.* Trans. M. Daniélo. N.p.:n.p. Reprinted from *Annales*
              *de philosophie chrétienne,* vol. 13, 1846.

Wilkins, Charles
1808          *A grammar of the Sanskrita language.* London: n.p.

Wilson, Horace Hayman
1858          Preface of the editor. In Mill 1858:vii–xiv.

Young, Arthur
1813          Review of J. C. Adelung, *Mithridates, oder allegemeine Spra-*
              *chenkunde. The Quarterly Review* 10, art. 12 (Oct.): 250–292.
              2d ed., London: John Murray, 1817.

# Index

Aarsleff, Hans, 39n, 41n, 128, 132n
Aborigines Protection Society, 166
Abu'l Fazl, 31, 53, 102, 105
Académie des Sciences, 85, 86
Alexander of Macedon, 32, 81, 108, 124, 126, 177, 180
Ali Ibrahim Khan, 218
Algebra of the Indians, 123
American Philosophical Society, 55
Ancient wisdom, 59–61, 62, 205
Andalusī, Ṣāᶜid ibn Aḥmad, 3n, 53, 224
*Āndhradīpaka*, 152–153
Anquetil-Duperron, Abraham Hyacinthe, 27, 30, 35–37, 47, 86, 126n, 169
Anthropological Society of London, 166–167, 179
Anthropology, 131, 132, 165–186
Anti-Semitism, 14, 15n, 178
Anville, Jean Baptise D', 48
Arberry, A. J., 29n
Archaeology, 143n, 184–185
Arya, Aryan, *ārya*, xi, xii, 2, 4–6, 11–16, 18, 27, 137, 159, 162, 163, 171, 172, 174–175, 180, 187, 195, 196, 202, 203, 207, 209, 211, 213–215; Aryan brethern, 172–178, 181, 187, 219–220; Aryanization of Europe, 185; Aryan race, 184–187; inclusive sense, xiii, 5
Asiatic Society, 22, 26–30, 90, 102, 112, 114, 115, 118, 127, 134, 135, 137–139, 158, 161, 218–222, 225, 228

*Asiatic researches*, 22, 29, 32, 38n, 65, 90, 93, 102, 137, 140, 146, 158, 169, 218
Aśoka, inscriptions of, 137
Astronomy of the Indians, 64, 84–89, 112, 123, 125, 129, 220
Aufrecht, Theodor, 189
Augustine, St., 55, 73
Avatars of Viṣṇu, 58–59, 78–80. *See also* Rāma
*Avesta*, 26, 30, 36, 47, 207

Bacon, John, 76
Ballantyne, James, 89n
Ballhatchet, Kenneth, 110n
Bailly, Jean-Sylvain, 85–86, 123
Bankimchandra Chattopadhyay, 220–221
Basham, A. L., xii–xiv
Bayer, Gottlieb Siegfried, 126
Bayly, Chris, 89n
Bentham, Jeremy, 117
Bentley, John, 88
Bernal, Martin, 15n, 51, 82, 132
Bernier, François, 30, 102, 105
Bernouf, Eugène, 139, 172
Berossus, 137
*Bhagavad Gītā*, 17, 32, 102, 105, 130, 220
Bharti, Brahm Datt, 218n
Bible, 41, 52, 57–59, 64, 70, 97, 100, 108, 121, 173, 188, 192, 193–194, 220, 226. *See also* Flood of Noah; Genesis; Tower of Babel
Binarism, 10–11, 223

| | |
|---:|:---|
| Compositor: | J. Jarrett Engineering, Inc. |
| Text & Display: | Sabon |
| Printer: | Thomson-Shore, Inc. |
| Binder: | Thomson-Shore, Inc. |